JONATHAN CLEMENTS
MONEY GUIDE 2015

ISBN: 150246361X
ISBN-13: 978-1502463616

PRAISE FOR THE
JONATHAN CLEMENTS MONEY GUIDE

"It's hard to imagine a finer place to begin your search for financial peace of mind than with *Jonathan Clements Money Guide 2015*. Yes, it's long. But so is the list of financial challenges faced by American families. Don't be intimidated. He's made it easy to navigate through these challenges, identify those where you need help, and successfully deal with them. Don't just scan this fine, readable, and insightful guide. Keep it by your desk and return to it as your circumstances change, as financial markets change, and as the world turns."
– John C. Bogle, founder, The Vanguard Group

"A comprehensive financial guide ranging from navigating health insurance alternatives to forming sensible investment portfolios. Clements is a first-rate financial writer who is a genius at making sophisticated advice accessible to everyone and a delight to read."
– Burton G. Malkiel, author of *A Random Walk Down Wall Street*

"Since the early 1990s, Jonathan Clements's columns taught his readers, profited them, and made them smile. Trouble was, you needed to have read all his *Wall Street Journal* articles. Until now, that is. His *Money Guide* wraps this bounty, and then some, into a tidy package, destined to be enjoyed and referred to over and over by readers for decades to come."
– William J. Bernstein, author of *The Investor's Manifesto*

"How do you get nearly 30 years of personal-finance wisdom and advice in an engaging, entertaining and easy-to-use format? Keep Jonathan Clements's *Money Guide* on your desk or tablet for instant answers to your essential money questions."
– Consuelo Mack, anchor, *Consuelo Mack WealthTrack*

"Would you like to have a friend who knew a lot and would share the straight scoop with you on any investment topic at any time in clear language, with candor and a wry sense of humor? Well, here it is. What a break!"
– Charles D. Ellis, author of *What It Takes* and *Winning the Loser's Game*

"As someone who has read just about every personal finance book ever published, I can honestly say this is the best money manual ever written—period! Jonathan Clements's *Money Guide* offers readers a host of brilliant insights on how to grow their money. It's required reading for anyone striving for financial independence."
– Allan Roth, author of *How a Second Grader Beats Wall Street*

FOR LUCINDA

CONTENTS

ACKNOWLEDGMENTS

While much of this *Money Guide* reflects the knowledge and insights I've collected during three decades of writing and thinking about money, it also covers a few topics I have never previously tackled. To fill in the gaps in my knowledge, I consulted innumerable sources and relied heavily on my tireless research assistant, who quickly responded to my every request without the slightest complaint. Google, I'm forever in your debt.

I also had the help of some humans. William Bernstein, Allan Roth and Jason Zweig were all kind enough to review the manuscript and offer their suggestions. Laura Saunders gave me her thoughts on the tax chapter and Rachel Silverman Robinson took a look at the estate planning section. Prudence Crowther assumed the arduous task of copyediting the book, David Glaubke designed the cover and the book's interior, Bill Blase helped with publicity and Samantha Steele redesigned my website, JonathanClements.com. Nicholas Clements and June Dosik gave the manuscript a final read. Many thanks to all of you. But as authors often say, any errors are mine. In a book this large, there are surely a few mistakes lurking somewhere in the pages that follow, and for those I apologize. Want to put me right? Write to ClementsGuide@gmail.com.

This book came together over the course of two hectic years, during which I left Citigroup to return to journalism, moved homes, got married and more. Along the way, nobody was more supportive than Lucinda, my lover, best friend and now wife. This book is for you.

PART I

INTRODUCTION
YOUR JOURNEY
BEGINS HERE

Welcome to the 2015 edition of the *Jonathan Clements Money Guide*. If I've done my job, this guide should make you smarter about money, tell you the latest financial numbers you need to know, and help you quickly answer life's crucial financial questions.

From here, you might peruse the first section, which is devoted to navigating this book. Next, consider heading to the sections devoted to today's economy, your human capital—and your goals. That's where your journey will begin in earnest. In this chapter, you can also learn a little about my biases.

Be warned: This is not a get-rich-quick book. You won't find a forecast for stock and bond returns in 2015. You won't find me proclaiming that some single investment—real estate, cash-value life insurance, gold—will answer all of your financial prayers. If that's what you are looking for, please ask for a refund—or perhaps give this book to that annoying colleague who keeps asking you financial questions.

In January 2016, I'll be back with a new edition of the *Money Guide*, which will include updated figures for the economy, markets and taxes. Wish this book had more details on a particular topic? Let me know at ClementsGuide@gmail.com and I'll try to build out that portion of the book for next year's edition.

In the meantime, enjoy your journey—and I hope you find what you're looking for.

1. NAVIGATING THIS BOOK

You could studiously work your way through this *Money Guide* from the first page to the last. But I've tried to design it so you can quickly zero in on the information you want.

Got a specific issue you need help with? While this book ostensibly has 14 parts, it's actually divided into 367 sections, each typically 250 to 350 words. This is section 1. At the end of Part XIII, you'll find section 367. The sections are listed in the detailed table of contents, which is akin to an index. Got a particular topic that's on your mind? Try heading to the back of the book and scanning the detailed table of contents.

Throughout, I have incorporated the latest numbers on the economy, markets and tax rates. I have also included statistics on how the typical American is faring financially, so you can see how you stack up against your neighbors. In addition, at the start of almost every chapter, you'll find a list of five steps to take in 2015.

While we tend to think of financial issues in different buckets—retirement, taxes, estate planning—one topic is often connected to another. When that's the case, I've tried to make it clear, and then direct readers to other relevant parts of the *Money Guide*. You will also find a slew of websites listed in the book, where you can find additional information and helpful calculators.

Finally, I have strong views on financial issues, and I realize not everybody shares my opinions. When I want to emphasize particular points or I figure my views may raise a few eyebrows, I have inserted them in a paragraph or two labeled "JONATHAN'S TAKE."

2. JANUARY 2015: WHERE WE STAND

Remember the financial panic of 2008 and early 2009? Like 9/11 for terrorism and Nixon's resignation for national politics, it was a watershed moment for the financial world—and we're still working through the consequences.

• The unemployment rate, which hit a high of 10 percent in October 2009, was 5.8 percent in November 2014.

• Real economic growth shrank at a -2.1 percent annualized rate in 2014's first quarter, but then surged 4.6 percent in the second quarter and 5 percent in the third.

• The savings rate in 2014 was running around 5 percent of personal disposable income. That's better than 2005's low of 2.5 percent, but the

Great Recession clearly hasn't brought on the new era of frugality that many expected.

- Total borrowing by Americans, including mortgage debt, hit a peak of $12.7 trillion in the third quarter of 2008. By 2014's third quarter, it was down to $11.7 trillion as Americans paid off debt and defaulted on loans. That's equal to $45,600 per household.

- Home prices remain 9 percent below their mid-2006 peak, as measured by the S&P/Case-Shiller U.S. National Home Price Index.

- The Standard & Poor's 500-stock index finished 2014 at 2059, or 204 percent above the March 2009 low. Despite that robust rally, the S&P 500 is just 35 percent above its March 2000 peak—a modest 2 percent annual price gain for the past 14-plus years.

- The benchmark 10 year Treasury note closed 2014 at just 2.17 percent, which means there remains far more room for rates to rise than fall.

- Buyers of certificates of deposit and savings accounts could see higher yields in 2015, though the Federal Reserve hasn't said for sure when it will lift short-term rates.

3. IT ALL STARTS WITH YOU

As you consider what financial steps to take in 2015, you might begin with your most valuable asset—yourself. Economists refer to our income-earning ability as our human capital. It should figure into many of our financial decisions, including how much debt we take on, how much emergency money we need, what insurance we purchase, and what mix of stocks and bonds we buy.

For instance, if you're a government worker with a steady job and a traditional pension upon retirement, you may not have huge lifetime earnings, but your paycheck doesn't involve much risk. That means you can probably take a fair amount of risk elsewhere in your financial life, including investing heavily in stocks and using an adjustable-rate mortgage to buy your home. But if you're a small-business owner, you are taking a lot of risk with your human capital—and you may want to favor bonds in your portfolio, keep your debts modest and build up a large emergency fund.

In the pages ahead, I'll encourage you to think about your human capital as you tackle four goals many of us share: paying for retirement, buying a home, putting the kids through college and protecting our family. Those four goals are the subject of the *Money Guide*'s next four parts.

As we pursue these goals, we'll do all manner of spending, saving, investing, taxpaying, borrowing and giving, which are discussed in the chapters that follow. I have also included a chapter on financial markets that's devoted to nerdy stuff about investing. Not everything fits neatly into these various categories. That's why I have a chapter on life events. To wrap up things, there's a final part with rules of the road for 2015.

4. YOUR GOALS

While most of us have four key goals—retirement, college for the kids, owning a home and protecting our family—that leaves plenty of room for interpretation. The house I dream of owning is no doubt quite different from the one you're imagining.

That is both good and bad. It's good because, if we can visualize our goals in great detail, we'll be more motivated to make the necessary sacrifices to achieve them. It is worth spending considerable time pondering our goals, so we strive for things we truly want.

That's where the bad part comes in. We just aren't very good at figuring out what we want. Maybe we hanker after a luxury sedan. But then the sedan turns out to be a disappointment. When we were kids, our parents always owned luxury cars and we remember our childhood as a happy, carefree time. But maybe it's the happy, carefree time we miss—and the expensive sedan is just a symbol in our air-brushed recollection.

How can you avoid such costly mistakes? Take your time before making major financial decisions. Don't impulsively buy the timeshare during the wonderfully relaxing vacation. Think hard about why you want something. Do you truly believe the pricey private school will give your children a better education—or are you drawn to the prestige or compensating for your perceived failings as a parent? Think about the potential headaches. The luxury sedan may be alluring. But what about the car payments?

Leading a thoughtful financial life can help you get the most out of your money. We all have limited means. If we waste money on goals that aren't important to us, we may not have enough for those that matter.

5. JONATHAN'S TAKE

I like to think of this *Money Guide* as an encyclopedia with attitude. Here are just some of the attitudes that permeate the pages that follow:

• It's a big mistake to view our homes, investment accounts, life insurance and other parts of our financial lives in isolation. Instead, we should take a broad view of our finances that encompasses our human capital, debts, stocks, bonds, real estate, financial obligations to family and more. This can help us to earn higher returns, avoid unnecessary risks and make sensible financial tradeoffs.

• All too many people hunt for the big win, whether it's with stocks, rental properties or lottery tickets. Many are disappointed. If your goal is financial success, a much surer path is managing risk, holding down investment costs and taxes, and saving diligently. Indeed, a healthy savings habit is the greatest of the financial virtues.

• Complexity might suggest sophistication. But in the financial world, it usually means high fees and befuddled investors. I would limit how many financial accounts you have and stick with simple investments that you truly understand, with a special emphasis on mutual funds and exchange-traded funds. What about individual company stocks? I don't think they should play a major part in the typical investor's portfolio.

• Money supposedly buys happiness—and yet many folks lead lives of financial anxiety and regret. They worry about having enough to pay the monthly bills and whether they're saving enough. They fret over their investments. They lust after new purchases, only to find themselves later disappointed. Want to be a contented investor and a happy consumer? You need to think hard about what unnerves you and what gives you a lasting sense of satisfaction.

6. ABBREVIATIONS

I strongly believe that sensible money management doesn't have to be complicated and, indeed, that simpler is usually better. Wall Street may try to bamboozle investors with jargon and needless complexity in an effort to justify its hefty fees. But in this guide, I've endeavored to avoid such nonsense and instead make the financial world understandable to the interested layperson.

With that in mind, I have avoided a lot of abbreviations. In each of the 367 sections, I try to spell out the full name on first reference, and only abbreviate on second and subsequent references.

But when it came to exchange-traded index funds and individual retirement accounts, this started to seem silly because there are so many references to these two items. So be prepared: You'll see a lot of mentions of ETFs and IRAs—and, fingers crossed, you'll remember what those initials stand for.

PART II

RETIREMENT

TURNING FOUR DECADES' LABOR INTO A HEAPING PILE OF DOLLARS

Imagine you are a freshly minted, penniless college graduate with alarming student loans and an unhealthy helping of credit card debt. Your net worth? It's likely measured in millions.

Over the next four decades, you might pull in tens and perhaps hundreds of thousands of dollars every year. To get a handle on how valuable that income stream is, consider how much you would need to invest in bonds or certificates of deposit to generate a comparable amount of annual income.

Of course, it's lucky you'll have all that income coming in, because ahead of you lies life's toughest financial task: amassing enough money so you can retire in comfort. In dry economic terms, your working career is about accumulating enough financial capital, so that one day you'll no longer need the income from your human capital. This is, alas, a task that most Americans are not good at.

Want to do better? To get you started, check out this chapter's five key steps to take in 2015. As you dig deeper and ponder how to pay for retirement, it's helpful to think about your life in three stages—your 20s, 30s and 40s, your 50s and early 60s, and age 65 and beyond—which is how the rest of this chapter is divvied up. Readers under age 50 might stick with the initial sections of the chapter and those already retired might head straight to section 23. What about those within 15 years of retirement? You should probably read both the part devoted to your 50s and early 60s and the sections geared to folks age 65 and beyond.

7. A WOBBLY THREE-LEGGED STOOL

Experts sometimes talk about the three-legged retirement stool, consisting of Social Security, traditional defined benefit pension plans and personal savings. The latter includes money stashed in 401(k) plans, individual retirement accounts and regular taxable accounts.

Cutting Social Security is a constant topic of conversation in political circles, with recent discussion focusing on adopting a new formula that will slow the annual increase in benefits because of inflation. Even without that change, benefits are already getting scaled back. The age at which retirees can claim full Social Security retirement benefits is gradually climbing. The full Social Security retirement age is 66 for those born between 1943 and 1954. It rises for those born in subsequent years, eventually hitting age 67 for those born in 1960 or later.

Meanwhile, traditional defined benefit pensions continue to disappear. These pensions, which pay eligible employees income every month throughout retirement, remain relatively common among public sector workers, despite recent cutbacks. Instead, the big falloff has occurred in the private sector. According to a Bureau of Labor Statistics study, just 18 percent of private-sector workers had pensions as of 2011, down from 35 percent in the early 1990s.

What about personal savings, the third leg of the retirement stool? Given the cutbacks elsewhere, this needs to be the strongest leg of the stool—but it also looks extremely wobbly.

8. TODAY'S RETIREMENT READINESS

How are Americans doing when it comes to retirement savings? Solid numbers are hard to come by. But the available statistics aren't encouraging. According to the Employee Benefit Research Institute's 2014 Retirement Confidence Survey, 50 percent of workers age 55 and older reported having savings of less than $50,000. This figure excludes the value of their home, Social Security and any defined benefit pension plan.

What if you include those items? For households approaching retirement age, the typical net worth is $598,700, calculates Boston College's Center for Retirement Research. That sounds more impressive—but 50 percent of this figure is represented by the value assigned to Social Security benefits, and another 26 percent by traditional pension plans, which are fast disappearing.

You can also get a glimpse of America's retirement readiness from the Federal Reserve's 2013 Survey of Consumer Finances. Among households headed by someone age 65 to 74, 85.8 percent owned their home. But 42.2

percent also had a mortgage, while 66.4 percent were carrying some kind of debt. Meanwhile, just 48 percent of this group had an IRA or similar retirement account.

Even if most folks aren't in good shape for retirement, presumably some are. How many? Each year, Phoenix Marketing International calculates how many U.S. households have $1 million or more in investable assets. Based on a 4 percent portfolio withdrawal rate, $1 million would give you $40,000 in first-year retirement income, on top of whatever you might receive from Social Security and any pension plans. That should be enough for a comfortable, though hardly lavish, retirement.

Phoenix calculates that there were 6.1 million households with $1 million or more in investable assets as of 2013. That's equal to 5.2 percent of all households. Maryland, New Jersey, Connecticut and Hawaii had the highest concentration of millionaire households, at more than 7 percent, while Mississippi, Arkansas, Idaho and West Virginia were at the bottom of the table, with less than 4 percent.

9. FIVE STEPS FOR 2015

Saving enough for retirement, and then turning those savings into a reliable stream of retirement income, is our life's great financial task. Want to start wrapping your head around what's involved? Start with these five tasks:

• Find out your life expectancy using the calculator at SocialSecurity.gov. Keep in mind that as you grow older, the average age to which you're expected to live also rises—and, of course, there's a 50 percent chance you'll live longer than that.

• If you're in the workforce, add up how much you saved for retirement in 2014, including any matching employer contributions to a 401(k) or similar plan. Are you socking away at least 12 percent of your pretax income?

• Consider whether you're shortchanging your retirement by devoting too much of your income to other goals. Can you truly afford private school for the kids? Can you really afford a second home?

• Give some thought to whether you could retire without immediately claiming Social Security. As you'll learn later in this chapter, Social Security is a hugely valuable income stream, and it often makes sense to delay benefits so you get a larger monthly check.

• Ponder what you'll do with your retirement years. Once you quit the workforce, what will get you out of bed in the morning and give a sense of purpose to your retirement?

10. YOUR 20s, 30s AND 40s

Most of us have all kinds of financial desires, including a nice home, a fancy car, a good education for the kids, a fun trip next summer. But retirement should take priority. Think of it this way: You can take out a loan to buy a house or car, and your kids can borrow to pay for college, and then slowly pay the money back. But when it comes to retirement, you'll need to start out with a heaping stack of dollar bills.

Moreover, retirement is significantly more expensive than these other goals, in part because you need to be so cautious when spending down your savings. Financial experts often talk about a 4 percent withdrawal rate. Translation: For every $100,000 you have saved by the time you quit the workforce, you can reasonably expect to pull out $4,000 in the first year of retirement. Want $60,000 in portfolio income during retirement? You will likely need to sock away something like $1.5 million. To amass that sort of money, you will probably have to save diligently starting soon after you enter the workforce.

Even if you're a good saver, that still leaves lots of decisions—including which accounts to stash those savings in, precisely how much to save every year and what investments to buy.

11. PUT RETIREMENT FIRST

Our hunter-gatherer ancestors were focused on surviving until tomorrow. We need to focus on retiring decades from now. Not surprisingly, this isn't something that comes naturally.

Our inclination is to deal with life's goals consecutively, rather than concurrently. In other words, we might save for the house down payment in our 30s, pay for the kids' college in our 40s and then finally turn our attention to retirement in our 50s. But if we do that, we could find ourselves in financial trouble. It's awfully tough to amass enough for retirement if we start saving in our 20s, let alone beginning at age 50.

Indeed, even as your attention is drawn to more immediate goals, don't shortchange retirement. Maybe you can't save 12 to 15 percent toward retirement in your 20s and 30s. But try to save at least some money every month.

The earlier you start saving, the longer your time horizon will be. In addition to having more years of saving regularly, you can take the risk of investing more in stocks and potentially earn higher returns. You may also get the chance to fund your employer's 401(k) plan and collect a matching employer contribution. That's free money—and you don't want to miss out.

Moreover, if you save a healthy sum from your 20s onwards, you will give yourself options. You may reach your late 40s or early 50s and discover that you are comfortably on track for retirement. At that point, you might opt to work less or switch to a less lucrative but perhaps more fulfilling career.

12. ARE YOU SAVING ENOUGH?

As a rule of thumb, you should probably save 12 to 15 percent of your pretax income toward retirement. If your employer has some sort of traditional defined benefit pension plan, which will pay you income every month in retirement, you can likely save less. Similarly, if your employer makes a matching contribution to its 401(k) or 403(b) plan, you might be able to trim your savings rate. Suppose your employer matches your 401(k) contributions at 50 cents on the dollar up to 6 percent of pay. To hit a 12 percent savings rate, you only need to sock away 9 percent, because you'll get 3 percent from your employer.

If you want to fine-tune this number by factoring in how far you are from retirement and how much you have already saved, try playing around with one of the many online financial calculators. But given all the uncertainty about market returns, you should take these projections with a grain of salt.

JONATHAN'S TAKE: While I'm not advocating a life of self-imposed poverty, I would strongly suggest saving as much as you reasonably can whenever you can. In today's brutal job market, you don't know when your ability to save may be disrupted by a bout of unemployment or if you might be forced to retire earlier than planned.

According to the Employee Benefit Research Institute's 2014 Retirement Confidence Survey, workers on average expect to retire at age 65. But it turns out the actual retirement age is 62. Many of those retirements aren't voluntary, with folks leaving the workforce because of ill health or layoffs. It might be ideal to save just enough every month for the retirement we want. But the reality is considerably messier: We retire with whatever we have managed to amass by that juncture—and the more we have, the easier our retirement will be.

13. FINANCIAL CALCULATORS

Are you saving enough for retirement? To find out, try the Retirement Planner at Dinkytown.net (named after a neighborhood in Minneapolis). You can quibble that the calculator is overly simplistic and easily abused: It presumes you earn the same return year after year, which is unrealistic, and delusional folks can make everything look rosy by assuming an absurdly high rate of return. Still, it does offer a quick look at your retirement readiness. If you have something akin to a 60 percent stock–40 percent bond portfolio, override the default investment returns: For the period both before and during retirement, plug in a 5 percent annual return and 3 percent for inflation.

What's the problem with assuming the same return year after year? Check out FIRECalc.com, which drives home a key concept every retiree needs to grasp: sequence-of-return risk. The bottom line: If you get rotten returns early in retirement, you can quickly end up in financial trouble, even if average returns over your retirement are just dandy.

Looking to dig deeper into retirement or other financial issues? TRowePrice.com has an impressive collection of retirement tools, including its Retirement Income Calculator, which uses something called Monte Carlo analysis to see how you might fare in a host of different market scenarios. Also check out the Retirement Income Calculator at Vanguard.com.

14. WHERE TO STASH YOUR SAVINGS?

You are saving diligently for retirement—but where should you invest those savings? You'll want to give careful thought to your so-called asset allocation, which is your basic mix of stocks, bonds and other investments. You will also want to consider whether to stash your savings in a taxable account, your employer's 401(k), a Roth IRA or elsewhere. You can get detailed help with these two issues in Part VIII, which is devoted to investing, and Part X, which discusses taxes.

You might start by thinking about your human capital. You have a paycheck to cover your daily living expenses, so there's less need to buy conservative, income-generating investments. That frees you up to invest for the long haul by buying stocks, which can offer wretched short-term performance but healthy long-run gains. Because you won't need to spend all your savings on the day you quit the workforce, your investment time horizon if you're in your 20s might be six decades or more, which should be plenty of time to ride out a few rough spells in the stock market.

Your long time horizon also means you can make full use of retirement accounts. These involve a long-term commitment: There are typically tax penalties if you withdraw money before age 59½. But in return for that commitment, you can enjoy some great tax advantages, as well as a potential matching contribution if you fund your employer's retirement plan.

15. YOUR 50s AND EARLY 60s

If you're within 10 or 15 years of retirement, the financial "to do" list can be daunting. This is your last chance to use the income from your human capital to prep your finances for life without a paycheck.

Between now and retirement, you probably want to save as much as you can and get all debt paid off. You need to decide whether to stay in your current home and, if you'll move, whether it makes sense to move now, while you have a paycheck to cover the costs involved. If you retire before you become eligible for Medicare at age 65, you have to figure out how to cover health care costs. You should also consider how you will cope if you end up needing long-term care. Health care issues are covered in Part V.

Pay particular attention to two key questions. First, will you have enough retirement income, and where will this income come from? That means assessing how much you will have saved by retirement, and considering what portfolio adjustments and other steps you should take to turn these savings into a reliable income stream. You should also weigh when to claim Social Security and whether it makes sense to continue working part-time once you leave your fulltime job.

Second, give some thought to what you will do with your retirement. This might seem laughably easy as you imagine sleeping late, lingering over the newspaper, heading out for lunch, taking a nap and so on through the day. But this is unlikely to make for a fulfilling retirement.

16. A FULFILLING RETIREMENT

We spend decades saving for retirement, but we often give scant thought to what we'll do with all that free time. This can be a huge mistake.

We might imagine that what we want is more time to relax. But we aren't built to relax. Rather, thanks to our hunter-gatherer ancestors, we're built to strive. We are here today because they never let up in their quest for survival. Result: We're often happiest when engaged in activities that we think are important, we're passionate about, we find challenging and which give us that pleasant sense we're making progress.

We also tend to be happiest when we feel we are part of a community—another inherited instinct. Studies have found that people are more satisfied and tend to live longer if they have a robust network of friends and family.

What does this mean for your retirement? The answer will be different for all of us. But as you contemplate what you might do with your final 20 or 30 years, try thinking back to the times in your life when you were happiest. What was it about those times that made them so happy? Maybe it was the friends you were with or the projects you were engaged in. If you can figure out what you find most fulfilling, you could have the roadmap for a great retirement.

17. WILL YOU HAVE ENOUGH TO RETIRE?

Are you on track for a comfortable retirement? Here's how to get a quick sense for where you stand:

• Add up the savings you have for retirement. Plug this number into the Retirement Planner at Dinkytown.net, along with how much you expect to save in the years ahead and when you expect to retire. Override the default investment returns, inserting 5 percent as your expected portfolio performance and 3 percent for inflation.

• Use the Retirement Estimator at SocialSecurity.gov to calculate your likely benefit.

• Find out how much you will receive from any traditional employer pensions. For many folks, the number will be zero because these plans, unfortunately, are now relatively rare.

On track? You might have the option of retiring early. Falling short? You'll need to play catch-up. Either way, you may want to make some portfolio adjustments, while also getting a firm grip on your living expenses.

18. ADJUSTING YOUR PORTFOLIO

In your 20s, 30s and 40s, you might have invested heavily in stocks because you had a paycheck to cover your living expenses. When you retire, you give up that paycheck—and that has big implications for your portfolio. Suddenly, you want not just growth from your investments, but also income.

Later in this chapter, when we talk about issues facing those age 65 and older, we'll discuss how you might generate income from your savings while fending off the threat from both short-run market declines and long-run inflation. But to prepare your portfolio and make sure your impending retirement isn't derailed by a stock market crash, you should probably scale back your investment risk over the last 10 or 15 years before you quit the workforce. An example: While you may have had 80 percent of your money in stocks in your early 40s, you might move toward a mix of perhaps 50 percent stocks and 50 percent conservative investments by the time you retire.

The precise percentages will depend on a host of factors. For instance, if Social Security and any pension income will cover a large portion of your retirement living expenses, you might take more risk with your portfolio. On the other hand, if the bulk of your retirement income will come from savings or you have little stomach for market swings, you might be somewhat more conservative.

19. ESTIMATING EXPENSES

Think about how much you spend during a one-week vacation. Now, imagine being on vacation 52 weeks a year. The implication: You'll likely find ample opportunities to spend whatever retirement income you have.

How much do you need for a happy retirement? One rule of thumb suggests that, to retire in comfort, you need 80 percent of your preretirement income. But a 2014 survey by T. Rowe Price Group found that retirees were, on average, living on 66 percent of their preretirement income—and they reported being quite content.

Your ability to splurge on travel, entertainment and eating out will depend not only on your after-tax income, but also on how much of that income gets chewed up by fixed costs, so you might take a shot at estimating what those will be. We're talking here about expenses such as utilities, groceries, car payments and insurance premiums. Potentially, your two biggest fixed costs will be housing and debt payments. You may want to spend your final years in the workforce getting those two under control.

To that end, consider whether you ought to trade down to a smaller home, which may cut your maintenance expenses, utility bills, homeowner's insurance and property taxes. It may also allow you to pay off any remaining mortgage debt and perhaps free up home equity that can then be added to your retirement savings.

For many folks, eliminating their mortgage is the sign that retirement is finally affordable. What if there's no way you can get your mortgage paid off by the time you quit the workforce—and you foresee carrying the loan for many years after that? You might refinance your existing loan balance with a new 30-year mortgage. That could slash your monthly payments, because you're extending the loan's repayment over a much longer period.

20. EARLY RETIREMENT

If you take early retirement, there are three key issues you need to worry about. First, and most important, do you really have enough saved? In this chapter, we've talked about a 4 percent portfolio withdrawal rate. But if you're quitting the workforce in your 50s, you might play it a little safer and assume not a 4 percent withdrawal rate, but 3 percent instead.

Second, if you retire before age 59½, you could potentially face tax penalties if you tap your retirement accounts. There are ways around that, as you'll learn in Part X. Still, if your goal is early retirement, you may want to sidestep potential problems by building up your regular taxable account.

Third, if you retire before you turn age 65 and become eligible for Medicare, you'll likely need to buy your own health insurance. That's become easier, thanks to the launch of health care exchanges in each state. You might also cover yourself for 18 months by taking advantage of the so-called COBRA coverage that may be offered by your employer. For more on both topics, head to Part V.

21. PLAYING CATCH-UP

Doesn't look like you'll have enough saved for retirement? Here's how you could get back on track:

• Save like crazy. You might take advantage of catch-up contributions to 401(k) plans and IRAs. You can learn more in Part X.

• Slash your expenses. Get all debts paid off. Trade down to a smaller home now rather than waiting for retirement.

• Delay retirement. Suppose you put off retirement from, say, age 65 to 67. That will give you two more years to save and two more years to earn investment returns. You can also put off claiming Social Security and buying an income annuity for two additional years, which will give you extra income.

• Annuitize more of your savings. The best annuity available is Social Security. Already planning to delay Social Security until age 70, so you get the largest possible monthly check? If you want more guaranteed income, you might buy an immediate fixed annuity when you quit the workforce. Retirees are often reluctant to buy income annuities. But this can be a good strategy if your goal is to squeeze maximum lifetime income out of your savings.

• Work part-time in retirement. Suppose you can make $10,000 a year working part-time. That is like having an investment portfolio that is $250,000 larger, assuming a 4 percent withdrawal rate.

One warning: Don't try to compensate for your modest savings by gunning for outsized investment returns. That risky approach may backfire or you might panic during a market decline, thus ruining any chance of a comfortable retirement. What if your situation seems hopeless? In the next section, check out one possible strategy for those in rough financial shape.

22. WHEN ALL ELSE FAILS

Let's suppose you have little or nothing saved for retirement. What to do? You might focus on one overriding goal: not claiming Social Security retirement benefits until age 70.

Social Security is a wonderful income stream: It's government guaranteed, at least partially tax-free, it rises every year with inflation, you get it for as long as you live and your spouse may receive your benefit as a survivor benefit. By delaying until age 70, you ensure that you will get the maximum possible monthly benefit. With any luck, that monthly check will allow you to retire in moderate comfort.

Of course, you might lose your job or your employer might compel you to retire before age 70. If that happens, look to continue working, even if it's at a modest wage, so you can delay Social Security. If you're married and you were the family's main breadwinner, you might "file and suspend" once you reach your full retirement age, so your husband or wife can claim spousal benefits. That will give you additional income. We discuss this strategy in greater detail later in this chapter.

Meanwhile, save what you can. Also look to slash your cost of living. In particular, consider trading down to a less expensive home and try to get all debts paid off by the time you retire. With maximum Social Security benefits, some savings and low living costs, you may be able to enjoy a modest retirement.

23. AGE 65 AND BEYOND

If amassing enough savings to retire is life's toughest financial task, managing that money in retirement is the trickiest. Consider the juggling act ahead: You need your money to last at least as long as you do, while fending off the threat from long-run inflation and short-term market declines. You also need to be prepared for unexpected expenses—and perhaps the biggest is long-term care, which we discuss in Part V.

No single financial product will accomplish all of these tasks. Instead, you'll want to figure out the best combination of Social Security, pension and annuity income, as well as the right mix of stocks, bonds and cash investments. To that financial toolkit, you might add part-time work, long-term-care insurance and the equity in your home.

Once retired, you'll also have a few other financial tricks at your disposal. For instance, you could temporarily cut back your spending if there's a major market decline. In addition, as a retiree, you have a great opportunity to manage your annual tax bill. You no longer have a regular paycheck coming in. Instead, you're creating your own paycheck. Each year, you can decide whether to take money from a taxable source, such as traditional IRAs, or from accounts that won't have any tax consequences, such as cashing out part of your savings account or Roth IRA. You can read more about this in Part X.

24. LIFE EXPECTANCY

What is retirement's biggest financial risk? Simply put, you don't want to run out of money before you run out of breath. Therein lies the great conundrum: You don't know how long you'll need to make your savings last.

To get a handle on the issue, don't look at life expectancies as of birth. Those are dragged down by all the folks who die before reaching retirement age. Instead, you might consider life expectancies as of age 65. According to the Social Security Administration, a 65-year-old man's life expectancy is age 84, while a 65-year-old woman can expect to live until 87. Bear in mind that these are medians. Half of retirees will die before these ages and half will live longer.

How much longer? Social Security estimates that a quarter of today's 65-year-olds will live beyond age 90 and 10 percent will live beyond age 95. If you're a couple, you have two tickets to the life-expectancy lottery—and there's a good chance that at least one of you will live to a ripe old age.

The Society of Actuaries estimates that there is a 51.8 percent chance that one member of a couple will survive to age 90 and an 8.7 percent chance that both will survive to that age. The Society notes that this may underestimate the odds, because there's evidence that married couples live longer than those who are single, divorced or widowed. Want to check out your life expectancy as of your current age? Try the Life Expectancy Calculator at SocialSecurity.gov.

25. INFLATION

Short-term market declines get all the attention. But long-run inflation can prove far more threatening.

In recent years, inflation has been relatively subdued. Over the 12 months through November 2014, consumer prices—as measured by CPI-U, the most popular inflation measure—climbed 1.7 percent, excluding food and energy. (With food and energy included, the rate was 1.3 percent, thanks to the sharp drop in oil prices.) Imagine inflation continued to run at 1.7 percent during a retirement that lasted 30 years. By the end of three decades, the purchasing power of $1 would be reduced to just 60 cents.

Moreover, CPI-U may underestimate how much seniors are affected by rising prices. The Bureau of Labor Statistics has a separate measure, known as CPI-E, which is designed to gauge inflation as experienced by households with folks age 62 and up. CPI-E assigns greater weight to housing and medical care. Both items tend to eat up more of the income of older Americans. Over the 29 years through December 2011, CPI-E rose 3.1 percent a year, versus 2.9 percent for CPI-U.

It gets worse. Even if retirees can generate an income stream that rises with inflation, they will likely find themselves lagging behind their neighbors who are still in the workforce. Why? The standard of living rises not with inflation, but with per capita GDP, which in the U.S. has grown 2 percentage points a year faster than inflation over the past 50 years.

The implication: Even as you strive to generate current income, you need to prepare for higher prices down the road. That might mean looking for income streams that are indexed to inflation, seeking capital gains with part of your portfolio or possibly setting aside a portion of each year's investment income to spend in future years.

26. MARKET DECLINES

While you had a job, it might have been unnerving when the stock market declined. But there was no immediate impact on your standard of living. You had a paycheck to cover your daily living expenses, so it wasn't like you needed to sell stocks to buy groceries.

In fact, a market decline represented an opportunity. You could funnel part of your paycheck into stocks, thus taking advantage of the lower prices. Want to amass a healthy retirement nest egg? If you're a rational investor who is unperturbed by market turmoil, you should hope for lousy returns while you are saving for retirement, followed by a huge bull market as you approach the day you'll quit the workforce. That way, you would buy investments when they are cheap and sell when they're expensive.

What if you aren't so lucky, and you retire and get hit with a bear market? You aren't saving regularly anymore, so tumbling markets no longer represent a great buying opportunity. True, you could take advantage of the decline by shifting some of your money from bonds to stocks. But instead of buying, you are far more likely to be selling as you seek to generate income.

Indeed, now that your human capital has stopped providing you with a paycheck, you'll need your portfolio to play that role instead. That means designing a financial strategy that focuses less on growth and more on income—and which can limit the damage done by sinking markets.

27. YOUR RETIREMENT INCOME

Where will your retirement income come from? You will likely rely on some combination of six key sources:

Savings. You will want to think carefully about how you'll extract income from your portfolio—and how much you can safely withdraw each year.

Social Security. When should you claim Social Security? Many folks opt for benefits at the earliest possible age. But relying solely on savings during your initial retirement years, while delaying Social Security to get a larger monthly check, is often the smarter strategy.

Pension plans. Not many people have traditional defined benefit pension plans anymore. Consider yourself lucky if you do. But also give some thought to the threat from rising living costs, because your pension is probably fixed rather than growing along with inflation.

Income annuities. Don't have a pension plan but like the idea of predictable monthly income? In addition to delaying Social Security, you might look into buying an income annuity.

Part-time work. Working a few days each week could greatly ease any financial strain, while adding richness to your retirement.

Home equity. Tapping your home's value to pay for retirement can be as simple as trading down to a less expensive place, or it could involve the hefty cost of a reverse mortgage.

This list isn't exhaustive: You might also receive income from rental properties, installment payments from the sale of a business and perhaps even an inheritance. You'll want to consider what role each of the above six income sources will play, and how their role may change over time. For instance, part-time work might be important early in retirement, while home equity could be your financial backstop if you live longer than you planned for.

28. PORTFOLIO WITHDRAWALS

Financial experts often suggest retirees use a 4 percent portfolio withdrawal rate. For instance, if you retire with $400,000 in savings, that would mean $16,000 in pretax first-year portfolio income. You might be able to generate that income by purchasing a collection of bonds that yield 4 percent. Problem is, that would leave you vulnerable to inflation, which will reduce the purchasing power of your bond interest with every passing year.

To fend off the threat from inflation, you might allocate part of your savings to stocks, which have the potential to deliver long-run inflation-beating gains. But that creates a new set of headaches, because you will likely have to cope with nasty short-term market declines.

What to do? Instead of investing for yield, try aiming for a healthy total return through a combination of interest, dividends and share-price gains. To generate that return, you might have perhaps 50 percent in stocks and 50 percent in bonds. Every year, to get your 4 percent portfolio withdrawal, you could spend your dividends and interest, while also cashing in some of your stock market and bond market winners. What if you don't have any winners to sell because you just got hit with a big market decline? As a precaution, consider rigging up a robust financial safety net.

29. YOUR SAFETY NET

It's a retiree's worst nightmare: Your stocks are hammered by a market crash. Your bonds are battered by rising interest rates. Yes, you have your dividends and interest. But to get more income from your portfolio, you might be compelled to sell stocks and bonds at the worst possible time.

To avoid that nightmare scenario, which many retirees faced in 2008 and early 2009, try dividing your portfolio in two. You might allocate 80 percent to a mix of stocks and riskier bonds designed to deliver healthy long-run growth. Meanwhile, consider earmarking 20 percent for a cash cushion that's stashed in savings accounts, certificates of deposit, short-term bonds and similar investments. That 20 percent is equal to five years of portfolio withdrawals, assuming a 4 percent withdrawal rate.

Every year, you would pull spending money from the cash cushion. In good years for the market, you could replenish your cash cushion by selling winners from the growth portion of your portfolio. In bad years, you wouldn't do any selling. Thanks to the five years of portfolio withdrawals in your cash cushion, you could ride out a long bear market without selling stocks and bonds at distressed prices.

Don't like the cash cushion approach? Alternatively, you might again invest for long-run growth, but ensure you have enough income from dividends, interest, annuities, pensions, Social Security and other sources to cover at least your fixed living costs. If markets crash, you might cut out discretionary spending and live solely off this income stream until you can, once again, sell stocks and bonds at reasonable prices.

30. FOUR PERCENT WITHDRAWAL RATE

By the late 1990s, with almost two decades of robust investment returns under their belts, investors would talk about 6, 8 and even 10 percent as a reasonable rate at which to draw down a retirement portfolio. But researchers begged to disagree—and the financial markets provided brutal confirmation, hitting stock investors with back-to-back bear markets in 2000–02 and 2007–09.

Today, 4 percent is considered a safe withdrawal rate (though even that number has been called into question). What does that 4 percent represent? Let's say you retired with $500,000. A 4 percent withdrawal rate suggests you would pull out $20,000 from your portfolio in the first year of retirement and thereafter step up that sum each year with inflation. For instance, if inflation ran at 3 percent a year, you would withdraw $20,600 in year two, $21,218 in year three and so on.

Any dividends and income you receive would count toward the annual sum withdrawn. Also, this 4 percent is pretax. After all those years of tax-deferred growth in 401(k) plans and IRAs, the tax bill comes due in retirement. Once Uncle Sam takes his cut, you will have less than 4 percent to spend.

Here's another way to look at that 4 percent withdrawal rate: If you know how much retirement income you want from your portfolio, you should aim to amass 25 times that sum by the time you retire. Need $20,000 in first-year retirement income from your portfolio? To generate that sum using a 4 percent withdrawal rate, you'd want 25 times $20,000, or $500,000, saved by retirement.

According to studies, a 4 percent initial withdrawal rate coupled with annual inflation adjustments should allow you to make it through a 30-year retirement without depleting your savings. This might seem like a meager income stream. But it's necessary because of a major danger: sequence-of-return risk.

31. SEQUENCE-OF-RETURN RISK

Consider this hellish scenario: You retire with what you imagine is plenty of money—and you're immediately hit with a brutal market decline, even as you pull out a growing sum from your portfolio each year to cover rising living expenses. You quickly deplete your savings. A few years later, the markets bounce back. But you don't benefit much because, by then, your portfolio has been whittled down by your need for spending money.

This is a key reason researchers have suggested a 4 percent withdrawal rate. In most financial situations imaginable, you should be able to withdraw that much initially, step up the annual sum withdrawn with inflation and still make your savings last through a 30-year retirement.

Problem is, a 4 percent withdrawal rate may not give you enough retirement income. Moreover, the whole premise seems a little absurd—that you would not simply withdraw the same sum each year, but robotically increase it along with inflation, no matter how terribly the financial markets perform.

What's the alternative? You might initially spend closer to 5 percent. But if the markets turn against you, you should stand ready to slash your portfolio withdrawals.

32. VARYING YOUR SPENDING

When we think about the financial tools available to us, we often overlook a key lever: our ability to control how much we spend. It's typically a lot easier to cut our spending than to increase our income. That is especially true once we are retired and no longer pulling in a paycheck.

No matter what, you'll always have to cover your fixed monthly costs. That is why it's important to know what that number is and keep it at a reasonable level. By contrast, it's pretty easy to cut out discretionary spending—things like eating out, going to the movies and taking vacations. This is discussed further in Part VI, the chapter on spending.

That brings us to your retirement-income strategy. While a 4 percent withdrawal rate is a good guideline, you might potentially spend more, but with one proviso: If the markets have a major downturn, you immediately slash your spending and hence your portfolio withdrawals.

In fact, you might try a variation on the 4 percent withdrawal rate, which assumes you increase the sum withdrawn each year along with inflation. As an alternative, you could simply withdraw a sum each year equal to 5 percent of your beginning-of-year portfolio balance. Any dividends and interest payments would count toward the 5 percent.

In good markets, your annual withdrawals will automatically go up along with your portfolio's value. In bad years, your withdrawals will go down. Because you're always withdrawing a percentage of whatever you have left, you would never run out of money, though a string of bad years could leave you with drastically reduced income.

33. INTRODUCTION TO SOCIAL SECURITY

In 2012, 45 percent of men and 51 percent of women claiming Social Security retirement benefits were age 62, the youngest possible age. (This calculation excludes those on Social Security disability benefits who were automatically converted over to retirement benefits.) If these 62-year-olds were in poor health, claiming benefits right away might have been the right choice. But many were likely making a mistake.

You can claim Social Security as early as age 62 or as late as age 70. The longer you delay, the larger your benefit will be. The amount of the increase will depend on the year you were born and hence your full Social Security retirement age. But waiting carries a cost, because you don't get benefits during the intervening years. The big risk: You die early in retirement and get nothing back after a lifetime of paying Social Security payroll taxes. Still, delaying Social Security will make sense for many retirees for three reasons:

• It provides insurance against living a surprisingly long time—and the later you claim benefits, the more insurance you'll have. Remember, Social Security payments are stepped up every year with inflation and paid for as long as you live. By delaying, you buy yourself more of this income, which could prove invaluable if you live longer than expected and run through your other savings.

• It can provide spousal benefits to your husband or wife, who may also want to delay, thereby getting more income.

• It can provide a survivor benefit to your spouse. By waiting, you can ensure more income for your husband or wife after your death. In fact, it may be worth delaying Social Security even if you're in poor health, because your benefit could live on after your death.

JONATHAN'S TAKE: Social Security is such a wonderful source of retirement income that most folks, I believe, should delay benefits so they get a larger monthly check. Retirement's big financial risk isn't dying young, with scant money collected from Social Security. Rather, the big risk is living so long that you deplete your savings—at which point a fat Social Security check could be your financial salvation.

34. SOCIAL SECURITY ELIGIBILITY

To be eligible for Social Security, you need to have worked and paid Social Security payroll taxes for 40 quarters, equal to 10 years. Your benefit is calculated based on your 35 years with the highest earnings. If you don't work for the full 35 years, you are still eligible for Social Security, but your benefit will be lower. The average retirement benefit is roughly $1,300 a month, while the average spousal benefit is $650 a month.

If you claim benefits before your full Social Security retirement age, which will be either age 66 or 67, your benefit will be reduced if you're still working and your earnings are above certain thresholds. This is the so-called retirement earnings test. At issue here are earnings from paid employment, not income such as interest from your bond portfolio or withdrawals from your retirement accounts.

In 2015, if you earn more than $15,720, you will lose $1 of Social Security benefits for every $2 you earn above this threshold. In the year you reach your full Social Security retirement age, the threshold is more generous. You will lose $1 of benefits for every $3 you earn above $41,880. The earnings test only applies up until the month you reach your full Social Security retirement age.

Sound bad? It isn't as bad as it seems: Once you reach your full retirement age, your monthly benefit will be increased to reflect the benefits that were lost because of the earnings test.

35. CLAIMING BENEFITS EARLY AND LATE

How much of a haircut will you take if you claim Social Security early? To find out, you need to know your full Social Security retirement age—a crucial piece of information, especially if you're married and trying to figure out the best strategy for claiming benefits.

If you were born between 1943 and 1954 and hence your full Social Security retirement age is 66, your benefit will be reduced by 25 percent if you claim benefits at age 62, 20 percent if you claim at 63, 13.3 percent at 64 and 6.7 percent at 65.

If you were born in 1960 or later and hence your full Social Security retirement age is 67, your benefit will be reduced by 30 percent if you claim benefits at 62, 25 percent if you claim at 63, 20 percent at 64 and so on. For those born between 1955 and 1959, the reduction will fall somewhere between these two numbers.

What if you claim benefits after your full retirement age? Your benefit will increase by 8 percentage points for every year you wait. For instance, if your full retirement age is 66, at which point you would be eligible for $1,000 a month, you could receive $750 if you claim at 62 or $1,320 if you claim at 70—a difference of 76 percent. Similarly, if your full retirement age is 67 and you'll be eligible for $1,000 at that point, you could receive $700 at 62 or $1,240 at 70—a difference of 77 percent. These figures don't reflect any increases because of inflation.

If you live to an average life expectancy, you should—roughly speaking—find that you fare equally well no matter when you claim benefits. This "actuarial equivalence," however, doesn't take into account three valuable benefits that tilt the argument in favor of delaying: spousal benefits, survivor benefits and the financial safety net that Social Security provides in case you live longer than expected.

36. SPOUSAL BENEFITS

If you are married, you can receive a spousal benefit equal to as much as half your husband's or wife's benefit as of his or her full retirement age. If you claim a spousal benefit before your full retirement age, your benefit will be reduced.

The reduction can be severe. Check out the spousal benefit calculator available at SocialSecurity.gov. If your full retirement age is 66, your spousal benefit will be reduced by 30 percent if you claim at 62, 25 percent at 63 and so on. What if your full retirement age is 67? The reduction at 62 would be 35 percent, while at 63 it would be 30 percent. On the other hand, don't claim spousal benefits any later than your full retirement age. Why not? You don't get any credit for delaying beyond that point.

Keep two key provisions in mind. First, if you file for benefits before your full Social Security retirement age, you will be deemed to have filed for both spousal benefits and any benefit owed based on your own earnings record, and you'll get paid the higher of the two. It's only if you're at your full retirement age or later that you can file just for spousal benefits, while leaving your own benefit to continue growing.

That said, if you file for benefits before your full retirement age, you can always get benefits based on your own earnings record, but you may not be able to claim spousal benefits. Why not? That brings us to the second key provision: You can't receive spousal benefits until your husband or wife claims his or her benefit. Confused? It's helpful to look at different strategies that couples might use.

37. CLAIMING STRATEGIES FOR COUPLES

What's the best strategy for claiming Social Security benefits if you're married? Much will depend on how big a benefit you're each eligible for, your relative ages and when you stop working.

Unless you are both in poor health, it often makes sense for the spouse with higher lifetime earnings to delay claiming benefits until age 70. Let's be politically incorrect and assume that's the husband. Delaying until 70 ensures not only the maximum possible monthly benefit for the husband, but also a handsome survivor benefit for his wife, assuming the husband dies first.

Meanwhile, the wife might claim benefits based on her own earnings record at age 62. Once the husband reaches his full retirement age of 66 or 67, he might "file and suspend"—apply for benefits but postpone taking them. This will allow his wife to claim spousal benefits. The resulting payment may be higher than the benefit the wife had been receiving based on her own earnings record.

Alternatively, suppose both spouses want to delay Social Security until age 70. To ensure a little income in the meantime, the husband might file and suspend at his full retirement age, which will allow his wife to claim spousal benefits. The wife would file a restricted application, requesting spousal benefits only—an option that's only available once you reach your full retirement age.

A third possibility: The husband might delay his own benefit until age 70, while the wife starts benefits earlier. Once the husband reaches full retirement age, he could claim spousal benefits based on his wife's earnings record. For this strategy to work, the wife would need to have started her own benefit.

What if the husband is younger than his wife? It could make sense for the husband to claim benefits before his full retirement age, so his wife can receive spousal benefits. The husband might then suspend benefits from full retirement age through to age 70, thereby earning delayed retirement credits and increasing his benefit. Claiming early may also make sense if you have children still at home.

Need additional help? Check out the Social Security Benefits Evaluator at TRowePrice.com or SSAnalyze at BedrockCapital.com.

38. BENEFITS FOR DEPENDENT CHILDREN

When you claim Social Security retirement benefits, it isn't just your spouse who can receive benefits based on your earnings record. If you still have dependent children, they too may receive Social Security.

Unmarried children are eligible to receive benefits if they are under age 18, up to age 19 if they're still in high school and at any age if they become disabled before age 22. Your children may be eligible to receive a sum equal to as much as half of your benefit as of your full retirement age. Moreover, a spouse of any age may receive benefits if he or she is caring for a child who is under age 16 or who is disabled. A child can be a biological child, adopted, a stepchild and sometimes even a dependent grandchild.

There is, however, a limit to Social Security's generosity. The total amount paid out to you and your family is typically capped at between 150 and 180 percent of your full retirement age benefit. Spousal benefits paid to an ex-spouse don't count toward the family maximum.

If you are age 62 and have children who would qualify for benefits, you may want to claim benefits right away, despite the many sound reasons for delaying Social Security. After all, your children will only get older—and, if you delay claiming benefits, they might not receive any money from Social Security. Once you reach your full retirement age, you could always opt to suspend benefits, so you receive delayed retirement credits from then until age 70. That would increase both your monthly benefit and the survivor benefit that could eventually go to your spouse.

39. FILE AND SUSPEND

It's often smart for the higher-earning spouse to delay claiming Social Security until age 70. That way, you ensure not only the maximum monthly benefit during your lifetime, but also your spouse could receive your benefit as a survivor benefit. In effect, your larger benefit could live on after your death, which is why even those in poor health might consider delaying Social Security.

But delaying creates a problem: Your husband or wife can't claim spousal benefits until you claim your benefit. To get around this, consider a strategy known as "file and suspend." You can use this strategy once you reach your full retirement age, which would be either 66 or 67.

(Suspending benefits shouldn't be confused with withdrawing your application for benefits. The latter is a onetime option that's available within 12 months of starting benefits. It can be used before or after your full retirement age, and can help those who realize they have claimed benefits too early. But there's a sizable price to be paid: You have to repay the benefits already received, including benefits collected by family members based on your earnings record.)

How does file and suspend work? You file for benefits. That allows your husband or wife to claim spousal benefits. You then suspend your benefit until age 70 to get the larger monthly benefit and potential survivor benefit.

File and suspend can even make sense for single individuals. If you file and suspend, and your health subsequently takes a turn for the worse at, say, age 68, you can immediately restart benefits—and also claim the benefits held in suspension between your full retirement age and whenever you restarted. That might mean receiving a lump sum equal to two or three years of benefits. The downside: If you claim the benefits held in suspension, your monthly benefit thereafter will be the benefit you would have received as of your full Social Security retirement age, and thus you won't receive a larger monthly check for delaying beyond your full retirement age.

Because file and suspend can be so lucrative, especially for couples, there's talk in Washington of limiting its use. The strategy was targeted in the fiscal 2015 budget released by the White House in early 2014.

40. SURVIVOR BENEFITS

If your spouse dies, you can receive his or her benefit as a survivor benefit. The larger your spouse's benefit, the more you receive.

Keep a few key details in mind. If you're at your full retirement age or later, you will be entitled to 100 percent of your spouse's benefit as a survivor benefit. If you claim earlier, there will be a reduction. There are slight differences between the full retirement age for regular Social Security benefits and the full retirement age for survivor benefits.

Unless you care for a child who is under age 16 or who is disabled, or you're disabled yourself, you can't claim survivor benefits before age 60. If you claim at age 60, your survivor benefit will be 28.5 percent less than your deceased spouse's benefit. Unmarried children may also be eligible for benefits, possibly up until age 19, or if they're disabled.

You can't receive both survivor benefits and a benefit based on your own earnings record at the same time, but you can switch between the two. One strategy: If you're in your 60s, you might claim survivor benefits right away—but put off claiming your own benefit until age 70, at which point it might potentially be larger than your survivor benefit, thanks to the credits you receive for delaying. Alternatively, you might claim benefits based on your own earnings record at age 62, while delaying survivor benefits until your full Social Security retirement age, which would be 66 or 67.

One modest financial item: A surviving spouse is eligible to receive a $255 onetime payment from Social Security.

41. DIVORCE AND SOCIAL SECURITY

You may be entitled to retirement benefits based on your ex-husband or ex-wife's earnings record, assuming your marriage lasted at least 10 years. If you remarry, however, you lose this right. Instead, you could potentially claim benefits based on your new spouse's earnings record.

Similarly, you may be eligible for survivor benefits based on your late ex-spouse's earnings record. Again, the marriage must have lasted at least 10 years. As with a married spouse, you need to be at least age 60 or older to receive survivor benefits. In this case, it's okay if you are remarried—as long as you didn't remarry until after age 60.

None of this should cause your ex-spouse any concern: If you claim benefits based on his or her earnings record, it won't affect either your ex-spouse's benefit or those of, say, his or her new wife or husband.

42. SOCIAL SECURITY'S FUTURE

Once again in 2014, there was talk of fixing Social Security so that the benefits paid out don't greatly exceed the Social Security payroll taxes that are collected. There are different fixes being bandied about, including changing the inflation measure used to increase benefits each year or raising the eligibility age for Social Security.

Eventually, there will likely be some fix made, but you shouldn't be too alarmed by that prospect. First, Social Security's unfunded liability is considerably smaller than that for Medicare, and thus it could probably be addressed without action that's too drastic.

Second, any major changes to Social Security will likely only apply to those under age 50 or 55, so younger workers should have plenty of time to adjust and potentially compensate by saving more for retirement.

What if you are already retired? It's almost inconceivable that any politician hoping to get reelected would vote to cut benefits for those who have reached retirement age. The outcry would be deafening. One implication: If you're, say, age 62, you shouldn't rush to claim benefits now, fearing the government will slash your Social Security benefit.

43. PENSION PLANS

If you're a participant in a defined benefit pension plan, ask yourself two questions. First, what happens if your pension plan doesn't pay as promised? Even if your employer seems committed to its pension plan today, much could change between now and when you retire—and perhaps even after you retire. If you're a public sector employee, maybe a fiscal crunch will force big budget cuts, including cuts to the pension plan. If you're a private sector employee who works for a seemingly healthy company, maybe there are financial shenanigans you're unaware of. Perhaps the company will get hit with a business-crippling lawsuit. Maybe your employer will get taken over in a leveraged buyout, the resulting debt proves too burdensome and the company ends up in bankruptcy.

Given all this uncertainty, it's prudent to have other retirement savings. If the pension plan doesn't come through, those additional savings could salvage your retirement. If the plan pays as promised, you will no doubt be happy to have the extra savings.

That brings us to the second question: What about inflation? Most pensions pay monthly benefits that aren't indexed for inflation. That means the benefit you receive at age 65 could have substantially less buying power by the time you're 80 or 85. To ensure your standard of living doesn't suffer too much as you grow older, you might save part of each pension check during the early years of retirement—or, alternatively, take the precaution of building up a decent pool of savings during your working years.

44. INCOME ANNUITIES

Social Security, with its guaranteed stream of inflation-indexed income, is arguably the best income annuity available. This is why you should give serious thought to delaying Social Security, so you get the largest possible check.

Even if you delay benefits, you may want more lifetime income. That's where income annuities come in. There are four types you might consider:

Immediate fixed annuities. These can provide a check every month for life, though—unlike Social Security—that check usually doesn't increase with inflation.

Charitable gift annuities. These are similar to immediate fixed annuities, except you buy from your favorite charity, not an insurance company. The downside: Charitable gift annuities typically pay less income. The upside: If you die early in retirement, your favorite charity stands to benefit, rather than an insurance company. Charitable gift annuities, along with charitable remainder trusts, are discussed in Part XII.

Longevity insurance. This provides lifetime income starting at a future date, thus addressing the financial risk of living a surprisingly long time.

Variable annuities that generate income. These are complicated products that offer the chance to generate lifetime income, while still investing for long-run growth. Some allow you to add a so-called living benefits rider, while others can be converted into immediate variable annuities.

JONATHAN'S TAKE: Retirees are often reluctant to buy income annuities, just as they're reluctant to delay Social Security. I think this is a mistake. Delaying Social Security and buying income annuities can be the key to a more comfortable, less financially stressful retirement. Both strategies make particular sense for those looking to squeeze maximum income out of their savings. Intrigued by income annuities? I'd check out longevity insurance and plain-vanilla, immediate fixed annuities.

45. IMMEDIATE FIXED ANNUITIES

With an immediate fixed annuity, you hand over a wad of money to an insurance company and, in return, the insurer sends you a check every month for a specified period. You can purchase annuities that will pay income for, say, 10 or 20 years. But if your financial worry is living longer than expected, you'll want to buy an annuity that pays lifetime income.

To get a sense for how much income an annuity might generate, check out ImmediateAnnuities.com and IncomeSolutions.com. Suppose a husband and wife are both age 70 and they use $100,000 of their savings to buy an annuity that pays the same income every year for life. According to ImmediateAnnuities.com, as of late December 2014, the annuity would pay $7,668 every year if the husband buys, $7,032 if the wife buys and $6,168 if the annuity pays income until the second spouse dies.

Insurers know that income annuities tend to be bought by folks who think they'll live longer than average, so the payout may not be as generous as you had hoped. As you'll see, the older you are when you buy, the more income you can receive. If you buy when interest rates are higher, that should also mean a larger monthly check.

You can get an annuity that pays income just for your life or for the life of both you and your spouse. You can also get various guarantees, such as payments made for a minimum number of years, even if you die earlier. You almost always pay a price for these guarantees in the form of lower monthly income.

Still, the guarantees highlight the big fear with immediate fixed annuities—that you'll make a big investment and keel over a few months later, having received little income from your big annuity investment. You might address this fear by making smaller annuity purchases over the course of perhaps five or 10 years. This will also allow you to buy from a variety of insurers, thus reducing the risk that your retirement will be imperiled by any one insurer going bankrupt, and perhaps purchase at higher interest rates, should they rise from today's modest levels. Alternatively, you might explore a charitable gift annuity, where the beneficiary of your early demise would be your favorite charity. These are discussed in Part XII.

46. LONGEVITY INSURANCE

Suppose you retired at age 65 and you knew it would all be over at 85. That would make generating retirement income relatively easy: You might spend 1/20th of your savings in year one, 1/19th in year two and so on. Problem is, there's a decent chance you will live beyond 85. That is where longevity insurance can help.

Longevity insurance, also called a deferred income annuity, is essentially an annuity that pays lifetime income starting at some future date. Because there's no guarantee that you will live that long, let alone collect a lot of income if you do, this has the potential to be a relatively low-cost way of dealing with longevity risk. For every $100 you invest in a deferred income annuity at age 65, you might receive $30 a year of income starting at age 85. You could use perhaps 15 percent of your savings to purchase longevity insurance that kicks in once you turn age 85. Meanwhile, you might spend down the other 85 percent of your savings between now and age 85 using the strategy described in the first paragraph.

You can purchase pure longevity insurance that pays only if you live to the specified age. But many folks, fearful they will die without getting any money back from their insurance purchase, opt for various guarantees. These guarantees carry a cost, which is paid in the form of lower future income.

Don't like the idea of longevity insurance? You could designate 15 or 20 percent of your portfolio for the post-age 85 period. If you live that long and you're in good health, you might use this money to buy an income annuity. If your health isn't so good, you could simply spend down your remaining savings. What if you don't live until age 85? The money could make a handsome inheritance.

47. LIVING BENEFITS

Variable annuities are tax-deferred savings vehicles, not unlike IRAs but more costly. We'll talk more about them in Part X. These variable annuities can be used to generate lifetime income, while still leaving you as owner of the account's assets, by adding a living benefits rider.

There are two types of rider that can provide lifetime income: a guaranteed lifetime withdrawal benefit (GLWB) and a guaranteed minimum income benefit (GMIB). With a GLWB, you might be assured annual income equal to 4 to 6 percent of your account's initial value, depending on your age when you begin withdrawals. If your investment choices perform well, your annual income can rise.

With a GMIB, there might also be a 4 to 6 percent initial guarantee, which you can take as a withdrawal or use to increase your "income base," which is an accounting device that's distinct from the account's actual value. The increased income base will mean higher income in future years.

What if you add a GMIB rider and then deplete the annuity's actual value through some combination of withdrawals and bad investment performance? After a waiting period, which is typically 10 years from the time you added the GMIB rider, you can swap into an immediate fixed annuity. That annuity will give you regular income for life based on your income base. This immediate fixed annuity may pay less income than the amount you were initially receiving based on the 4 to 6 percent.

The big problem with living benefits: Not only are they complicated, but also the annual costs are high. Those costs crimp performance, so there's a risk your income won't increase over time. What to do? In an effort to boost performance, you might invest the annuity heavily in stocks. That way, you are also taking advantage of the downside protection that's costing you so much. If your investment bets go wrong, you can always fall back on the annuity's guaranteed minimum.

48. IMMEDIATE VARIABLE ANNUITIES

Instead of adding a living benefits rider, you can squeeze income out of a tax-deferred variable annuity by converting it to an immediate variable annuity. But there's a crucial difference between the two. A variable annuity with living benefits leaves you as owner of the account's assets. With an immediate variable annuity, you surrender ownership to the insurance company.

Indeed, immediate variable annuities are an odd beast: As with an immediate fixed annuity, you hand over a lump sum to an insurance company in return for lifetime income. But unlike with an immediate fixed annuity, you still get to call the shots on how the immediate variable annuity is invested. As with other variable annuities, there's a menu of investment options you can choose from.

Your goal: Pick investments that beat a hurdle rate of return, known as the "assumed interest rate," which typically ranges from 3 to 7 percent a year. The higher the AIR and the older you are when you buy the annuity, the more income you initially receive. But a high AIR has a drawback: For your income to grow, the investments you select within the variable annuity need to generate annual returns that outpace this hurdle rate. What if you fall short? Your monthly income will decline.

You also need to pay close attention to a variable annuity's costs. The higher those costs, the harder it will be for your investments to earn decent performance and thereby outpace the hurdle rate of return.

49. SPENDING HOME EQUITY

If your retirement savings are on the skimpy side, you might tap into the value of your home. Consider three strategies.

The safest strategy is to trade down to a less expensive home. Selling one home and buying another can be both costly and a hassle. Still, this has the potential not only to free up home equity that you can then spend, but also it may lower your living costs, including property taxes, utilities, homeowner's insurance and maintenance expenses.

The least expensive but riskiest strategy is to refinance your home by taking out a 30-year mortgage for as much as the bank will let you borrow. Thereafter, you'll have to make regular mortgage payments again, presumably drawing on the money you got in the refinancing. But if you do the refinancing late in retirement and your life expectancy is 10 years or less, the refinancing should leave you with money for other expenses. The risk: If you live longer than expected or you spend too freely, you might end up without money to pay the mortgage—and you'd be in a heap of trouble.

Finally, you might take out a reverse mortgage. With all the fees involved, coupled with the need for you or your heirs eventually to sell the house, this has the potential to be the costliest strategy. But as long as you're careful, a reverse mortgage should allow you to stay in your home for the rest of your life.

50. REVERSE MORTGAGES

A reverse mortgage lets you borrow against the value of your home without paying back any of the loan during your lifetime. Instead, the loan is repaid when you move permanently or, more likely, after your death. At that juncture, the total amount owed, including all accrued interest, can't exceed your home's value. You can typically borrow more if you're older, interest rates are low or your house is appraised at a high value. The money received is tax-free.

The big downside is cost. To get a handle on the expenses involved, try playing with the calculator offered at ReverseMortgage.org, which is the website of the National Reverse Mortgage Lenders Association. At the bottom of the calculation, you'll see a figure for "Total Fees & Costs." This doesn't, however, tell the entire story. At the top of the estimate, check out the initial loan interest rate—which will likely be higher than on a conventional mortgage —and the charge for mortgage insurance that's layered on top of that.

In addition, keep in mind that you still have to handle the home's maintenance, property taxes and insurance. If those expenses prove too burdensome, you may be compelled to move, at which point the reverse mortgage has to be repaid. There have also been problems because just one spouse was listed on the reverse mortgage, that spouse dies or moves to a nursing home, and the surviving spouse has had to deal with demands to repay the loan.

JONATHAN'S TAKE: Despite all the drawbacks, I wouldn't rule out a reverse mortgage. Let's face it: You get only one shot at retirement and you should make the most of it, even if it means spending assets you had hoped to bequeath to your children. That said, I would consider a reverse mortgage a last resort, not your first choice.

PART III

HOUSES
BUYING FOR THE WRONG REASONS, STAYING FOR THE VIEW

Don't own a home? Eventually, you should probably make the switch from renter to owner—for five reasons.

First, with a fixed-rate mortgage, you lock in your housing costs and thereby protect yourself against a booming real estate market that drives up rents and property prices. An adjustable-rate mortgage doesn't offer the same degree of certainty, though typically there are caps on how much your monthly payment can increase.

Second, as you pay down your mortgage, you come to own a valuable asset outright. Think of a mortgage as forced savings, with a portion of every monthly payment going toward reducing your loan's principal balance.

Third, once your mortgage is paid off, you eliminate a major expense, making it easier to retire because you can now live "rent-free."

Fourth, home prices historically have increased slightly faster than consumer prices, acting as a hedge against inflation. Inflation also effectively trims the cost of your mortgage, because it allows you to pay off the loan with dollars that are less valuable.

Finally, Congress has showered homeownership with tax breaks. You can deduct your mortgage interest and property taxes. Up to $500,000 of your home's price appreciation may be tax-free when you sell. There's also a less obvious advantage: If you rented out your home, you would have to pay taxes on the rent you receive. But there's no tax owed when you rent to yourself.

Yet, even with these five advantages, things can go terribly wrong. While 2014 was a good year for housing, many homeowners are still underwater thanks to the bust that began in mid-2006. Want to avoid making major mistakes? Check out this chapter's five key steps to take in 2015—and then read about the housing myths you ought to avoid.

51. TODAY'S REAL ESTATE MARKET

How did the property market fare last year? Let's look at the numbers:

• Home prices rose 4.6 percent over the 12 months through October 2014, as measured by S&P/Case-Shiller's U.S. National Home Price Index.

• The national median sales price for an existing home was $205,300 as of November, reports the National Association of Realtors. This average disguises huge variations, with even modest homes in cities on the two coasts often costing three or five times as much. Home sales rose 2.1 percent over the past year, while the inventory of homes for sale increased 2 percent.

• As of year-end 2014, a 30-year fixed rate mortgage cost 4.04 percent, down from 4.68 percent at year-end 2013.

• Housing has become slightly less affordable over the past year, calculates the National Association of Realtors. Affordability is assessed by looking at the typical home price, typical family income and current mortgage rates.

• Homeownership remains widespread, with 65.2 percent of American families owning their home and 13.2 percent owning a place that isn't their main residence, according to the Federal Reserve's 2013 Survey of Consumer Finances. That 13.2 percent includes second homes, rental properties and time shares. The survey also found that, among homeowners, 65.9 percent have a mortgage or other debt that's secured by their home.

52. FIVE STEPS FOR 2015

Want to take a fresh look at your housing situation? Start with these five steps:

• If you currently rent, use the mortgage calculator at Bankrate.com to figure out how big a mortgage you could support with your monthly rent payments. That will give you a sense for whether homeownership is within reach.

38

• If you currently own, calculate your mortgage payment, including property taxes and homeowner's insurance, as a percentage of your pretax monthly income. If the number is well above 30 percent, you may have bought more house than you can comfortably afford. We discuss debt ratios further in Part XI.

• Think about the rooms in your house. Besides any bedroom set aside for guests, are there rooms you rarely or never use? That may be a sign you own more house than you really need—and perhaps you ought to trade down.

• Planning to buy a home in the near future? Get your finances in shape, including checking your credit reports and credit score. After you read this chapter, consider heading to Part XI, which is devoted to managing debt, including mortgages.

• Looking to sell your house in the near future? Get the place in shape. With the need to clear out any clutter, touch up the paint, spruce up the yard and more, this could take many months.

53. HOUSING MYTHS

Housing is a source of endless confusion—which isn't surprising given that there are so many issues to consider, including attractive tax breaks, fluctuating property prices, leverage from any mortgage debt, and the monthly mortgage payment's shifting mix of interest and principal. Here are five common myths:

"You can't go wrong with real estate." You heard this often before and during the real estate bubble, but far less frequently since the brutal decline that saw homes lose more than a quarter of their value between mid-2006 and early 2012. The potential for another decline should factor into your decision about whether to rent or buy.

"My house is the best investment I've ever made." Paying down a mortgage forces people to save and owning a house gives them a place to live. But what about home price appreciation? Historically, that's been modest and largely offset by the costs of homeownership.

"The bank owns half my house." Not true. The bank merely lent you money. Unless you plan to go into foreclosure, you own 100 percent of your home—and benefit from any price increase and suffer any decline.

"You should take out the largest mortgage possible." Many homeowners think mortgage interest is some sort of financial freebie. Think again. If you're in the 25 percent federal income tax bracket, pay $1 of mortgage interest and itemize your deductions, you'll save just 25 cents in federal taxes—which means the other 75 cents is coming out of your pocket.

"Our new kitchen added $100,000 to our home's value." The home may have climbed in value. But the boost from the new kitchen was almost certainly less than its cost. When homeowners sell, they typically don't fully recoup the full cost of their remodeling projects.

54. BUY OR RENT?

Homeownership offers many advantages, which we detailed at the start of this chapter. But there's no guarantee you will make money, especially if you own a house for just a few years. Thinking of purchasing a home? Here are four caveats.

First, given the risk of declining property prices, you shouldn't buy unless you can see staying put for at least five years and preferably seven years or longer. Even now, more than eight years after the real estate market peaked, prices in many places are below the heady levels of mid-2006. While it's hard to imagine we will suffer another decline of similar magnitude any time soon, a smaller drop is entirely possible.

Second, homes are horribly expensive to buy and especially sell, which is another reason you need a long time horizon. There's the mortgage-application fee, home inspection, title insurance and legal fees when you buy—and the 5 or 6 percent real estate brokerage commission and local transfer taxes when you sell. Suppose your home's price rises a few percentage points a year, but you end up selling after just five or six years. Once you figure in all the costs of buying and selling, you may not make money.

Third, homeownership involves hefty ongoing costs. On top of the mortgage payments, you'll have property taxes, homeowner's insurance and regular maintenance.

Finally, if you can't make the regular payments on your home, your financial life can unravel fast. That's why, before you buy, it is important to have a strong sense that your job is secure and a backup plan in case you're wrong. That plan might include not only a healthy emergency fund, but also a list of expenses you'll slash if your income suddenly drops. Both topics are discussed in Part V.

55. REAL ESTATE RETURNS

Folks are fascinated by what their homes are worth. Along the way, they make all kinds of dubious claims about how much they've made—and they miss the big story. Want to get a better grip on your home as an investment? For the moment, forget about your mortgage and focus just on home price appreciation.

Historically, homes have not been a great source of price appreciation. According to Freddie Mac, U.S. home prices climbed 3.7 percent a year over the 30 years through September 2014, not much ahead of the 2.8 percent inflation rate.

Next, think about all the ongoing costs that homeowners incur, such as maintenance expenses, homeowner's insurance and property taxes. These costs will vary widely. Property taxes are much steeper in some parts of the country than others. Insurance can be significantly higher if there's a risk of extreme weather, flooding or earthquakes. Regular maintenance—not to be confused with home improvements—will be greater if you own an older home.

If you add up all these expenses, they might equal 2 or 3 percent of a home's value each year. Deduct these costs from a home's price appreciation and many homeowners will find they are lagging far behind inflation, and perhaps barely breaking even.

Unfortunately, the expenses don't end there. There are the costs to buy a home, including mortgage-application fees, lawyers, title insurance, home inspections and possibly private mortgage insurance. You'll pay even more when you sell, notably a substantial commission to the real estate agents involved.

All of this might be true, you concede. But what happens once you figure in the mortgage? That mortgage can potentially take even modest gains and leverage them into big money.

56. LEVERAGE

Suppose you purchase a $300,000 home. To avoid taking out private mortgage insurance, you make a 20 percent down payment, equal to $60,000. You borrow the other $240,000 using a 30-year fixed-rate mortgage with a 5 percent interest rate. Five years later, your home is worth $360,000, or 20 percent more than you paid.

Your gain, however, looks considerably larger. Your home equity, which was initially $60,000 thanks to your down payment, has grown to $120,000. That's the wonder of leverage: A 20 percent rise in your home's value translated into a 100 percent increase in your home equity. In fact, your home equity would be closer to $140,000, because you would have whittled down the $240,000 mortgage balance to almost $220,000 with your first five years of monthly mortgage payments.

But leverage is not always so kind. From the mid-2006 peak to the early 2012 trough, home prices tumbled 27.4 percent, as measured by the S&P/Case-Shiller U.S. National Home Price Index. In the above example, that decline would have left you underwater, wiping out both your $60,000 down payment and the $20,000 you had trimmed from the mortgage balance with your five years of monthly payments.

Moreover, even if your home's value had climbed by 20 percent to $360,000, you would have paid a high price for that appreciation. Over those first five years, you would have coughed up almost $58,000 in mortgage interest, as well as homeowner's insurance, property taxes and maintenance expenses. Sound bad? It gets worse: If you tried to cash in your gain and paid a 5 percent real estate commission to sell your $360,000 home, you would immediately lose $18,000.

Yet none of this should dissuade you from buying a house. We're still missing the final piece of the puzzle: the so-called imputed rent.

57. IMPUTED RENT

Okay, real estate price appreciation is nothing to write home about. Okay, the benefits of leverage might be offset by the cost of the mortgage. In fact, once you figure in all the expenses involved in buying, owning and selling a home, there's a good chance you are losing money big-time. But you get to live in the place, right?

That is, indeed, the big payoff from homeownership. If you live in your own home, you are essentially renting the place to yourself. Think about how much you might pay each year if you didn't own your current home and instead had to make monthly payments to a landlord. While your home might appreciate just 3 percent a year, the annual value of this imputed rent could be equal to 7 percent of your home's value. That 7 percent is the big allure of investing in rental properties.

But if you're the person living in the house, nobody is paying you this 7 percent. In essence, your home is part consumption—you get to live there—and part investment, which is the price appreciation. And the consumption part is significantly more valuable than the investment part.

JONATHAN'S TAKE: Whether you're buying a principal residence or a vacation property for your own use, you need to keep in mind the crucial distinction between price appreciation and imputed rent. You are unlikely to make much from home price appreciation, once you factor in all costs. You will enjoy large sums of imputed rent, but you're the one consuming that imputed rent. The implication: You should focus on buying homes that you can comfortably afford and that'll give you a lot of pleasure—because that pleasure is the big return from owning real estate.

58. BUYING A HOME

Thinking of buying a home? Before you start bidding on properties, ask yourself five questions:

How long will you stay put? If you think you'll move within five years, perhaps because of your job or because the house you can currently afford won't really be big enough, buying may not be smart. It would likely be better to wait until you can purchase a place you'll be happy with for the long haul.

How much can you borrow? A mortgage lender may be willing to let you take on total monthly mortgage payments, including principal, interest, homeowner's insurance and property taxes, equal to 28 percent or so of your pretax monthly income. We have more on mortgages in Part XI.

How much can you put down? Ideally, you should save enough to put down 20 percent of the purchase price, so you avoid taking out private mortgage insurance. Even if you can't scrape together 20 percent, the more you put down, the less you may have to pay in private mortgage insurance. Coming up short? You might be eligible for a $10,000 penalty-free withdrawal from your individual retirement account, which we discuss in Part X.

The down payment isn't the only cost you will incur. Mortgage application fees, legal costs, a home inspection and title insurance could easily amount to $3,000 to $6,000, and maybe more.

Where should you buy? In tackling that question, give particular thought to two issues. First, are the schools good? If not, you might find yourself paying for private schools, which is an expensive proposition. Even if you don't have children, good schools can bolster property prices. Second, how long will your commute be? Research suggests that a long commute is one of the biggest causes of unhappiness.

What other costs will you face? Beyond the down payment and closing costs, give some thought to other expenses you might incur. What are the property taxes? Will you need to spend substantial sums on remodeling, either immediately or within the first few years?

59. SELLING A HOME

Prepping a home for sale can take months, so give yourself ample time. What needs to be done—and what shouldn't you do? Here are some pointers:

Skip the remodeling. Most home improvements are money losers, so you shouldn't undertake extensive remodeling with a view to turning a profit when you sell. On the other hand, smaller improvements—a fresh coat of paint, a tidier garden, refinishing the bathtub—could be worthwhile, because they may make your home easier to sell.

Go neutral. If you paint the bedrooms or retile the kitchen or bathroom, favor colors and patterns that are less likely to offend. No matter how tasteful you think your decorating is, many potential buyers will likely disagree. When you ready your home for sale, you should also remove personal pictures and get rid of clutter. The goal: Organize your home so buyers can see themselves living there, not you.

Negotiate the commission. The 6 percent real estate agent's commission, once standard, is fast becoming history. You should pay less than 6 percent unless there's something about your home that will make it extremely difficult to sell, such as the need for major repairs or an environmental problem.

Price realistically. To win your business, an agent might suggest your home is worth some fancy price. But do your own research, including checking listings for comparable homes.

If it's clear you are asking too much, move quickly to lower the price to a more compelling level, rather than making a series of small price drops that might make your home seem like tainted goods to potential buyers. That's especially true if your home is sitting empty. You aren't getting any use from the house, but you are incurring all the carrying costs, plus the equity tied up in the house could be invested elsewhere and earning gains.

60. SELLING YOURSELF

The precise number is a matter of some debate: Still, each year, it seems 10 to 20 percent of homes are sold directly by owners, rather than through a real estate agent. Should you, too, try selling your own home?

Sellers can list their homes using sites such as BuyOwner.com, ByOwner.com, ForSaleByOwner.com, Owners.com and Zillow.com. Many of these sites charge if you want more than a basic listing. Even so, with traditional real estate agents often taking 5 or 6 percent of the proceeds from a sale, the potential savings are huge.

The potential hassles, however, are also great. You need to be available to show your home at any time, often on short notice. Buyers are frequently suspicious of homes that are listed without an agent, fearful that the properties may have undisclosed problems. Many sellers also hurt their cause by pricing their homes too high. Before you list your home, be sure to study the local property market and carefully prepare your home for sale.

Among folks who endeavor to sell on their own, many throw in the towel and end up using an agent. But if you aren't in a rush, trying initially to find a buyer by yourself could be a smart move. Want to learn more? You can find an extensive library of articles at BuyOwner.com,

ForSaleByOwner.com and Owners.com.

61. REAL ESTATE AGENTS

Despite the cost involved, the vast majority of homeowners continue to use a broker when they sell. Real estate commissions were once a standard 6 percent of the proceeds from a home's sale. Today, 5 percent is increasingly common, with the commission set at perhaps 4 percent if the seller's agent also manages to find the buyer, without involving another agent. But whether it's 6, 5 or 4 percent, it's a lot of money, though maybe not as lucrative to the broker as you imagine.

Suppose you're selling your home and you have negotiated a 5 percent commission with your real estate agent. If the house sells for $400,000, the commission will nick $20,000 out of your proceeds. Your agent will have a big payday, but he or she won't be getting the full $20,000. The commission will have to be split with the buyer's agent, and the real estate brokerage firms that employ the two brokers will also get their take. Result: Your agent, especially if he or she isn't a high producer, might personally pocket just $5,000, or 1.25 percent of the gross proceeds.

Because the percentage is so small, your agent's greatest incentive isn't to garner the highest possible price, but rather to get the deal done as quickly as possible. Suppose you hold out for an extra $20,000 and it takes an extra six weeks to sell your home. You'll pocket perhaps $19,000 more, which you would no doubt be happy about. But your agent may collect just a few hundred additional dollars, despite weeks of extra work.

62. ASSESSING THE LOCAL MARKET

As 2015 begins, the national housing market appears to be at a comfortable midpoint, neither as crazed as it was in 2005 nor as depressed as it was in 2011. Still, it's not terribly helpful to talk about the national market, because there's so much variation across the country.

For instance, according to the S&P/Case-Shiller real estate indexes, the Miami and San Francisco markets posted gains of more than 9 percent in the year through October 2014, while prices in Charlotte, Chicago, Cleveland, Minneapolis, New York, Phoenix and Washington, DC, were up less than 3 percent.

How can you get a handle on the local property market? Ask a local real estate agent for details on recent sales, including how long it's taking properties to sell and how final selling prices compare to list prices. Visit real estate sites such as Realtor.com, Trulia.com and Zillow.com. Go to open houses in your neighborhood—even if you're looking to sell, not buy. That way, you can get a reality check on whether you are pricing your home properly.

If you are looking both to sell and buy within the same local market, you shouldn't be too bothered if the market is buoyant or depressed. Even if you're suffering on one side of the transaction, by receiving too little or paying too much, you presumably are benefiting on the other side.

Buying in a market that's overly exuberant? Think twice before getting into a bidding war. You could end up suffering from the so-called winner's curse. What's that? Winners of bidding wars often discover they paid too much, while those with cooler heads had a better handle on the home's value. Before you blithely boost your bid by $20,000, think about how many months you would have to work to save that sort of money.

63. REMODELING

When you sell your home, you might make back 60 to 80 percent of the money spent on remodeling projects. For proof, check out Remodeling magazine's annual survey at CostvsValue.com. The survey is based on selling your home within a year of making the improvements.

For example, according to the 2014 survey, a bathroom addition costs an average $38,186, but you might recoup just $22,940, or 60.1 percent, if you sell soon after. The longer you wait to sell, the less you are likely to recoup, because your improvements will no longer look spanking new.

In other words, as with homeownership in general, remodeling is part consumption and part investment. With that in mind, you should go ahead with remodeling projects only if they will give you pleasure commensurate with the dollars spent and not because you think they will boost your home's value.

That said, if you're concerned about your home's resale value, you should probably avoid fixing up your home to the point where it's fancier than most others in the area. Instead, you are more likely to get a fair price if your house is comparable to others in the neighborhood.

In the market for a new home? Because remodeling projects tend to be money losers, you might look for a home that has been fixed up to your liking. That way, you may be able to buy the owner's home improvements at a discount.

64. RENTAL PROPERTIES

For many ordinary Americans, buying properties and renting them out has been a road to financial success. Typically, the strategy is to find places where the rental income can cover the mortgage payments and other ongoing costs. That way, the tenant effectively pays off your loan, plus you also benefit from any price appreciation. As you raise the rent over time, you can get to the point where you aren't merely covering costs, but pocketing a tidy sum each month.

Sound attractive? Keep three drawbacks in mind. First, your tenants won't treat the place the way you would. In shopping for rental properties, you might favor homes that are somewhat rundown. That way, it will matter less if the tenants are a little rough on the place.

Second, being a landlord is hard work. You will occasionally have to find new tenants and you will have yet another home to maintain. Even if you don't do the maintenance yourself, you'll need to find others to do the work—and that means not only extra costs, but also extra hassles. You could hire a property management firm to handle all these issues, though that might cost you 10 percent or more of your rental income.

Third, a rental property represents a big undiversified bet. Your tenants may fail to pay the rent, at which point you'll have no help when it comes to meeting the mortgage and paying other costs. Even if your tenants are well-behaved, they may not stick around for long. That means you may have short periods without any rental income.

65. TAXES WHEN SELLING A HOME

When you sell your primary residence, you can avoid capital gains taxes on $250,000 of appreciation, or $500,000 if you're married filing jointly. To qualify for the $250,000 or $500,000 exclusion, you need to have lived in the house for at least 24 months during the prior five years.

What if your capital gain is more than these sums? You can add certain items to your home's cost basis, such as some of your closing costs and the amount spent on home improvements. That will trim your taxable gain.

Things are trickier if you sell a second home. In the past, you were able to move into a vacation property, live there for two years and get the full benefit of the $250,000 or $500,000 exclusion. That ploy no longer works. For instance, if you owned the place for five years but used it as your principal residence for just two years, only 40 percent of any gain is eligible for the exclusion—and you would owe capital gains taxes on the other 60 percent.

The new rules apply to 2009 onward. What if you owned a second home prior to 2009? You get some tax relief. To figure out what percentage of your gain isn't eligible for the exclusion, you take the amount of time the property wasn't your primary residence in the period since 2009 and divide it by the total number of years you owned the property—including the years prior to 2009.

PART IV

COLLEGE

IT COULD MAKE YOUR KIDS RICH AND COST YOU A FORTUNE

E arning a college degree isn't just an enriching experience that sets you up for a potentially more interesting career. It also makes your human capital substantially more valuable.

According to a June 2014 White House report, the median annual income in 2013 for those with at least a bachelor's degree was $62,300. That was $28,300 more than the median earnings for those with only a high school diploma. These figures reflect those age 25 and older who are working fulltime. College graduates were also less likely to be unemployed, at 4 percent, versus 8 percent for those who only graduated high school.

Problem is, this enhanced earning power doesn't come cheap. If you have a newborn, you face four daunting tasks. First, you need to save for college over the next 18 years, while juggling other financial goals like retirement and buying a home. Second, as your teenager struggles with college applications, you get to struggle with the financial aid forms—and you'll both be on tenterhooks awaiting the outcome. Third, there's paying for the college years, which often involves a patchwork approach. You might dip into savings, receive some grant money, take out loans and pay part of the cost out of your regular paycheck.

Finally, there's the aftermath, which may see your college graduate grappling with student loans, even as you work to pay off the money you borrowed. Figures from the Federal Reserve Bank of New York show education borrowing up 241 percent over the past 10 years—and some observers think this is the next debt crisis in the making.

66. TODAY'S COLLEGE COSTS

According to the College Board, it costs an average $18,943 in tuition, fees, room and board to send a child to an in-state university for the 2014–15 academic year. Even after subtracting out inflation, that's 1 percent higher than the year before and up a cumulative 12 percent over the prior five years.

For a private college, the average tab for 2014–2015 was $42,419, a 1.6 percent increase from a year earlier and up 9 percent over the preceding five years. Again, these are increases over and above inflation. Sound steep? At some elite private colleges, the cost is now approaching $60,000.

Some have contended the real cost hasn't climbed nearly as fast as the sticker price, thanks to financial aid. Still, as published college costs have increased, so too have education loans. The College Board says 60 percent of recent four-year college graduates borrowed to pay their education costs, with their debts averaging $27,300.

It isn't just undergraduate borrowing that is increasing. A March 2014 report from the New America Foundation estimated that 40 percent of the roughly $1 trillion in outstanding student loans represented borrowing by students pursuing graduate and professional degrees.

67. FIVE STEPS FOR 2015

Got college-bound kids and want to get yourself on track financially? Here are five steps to get you started:

• Save something, even if it's just $25 a month. Whatever you can put aside will come in handy once the college bills start rolling in.

• Use the EFC calculator available at CollegeBoard.org to figure out how much financial aid you might receive. In all likelihood, you will be unpleasantly surprised. EFC is an abbreviation for expected family contribution.

• If you have money earmarked for college sitting in custodial accounts, consider shifting it to a 529 plan. While that switch might trigger an immediate capital gains tax bill, it could save you on taxes in the years ahead and improve your chances of receiving financial aid.

• Set up a home equity line of credit as a backup source of college money. You can read more about credit lines in Part XI.

• Talk to your children about how much financial help you'll give, not only with college costs, but also with other expenses like weddings and house down payments.

68. MANAGE EXPECTATIONS

We all want the best for our children. But what can you reasonably afford? If you're struggling to save enough for retirement, it may be unrealistic to think you can also help with college costs.

If that's the case, you should tell your children early on and preferably no later than the freshman year of high school. You don't want your kids to spend years imagining they will go to a college that you simply cannot afford and that, even with financial aid, is probably out of reach. Moreover, if you tell your children in time, it will give them the chance to work part-time jobs and perhaps save a little money toward college costs. Even if you can't offer financial help, you can offer advice. For instance, if your children plan to pursue careers that won't be especially lucrative, you should discourage them from attending a college that will necessitate taking on hefty student loans.

What if you can help financially? Let your children know how much assistance you can provide—and where you'll draw the line. Many parents help with undergraduate costs, but tell their children that they're on their own when it comes to graduate school.

You should also talk to them about any other financial help you will—or won't—provide. If you can assist with a house down payment and a lavish wedding, that's wonderful. But if that sort of help isn't in the cards, you should say so. These financial conversations shouldn't just happen when your children are teenagers and they shouldn't be focused solely on the help you'll give them in their teens and 20s. Once they're adults, you might occasionally discuss your own retirement finances, how much they might inherit and what end-of-life decisions you would like made on your behalf.

69. SAVE SOMETHING

Take the figures from the College Board—the $18,943 average cost for a child at an in-state university for the 2014–15 academic year and the $42,419 for a private college. Multiply those sums by four years, throw in 3 percent annual inflation for 18 years, and you are looking at $129,000 for an in-state university and $289,000 for a private college. That's how much it might cost to send today's toddler to college.

To amass those sums, you would need to save $290 a month for 18 years for the in-state university and $650 for the private college, assuming a 5 percent annual return and assuming you stepped up the sum saved each year with the 3 percent inflation rate. For most parents, that simply isn't doable, especially because they also need to save for their own retirement. In fact, retirement should take precedence: Your kids can take out loans to pay for college, but for retirement you'll need to start out with a heap of cash.

Still, save what you can. When it comes time to pay those college bills, you'll be grateful for any cash you have set aside. Where will the rest of the money come from? If you're like most parents, you will muddle through, paying college costs out of current income, perhaps getting some help from the grandparents, asking your children to take on loans and also borrowing money yourself.

If you put aside at least some savings, it may allow your children to graduate without crippling amounts of student debt. But that still leaves two questions: How should you invest your children's college savings—and what sort of account should you use?

70. INVESTMENT STRATEGY

You should probably be more conservative with your children's college savings than with your own retirement nest egg. Sound counterintuitive? Remember, your kids likely have no more than 18 years until they head off to college, while you may have decades until you quit the workforce—and you'll likely live a few decades beyond that.

The implication: While you might initially invest your children's college savings heavily in stocks, you should probably start moving toward bonds even before they enter high school. Let's assume you plan to put a quarter of your children's college fund toward each of the four years needed to earn an undergraduate degree.

With that in mind, you might look to have a quarter of your children's savings in certificates of deposit, short-term bonds or similar conservative investments when they're five years from their freshman college year. You might aim to have another quarter in conservative investments when they're five years from their sophomore year, and so on.

Why this caution? Over some five-year stretches, stocks have lost money. Another reason: While you might spend your retirement money over 20 or 30 years, the deadline is a lot harsher with your children's college savings, because the money is spent over a brief four-year period.

As you invest your children's college savings, also think about what sort of account to use, whether it's a 529 college savings plan, prepaid tuition plan, Coverdell education savings account or custodial account. As an alternative, some parents keep the money in their own name, perhaps stashing it in a regular taxable investment account, putting it in savings bonds or even using an individual retirement account.

71. SECTION 529 COLLEGE SAVINGS PLANS

While 529 college savings plans have drawbacks, they have emerged as perhaps the best choice for parents looking to sock away money for college.

These plans, named 529 after the relevant section of the federal tax code, allow you to save huge sums every year. Moreover, you can contribute no matter how high your income. Your savings grow tax-free as long as the money is used for qualified education expenses. Many states even offer state tax deductions or credits for contributing. For financial aid purposes, the plans are typically considered a parental asset, which means their impact on aid eligibility is far less than if they were deemed the student's asset. If you don't use all the money for one child's education, you can change beneficiaries and use the account to help another child. To learn more, go to SavingforCollege.com.

For well-heeled parents, 529 plans can be especially attractive. In 2015, you can't give another person more than $14,000 without worrying about the federal gift tax. But with a 529 plan, both parents could contribute five times that sum, or $70,000 each, and count it as their gift for the next five years. That gets the money growing tax-free more quickly, which potentially is a significant benefit. This might also be a smart strategy for wealthy grandparents.

What about the drawbacks? Some plans have high expenses, but you can sidestep that problem by favoring lower-cost plans. You can change your investment selection just twice a year, which means 529 plans aren't a good choice for those inclined to trade. Finally, if you don't use the money for education and instead simply withdraw it, you'll face income taxes and tax penalties on the tax-deferred growth.

72. GRANDPARENTS AND 529s

If you have grandchildren, funding 529 plans is an intriguing option with three big benefits and one significant problem. First, as mentioned in the previous section, you can gift as much as $70,000 in 2015 and count it as your gift for the next five years. That can get a big chunk of money, as well as its future investment growth, out of your estate. If, however, you die before the five years are up, a pro-rated share of the gift will be added back to your estate.

Second, if you open the account rather than funding a 529 opened by the parents, you remain in control of the money. That means that, if your grandchildren's parents divorce, there's no risk the money will get divvied up and spent.

Third, unlike with other education accounts, your contributions to a 529 aren't irrevocable. In other words, if you later discover that your retirement portfolio is becoming depleted, you can reclaim the money in your grandchildren's 529s, though you'll owe income taxes and tax penalties on any investment growth.

What's the problem? If it turns out your grandchildren are eligible for financial aid, you'll want to time your 529 withdrawals carefully. When applying for financial aid, a grandparent-controlled 529 doesn't show up as an asset belonging to either the parents or the child, which is a plus. But when a grandparent makes a 529 withdrawal to pay college expenses, it counts as income for the student, which can badly hurt aid eligibility.

To get around this problem, you might use the 529 to pay college expenses starting in the second half of your grandchild's junior year. At that point, your grandchild should have made his or her final aid application, so the 529 withdrawal won't affect aid eligibility.

Problem solved? Maybe not. If your grandchildren go to a private college that requires the CSS Profile financial aid form, they may be asked to disclose whether they are beneficiaries of a 529—including those funded by grandparents.

73. PREPAID TUITION PLANS

Prepaid tuition plans are a type of 529 plan. But unlike a 529 college savings plan, where you aim to earn healthy investment gains by picking from among a menu of mutual funds, a prepaid tuition plan is designed to let you lock in future tuition costs at today's price. In effect, your rate of return should equal the percentage by which tuition costs increase between now and when your kid heads off to college.

In practice, you may earn less than the rate of tuition inflation, because many prepaid plans charge a premium price for these future tuition credits. Moreover, the credits can only be used at certain colleges, so you should read the small print to see what happens if your child opts to go elsewhere.

In recent years, prepaid plans in some states have struggled financially and been closed at least temporarily to new investors. While state prepaid plans in states such as Florida, Massachusetts, Mississippi and Washington are backed by the full faith and credit of the state, other plans don't have that sort of backing, which means payouts could be scaled back if the plan doesn't earn a high enough return when investing participants' money.

As with a 529 college savings plan, parent-controlled prepaid tuition plans are treated as a parental asset for financial aid purposes and the gains are tax-free at the federal level as long as the money is used for qualified education expenses. You may also be eligible for special state tax breaks. To research plans, head to SavingforCollege.com.

74. COVERDELL EDUCATION SAVINGS ACCOUNTS

A Coverdell education savings account can give you tax-free growth if the money is used for qualified education expenses, just like a 529 college savings plan. It's also typically treated as a parental asset for financial aid purposes—another attractive feature.

But there the similarities end. While 529 college savings plans restrict you to the plan's menu of investment options, you have a much wider choice with a Coverdell, which means you could potentially slash your investment costs by, say, favoring index funds with rock-bottom annual costs. You can also use the Coverdell to pay for education expenses from kindergarten through college, while a 529 plan is restricted to college costs only.

But those advantages are offset by a few notable disadvantages. You can invest just $2,000 a year in a Coverdell. The amount you can contribute in 2015 phases out if your modified adjusted gross income is between $190,000 and $220,000 and you're married filing jointly, or between $95,000 and $110,000 and you're filing as single or head of household. Above these income thresholds, contributions aren't allowed. These income eligibility thresholds do not rise each year with inflation.

You could sidestep the limits by having a family member with less income make the annual contribution. Indeed, you need to be aware of what others are doing, because the $2,000 annual limit is a total amount per child. Thanks to these various drawbacks, the Coverdell hasn't proven that popular, and some financial firms have stopped offering them, instead focusing their efforts on 529s.

Once the beneficiary of a Coverdell turns age 18, you can't make further contributions. The account needs to be emptied within 30 days of the beneficiary turning age 30. But if, as that deadline approaches, there happens to be money left in the account, you can keep the tax-free growth going by switching the account's beneficiary to another family member who is under age 30.

75. CUSTODIAL ACCOUNTS

If you open a regular investment account for your child, you need to set it up as a custodial account under your state's Uniform Transfers to Minors Act or Uniform Gifts to Minors Act. With an UTMA or UGMA account, you typically name yourself as custodian. That means you call the shots on how the account is invested. The money you put in the account is an irrevocable gift to your kid. To fund the account, you might take advantage of the annual gift-tax exclusion, which means you could contribute as much as $14,000 in 2015 without worrying about the gift tax.

There are three big drawbacks with custodial accounts. First, while investment earnings in the account of up to $2,000 in 2014 and up to $2,100 in 2015 would be taxed at a modest rate, gains above that level are taxed at the parents' rate, thanks to the so-called kiddie tax. That could mean a steep tax rate and, perhaps more important, some additional hassles at tax time.

Second, once your child reaches the age of majority, which is typically 18 to 21 depending on the state where you live, your kid can take control of the account—and the money could end up being spent on a fast car rather than a good education.

Third, in the financial aid formulas, a custodial account is considered a child's asset, rather than a parental asset, which means it could cost you dearly in financial aid.

JONATHAN'S TAKE: If you're saving for a child's college costs, a custodial account seems like a poor alternative to 529s and Coverdells, with their tax-free growth and favorable financial aid treatment. Got college money in a custodial account? You might move it to a 529, though that could trigger a big capital gains tax bill when you sell the custodial-account investments. What if you're confident your family won't qualify for financial aid and you want to invest for your child, so he or she will later have money for, say, a house down payment? In that scenario, a custodial account might make sense.

76. KIDDIE TAX

The kiddie tax is designed to prevent parents from transferring large sums to their children with the goal of saving on taxes. In 2014, the first $1,000 of a child's investment gains are tax-free and the next $1,000 are taxed at the child's rate. For 2015, these two figures rise to $1,050. Any investment gains above $2,000 in 2014 and above $2,100 in 2015 are taxed at the parents' rate.

The kiddie tax typically applies to children under age 18 or, if they don't have much income from employment, under age 19. It also applies to young adults under age 24 who were fulltime students as of year-end. Instead of filing a separate tax return for a child, parents may be able to include the kid's investment gains on their own tax return. That way, you avoid filing an extra tax return, but arguably it isn't any simpler.

While the kiddie tax was a big issue in the 1990s, when many parents used custodial accounts to save for college, it shouldn't be as big an issue today. Why not? If you save for college, you now have two great college savings options available to you: 529 college savings plans and Coverdell education savings accounts. Neither account, with their potential tax-free growth, would trigger the kiddie tax.

What if you want to invest in a child's name with the goal of helping him or her save money for after college? You might invest in a way that's likely to generate less than $2,100 a year in annual investment gains. For instance, you could favor tax-efficient investment vehicles like stock index mutual funds or tax-managed stock funds.

77. COLLEGE SAVINGS IN THE PARENTS' NAMES

There's no law that says college savings have to be in a special education account. Yes, these offer tax advantages. Using a specially designated account also appeals to our mental accounting: We like the idea that the money is segregated, and the separate account makes it less likely we'll spend the savings on something else.

Still, for many parents, keeping college savings in their own name often makes sense. You might stash the dollars in a regular taxable investment account, savings bonds, a retirement account or perhaps use it to pay down your mortgage. If your income is modest and there's a good chance your family will receive financial aid, you should probably focus your spare cash on other goals, such as buying a home and investing for retirement. If it turns out your income is higher than expected and hence your aid eligibility is less, you could always pay for college by, for instance, borrowing against your home's value or withdrawing your Roth IRA contributions.

Sticking college savings in a traditional IRA might also make sense, especially if you have children later in life. But if your kids qualify for financial aid, you should think carefully about when to make your traditional or Roth IRA withdrawals.

In addition, keeping college savings in your own name might be appealing if you favor flexibility. The fact is, you don't know whether your kids will go to college, whether you'll need the money for your own retirement, or what will happen to the tax code and financial aid formulas in the years ahead. Set against that is the tax-free growth offered by a 529 or a

Coverdell. But given the relatively short time you have to invest for a child's college education, you might decide the tax savings won't be that significant.

78. RETIREMENT ACCOUNTS

If you're paying qualified education expenses, you can withdraw money from an IRA and avoid the usual 10 percent tax penalty levied on those under age 59½. Problem is, if you withdraw from a retirement account—and that includes taking tax-free withdrawals from a Roth IRA—you'll increase the income you have to report on your next financial aid application and potentially reduce aid eligibility.

One solution: You might borrow during the early college years and then withdraw from your IRA to repay the loans after your child has submitted his or her final financial aid application, which will likely be January of your kid's junior year. If you're over age 59½ at that juncture, you won't have to worry about the tax penalty.

What if you're under age 59½? If you're simply withdrawing contributions to a Roth IRA, the tax penalty won't be an issue. But if you're withdrawing from a traditional IRA or the investment earnings from a Roth IRA, you'll want to calculate how much in qualified education expenses you have for that year and then withdraw no more than that amount, so you avoid the 10 percent tax penalty.

Keep in mind that your qualified expenses will be less than the sum of tuition, fees, room and board if part of these costs was covered by other financial assistance, such as a Coverdell withdrawal or a Pell grant.

79. SAVINGS BONDS

At one time, it was popular to buy savings bonds to pay for a child's college costs. These days, you don't hear savings bonds discussed that often, partly because 529s and Coverdells seem like better alternatives and partly because yields on savings bond are now so modest. There's more about savings bonds in Part IX.

Still, for those who qualify, savings bonds can be a low-risk, tax-free way to save for college. You can cash in savings bonds and avoid income taxes on the accumulated interest if you use the money for tuition and fees at a qualified educational institution for yourself, your spouse or your child. In 2015, this tax break phases out if you are married filing jointly with modified adjusted gross income between $115,750 and $145,750. For other taxpayers, the phase-out range is $77,200 to $92,200.

To get the tax break, there are a few other conditions. The bonds need to be owned by one or both parents and you need to have been at least 24 years old when you bought the bonds. The bonds need to be either EE bonds issued after 1989 or Series I bonds. To qualify for the tax break, you also can't be married but filing separate tax returns.

80. FINANCIAL AID

College financial aid is a source of great hope, frequent confusion and often bitter disappointment. To get a handle on the topic, start by considering three points:

• While there are scholarships available for the academically and athletically gifted, much financial assistance consists of aid that is based on a family's financial need. This need is captured by a notion known as EFC, or expected family contribution.

• Financial aid can take the form of subsidized loans, unsubsidized loans, work study and grant money. If your children qualify for financial aid and they're desirable to colleges because of their academic brilliance, athletic abilities or some other quality, colleges may tweak an aid package to include more grant money. Indeed, if you are disappointed with the aid package that your child is offered, consider appealing to one of the college's financial aid officers. Such appeals are often successful if your child is the type of student the college is looking to recruit. In 2013–2014, undergraduates received an average $14,180 in financial aid, $8,080 of which was grant money, according to the College Board.

• While folks often talk about the financial aid formula, there are actually two formulas. One is used by the federal government, which is the biggest source of financial aid and which assesses aid eligibility using information you provide in the FAFSA, or Free Application for Federal Student Aid, a daunting form with more than 100 questions. The other formula, known as the institutional methodology, is used by many private colleges when doling out their own money. These schools require that you also fill out the CSS Profile form, which includes additional details not included on the FAFSA. (CSS stands for College Scholarship Service.) While federal grants typically go to poorer families, private colleges use their endowments to distribute significant amounts of grant money to middle-class families.

You typically file for financial aid in the first two months of the year. If your child is a senior in high school, you should hear about financial aid when you hear whether your child has been accepted, which is usually around April 1 or shortly thereafter. To learn more about college financial aid, check out FinAid.org, an independent website, and also the U.S. Department of Education's StudentAid.ed.gov.

81. EXPECTED FAMILY CONTRIBUTION

The amount you're expected to pay toward college costs is reflected in a number known as your EFC, or expected family contribution. Many parents are shocked by how much they're expected to cough up each year toward college costs. You can calculate your expected contribution under both the federal and institutional aid formulas using the EFC calculator available at CollegeBoard.org.

Let's say your EFC is $15,000 a year. If your teenager goes to a college that costs $20,000, you should receive $5,000 a year in financial aid. What if your kid goes to a $50,000-a-year college? You should receive $35,000 in aid.

The implication: You shouldn't dissuade your children from applying to colleges because they appear to be too expensive. Sure, if a college costs less than your expected family contribution, your out-of-pocket cost will be less. But if your teenager is choosing between two colleges, one that costs $2,000 more than your EFC and another college that costs $20,000 more, you should—in theory—be indifferent, because your out-of-pocket cost will be the same.

In practice, a lot will depend on the composition of the aid package. If the more expensive college offers an aid package that includes a substantial amount of student loans, you may want to favor the less costly college rather than send your children out into the world burdened by debt. In addition, not all colleges offer aid packages that fill the full gap between your EFC and the college's cost, and that could leave you scrambling to make up the shortfall.

82. AID ELIGIBILITY

The aid formulas take into account a host of factors, such as family size and whether you have more than one child in college at the same time. Still, much hinges on four key drivers of aid eligibility: the parents' income, the parents' assets, the child's income and the child's assets.

Under the formulas, parents are expected to contribute as much as 47 percent of income and as much as 5 to 5.6 percent of assets toward each year's college costs, though only higher-earning and wealthier parents will be assessed at such high rates. Students are expected to contribute as much as 50 percent of income and as much as 20 to 25 percent of assets.

For most families, the parents' income will be the biggest determinant of aid eligibility. While it doesn't make sense to ask your boss for a pay cut, you might take steps to hold down your income, including your investment income, during the four calendar years that will be used to gauge your aid eligibility. Aid eligibility is reassessed each year. The so-called base year—which covers the second half of your teenager's junior year in high school and the first half of the kid's senior year—is especially important.

You might also look carefully at the assets held by both parents and students, as well as what counts as an asset. In addition, if your child is applying to private colleges, you should pay attention to differences between the federal and institutional aid formulas.

83. FEDERAL VS. INSTITUTIONAL METHODOLOGY

The federal financial aid formula and the institutional formula used by many private colleges differ in notable ways, including how heavily they assess the income and assets of parents and students. But you may want to pay particular attention to two key differences.

First, while the federal formula ignores home equity, it's considered in the institutional methodology. You hear about parents who use their savings to buy an overly large home or undertake elaborate remodeling projects with an eye to increasing aid eligibility. That may help with the federal methodology, but it may not increase aid eligibility if your children plan to attend a private college.

Second, if a couple is divorced, the federal formula focuses solely on the finances of the custodial parent and, if remarried, the finances of his or her new spouse. The custodial parent is typically the parent with whom a child has spent the most nights over the past year or who provides the bulk of the child's financial support.

By contrast, with the institutional methodology, both parents may be considered, as well as the finances of any new spouses. One implication: If your child isn't likely to attend a college where the institutional formula is used, you should give careful thought to who should be listed as the custodial parent.

84. INCREASING AID ELIGIBILITY

Want to increase aid eligibility? Consider these strategies:

• Use taxable account savings to pay down debt. Consumer debts such as credit card balances and auto loans are ignored by the aid formulas, so they won't make you appear needier, while paying them off will reduce the money you have in regular taxable accounts, which is assessed. You might also use spare cash to pay down mortgage debt and make necessary purchases, such as buying a new car or replacing the roof.

• Stash college savings in the parents' names or in Coverdell and 529 plans. Don't use UGMA or UTMA accounts, which are considered the child's asset and assessed more heavily for financial aid purposes. If you have money in your child's name, consider spending it before applying for financial aid by using it to pay for items, such as summer camp, that are not considered part of the usual parental obligation. You could also liquidate the UGMA or UTMA account and use the proceeds to fund a 529 plan, though this may trigger a big capital gain, part of which could be taxed at the parents' rate because of the kiddie tax.

• Hold down your income during the years used to assess aid eligibility. Avoid realizing capital gains in your taxable accounts or, if you do, try to take offsetting capital losses. Also avoid tapping retirement accounts to pay college expenses. See if your employer will postpone paying your year-end bonus. These various steps are especially important in the base year for assessing financial aid eligibility, which is typically the calendar year that covers the second half of your student's junior year and the initial months of his or her senior year.

• Max out savings in retirement accounts. Tax-deductible contributions won't reduce your income for aid purposes, but it will help when it comes to assessing your assets. Money in retirement accounts is typically ignored in the aid formulas, while taxable account savings will reduce aid eligibility, so you might focus on fully funding 401(k) plans and IRAs in the years running up to college.

85. HELP FROM FAMILY

Family members, especially grandparents, often chip in to help with college costs. If your children are eligible for financial aid, you should discuss the best way to give this financial assistance.

For instance, while the annual gift-tax exclusion is $14,000 in 2015, there's no limit on the help you can provide with education costs, as long as the money is sent directly to the educational institution. Problem is, if the grandparents or others do this, it can result in a dollar-for-dollar reduction in financial aid.

Instead, family members might gift the money to the parents, who can then use it to pay college costs. Alternatively, family members might help with college costs after the final financial aid application is filed, which will typically be January of the student's junior year, or they could assist the student with paying off education loans after graduation.

Family members might also contribute to a 529 plan that the parents have established. This avoids the financial aid problems that can arise with 529 plans set up by grandparents and other family members, though it also means giving up control of the money.

86. EDUCATION BORROWING

According to the College Board, 60 percent of students graduating from four-year colleges during the 2012–13 academic year had borrowed to pay their education costs. The average amount borrowed was $27,300. The Federal Reserve Bank of New York calculates that, over the five years through 2014's third quarter, student loans outstanding soared 62 percent, even as overall household debt declined. Among the different types of financial aid given out during the 2013–2014 academic year, loans accounted for 37 percent, grants for 54 percent, and education tax breaks and work study for 9 percent.

The jump in education borrowing has been driven partly by rising college costs and partly by declining financial help from parents. Can't afford to help your children with college costs? Consider counseling them to avoid costly colleges that will leave them heavily in debt, especially if their planned career will pay them a modest income.

You might also suggest strategies that can hold down college costs, such as attending a community college for the first two years and then transferring to a more prestigious school, which they would then graduate from. Alternatively, you might suggest attending a nearby college and saving money by living at home initially. Room and board are a major college cost, accounting for an average 42 percent of total costs for in-state students at public universities, according to College Board figures.

While education loans are available from some banks, students should probably focus on federal loans. Parents might consider the federal loan program for parents, a home equity line of credit or possibly a 401(k) loan.

87. STUDENT LOANS

To receive federal loans, you have to file the Free Application for Federal Student Aid, or FAFSA. There are three main federal student loan programs:

Subsidized Stafford loans. These loans, which are awarded based on financial need, don't incur interest while a student is in college. Repayment begins six months after graduation or, alternatively, if a student starts attending college less than halftime.

Unsubsidized Stafford loans. These loans, which aren't awarded based on need, incur interest while a student is in college, though the interest can be added to the loan balance if a student is still attending school.

Students often end up with a mix of subsidized and unsubsidized loans, both of which charge 4.66 percent interest if disbursed during the 12 months through July 1, 2015. The total amount that can be borrowed is capped each year. For instance, for a first-year undergraduate who is considered a dependent student, total subsidized Stafford loans are capped at $3,500, with the possibility of borrowing another $2,000 in unsubsidized loans.

What if a student isn't eligible for subsidized Stafford loans? He or she can always take out unsubsidized loans instead, potentially borrowing as much as $5,500 during the first year of college. In subsequent years, the annual amount that can be borrowed increases.

Perkins loans. These currently carry an interest rate of 5 percent. They are only awarded to students with exceptional financial need—and yet they now charge a higher rate than Stafford loans.

Student loans may also be available from the college itself. The interest rate charged may be less than on federal loans. In addition, some states have set up agencies or nonprofit organizations that provide loans to students who are residents or who go to in-state colleges, and loans are also available from private lenders. For more information, check out FinAid.org, StudentAid.ed.gov and StudentLoanNetwork.com.

88. PARENT LOANS

The federal government offers not just student loans, but also loans to parents through the PLUS program. PLUS loans incur interest immediately, but parents of undergraduates can defer all payments until six months after their child graduates. The interest rate is 7.21 percent for loans disbursed during the 12 months through July 1, 2015. You can borrow up to the cost of your child's college, minus any other financial aid received. To borrow through the PLUS program, parents are subject to a fairly lenient credit check, and you have to file the Free Application for Federal Student Aid.

Instead of a PLUS loan, you could borrow through a home equity line of credit, which may charge a lower interest rate. The interest on both PLUS and home equity loans is potentially tax-deductible. If you opt to borrow against your home, favor a home equity line of credit, which you can draw on as needed, rather than a home equity loan. The latter involves borrowing a lump sum, which will then show up as additional money in your regular taxable account—and possibly hurt you when you next apply for financial aid.

You might also borrow from your 401(k) plan. Such loans are typically limited to half your account balance, with the amount borrowed capped at $50,000. Some folks are attracted to 401(k) loans because the interest you pay ends up in your account, so you're effectively paying interest to yourself. Nonetheless, there is a real cost. The money borrowed is removed from your account, so the true price of these loans is the investment gains the money could have earned.

Finally, you might investigate taking out an education loan from a bank. If you have an excellent credit score, the interest rate may be below the 7.21 percent charged for PLUS loans. But if your credit score isn't so good, you would likely be better off with the federal PLUS program.

89. REPAYING EDUCATION LOANS

If you're struggling to pay your federal student loans or you're simply overwhelmed by the number of loans you have to pay each month, consider consolidating your federal loans through StudentLoans.gov. The interest rate on the consolidated loan will be based on the weighted average interest rate of your existing loans.

When consolidating, look into extending the term on the loan. Most federal loans are for 10 years, but you may be able to increase the repayment period to as long as 30 years, depending on the total sum involved. This will reduce your monthly payment, simply because you're extending the loan's repayment over more years. But thanks to that longer repayment period, you'll also end up paying more in total interest. Among the loans that can be consolidated are Stafford, Perkins and PLUS loans.

If you need further relief, investigate the federal government's income-based repayment program, which can lead to lower monthly payments, depending on your income and family size. An expansion of eligibility for the Pay As You Earn Repayment Plan is slated to take effect later in 2015. You might also be able to get your student loans forgiven if you work for 10 years in the public or nonprofit sector. Others in the income-based repayment program may be eligible to have their student loans cancelled after 20 years. For more information, head to StudentAid.gov.

What about private loans? If you refinance, you may be able to lower your interest rate or at least extend the term of the loans, thereby reducing your monthly payment. To refinance, often you will need a good credit score and a cosigner on the loan, who is typically a parent, especially if you're applying to refinance soon after graduating.

90. EDUCATION LOAN INTEREST DEDUCTION

You can deduct the interest charged on your education loans, just like you can deduct the interest on a mortgage and on margin loans. But in the case of education loans, the tax break comes with limitations.

For starters, in 2014 and 2015, you can only deduct up to $2,500 in interest on qualified education loans. In addition, the ability to claim the deduction is subject to an income test. In 2014 and 2015, the deduction phases out if your income is between $130,000 and $160,000 and you're married filing jointly, or between $65,000 and $80,000 and you're single or you file as head of household. You can't claim the deduction if your tax-filing status is married filing separately.

Some good news: The deduction is claimed directly on your 1040, the main page of your federal tax return. That means you can get the tax savings even if you don't itemize your deductions on Schedule A.

91. AMERICAN OPPORTUNITY TAX CREDIT

The American Opportunity Tax Credit is a tax break available to help pay for up to four years of higher education for yourself or your dependents. For those eligible, it can be hugely valuable. Remember, a tax deduction shrinks your taxable income, so that a $1,000 tax deduction might save you $250 in taxes, assuming you're in the 25 percent federal income tax bracket. By contrast, American Opportunity is a tax credit, which means it gives you a dollar-for-dollar reduction in your total tax bill.

In 2014 and 2015, the American Opportunity credit could reduce your tax bill by up to $2,500 per student. The credit consists of 100 percent of the first $2,000 of qualified education expenses, including tuition, fees and course materials, and 25 percent of the next $2,000. What if your total tax bill is less than the total credit you're claiming? The American Opportunity credit is partly refundable.

You can't claim the American Opportunity Tax Credit at higher income levels. In 2014 and 2015, the credit phases out if you're married filing jointly and your income is between $160,000 and $180,000. If you're single or head of household, the phase-out range is $80,000 to $90,000. The credit can't be claimed if you're married filing separately.

You also can't claim the American Opportunity Tax Credit and the Lifetime Learning Credit, discussed next, for the same student in the same tax year. If you're eligible for both, you'll probably want to take the American Opportunity credit, which is more valuable. The Lifetime Learning Credit is more likely to be claimed by graduate students, who may have already used up their four years of the American Opportunity credit.

92. LIFETIME LEARNING CREDIT

The American Opportunity Tax Credit is designed to help students pay for four years of undergraduate education. The Lifetime Learning Credit is geared toward those studying later in life: While it can be claimed for undergraduate expenses, it's more likely to be used for graduate school or professional degree courses. There's no limit on the number of years that you can claim the Lifetime Learning Credit.

The credit is worth up to $2,000 in 2014 and 2015. To hit the maximum, you would need $10,000 of qualified expenses, on which you can then claim a 20 percent tax credit, which is how you get to $2,000. Unlike the American Opportunity Tax Credit, the Lifetime Learning Credit is a per-tax-return credit, not per student, and it isn't refundable if it exceeds your tax liability.

The Lifetime Learning Credit isn't available to taxpayers with higher incomes. In 2014, the credit phases out if your income is between $108,000 and $128,000 and you're married filing jointly, or between $54,000 and $64,000 and you're filing as single or head of household. In 2015, the credit phases out between $110,000 and $130,000 if you're married filing jointly, and between $55,000 and $65,000 if you're single or head of household. You can't claim the credit if you're married filing separately.

If you have exhausted your four years of the American Opportunity Tax Credit and your income is too high for the Lifetime Learning Credit, check to see whether you might be eligible for the Tuition and Fees Deduction, which allows you to deduct up to $4,000 of qualified education expenses. The Tuition and Fees Deduction, which can be used in 2014 but will disappear for the 2015 tax year unless Congress acts, is available at somewhat higher income levels than the Lifetime Learning Credit. The deduction phases out between $130,000 and $160,000 if you're married filing jointly and between $65,000 and $80,000 if you're single or head of household.

PART V

FAMILY

MAKING SURE EVERYBODY'S OKAY
WHEN EVERYTHING GOES WRONG

There's a certain pleasure associated with saving for retirement, college or a house down payment. You get that pleasant sense of progress as you watch your account balances balloon, plus the goals themselves are exciting.

There is, alas, no such pleasure when rigging up your family's financial safety net. It's all about thinking through the bad stuff that might happen and then playing defense as best you can. That brings us to a crucial notion many folks fail to grasp: When we talk about protecting your family, we're talking about fending off major financial threats to you and those who depend on you financially.

For instance, the death of a child is a terrible thing. But unless your children are Hollywood stars, probably neither you nor anybody else depends on them financially. That means it doesn't make sense to buy insurance on your children's lives. Insurance salves financial wounds. It doesn't fix broken hearts.

Similarly, it would be bad if your television went kaput. But in all likelihood, you can afford to buy a new one, so you probably shouldn't buy the extended warranty. Insurance is about getting somebody else to shoulder risks you can't afford to shoulder yourself. A bum television doesn't fall into that category.

Your goal: Rig up a financial safety net that protects your family against major threats—and then stop there, knowing that money devoted to your safety net is a cost that will leave you with less for other goals. So what steps should you take to protect your family? Consider focusing on four areas: preparing for financial emergencies, getting the right insurance coverage, protecting against lawsuits and organizing your estate. The first three topics are tackled in this chapter. Estate planning is dealt with in Part XII.

93. FIVE STEPS FOR 2015

Want to make sure your family is adequately protected against financial disaster? To get you started, consider these five steps:

• Ponder how you would cope financially if you lost your job and it took six or even 12 months to find work. How much money would you need each month to cover your living costs—and where would you get this cash?

• Think about what sort of financial shape your family would be in if you died tomorrow. Would they have enough money, or should you buy more life insurance?

• Give some hardheaded thought to nursing home costs. Can you afford to pay out of pocket, should you buy long-term-care insurance, or will you deplete your assets and then fall back on Medicaid?

• Look at the fine print on your homeowner's and auto policies. Could you save money by raising the deductibles? If your house burned down, would your homeowner's policy pay enough to allow you to rebuild?

• Find out which of your assets would be protected if there were a large legal judgment against you because, say, someone had an accident at your home or you caused a car crash. Federal law would likely protect much or all of your retirement account money. But what additional protections are offered by state law?

94. EMERGENCY PLAN

Your plan for financial emergencies might have three components: a cash reserve, credit lines and low fixed living costs.

One rule of thumb says that, as an emergency reserve, you ought to keep six months' living expenses in conservative investments, such as a savings account or a money-market fund. This can be a heap of dough. For instance, if you make $75,000 a year, you might need to set aside $15,000 or $20,000 to cover your living expenses for half a year. Even if you're a diligent saver, it would likely take you at least a few years to accumulate that money. And once you have the money, it will probably languish in a savings account or a money-market fund earning precious little interest.

Could you make do with a smaller emergency reserve? You might hold less emergency money if you have easy access to borrowed money. We discuss credit lines and other ways to borrow in Part XI.

In addition, you might keep a smaller emergency reserve if you focus not on covering your family's total monthly living expenses, but on putting aside enough to cover your family's fixed costs. The idea: If you lose your job or have some other type of financial emergency, you would slash discretionary spending and instead limit yourself to expenses that are absolutely necessary. The lower these fixed costs are, the less emergency money you would need. This notion is tackled in Part VI.

In the end, the size of your emergency fund will likely hinge on one question: How secure is your job?

95. HOW BIG AN EMERGENCY FUND?

Do you really need an emergency fund equal to six months' living expenses? Partly, that's a matter of personal preference and hence how much you need to set aside to feel financially secure. But you should also give some thought to your job situation.

While you might tap your emergency fund to pay for a major car or home repair, the No. 1 reason to have an emergency fund is to cover a prolonged period of unemployment. Indeed, if you're retired and don't rely on a regular paycheck, you arguably don't need a separate emergency reserve.

Still in the workforce? If your job is tenuous, you may need the full six months of emergency money and perhaps more. But if your job is reasonably secure, you might keep just three months' living expenses in a savings account. Similarly, you might opt for a smaller emergency fund if your spouse also works, unless there's a risk you could both lose your jobs at the same time because you work for the same company or in the same industry.

JONATHAN'S TAKE: As you save for retirement and other goals, you may find yourself socking away money not just in 401(k) plans and individual retirement accounts, but also in a regular taxable account. You can tap that taxable account at any time without worrying about the 10 percent tax penalty that's typically levied on retirement account withdrawals before age 59½. As your taxable account grows, keeping a separate emergency fund may seem unnecessary. After all, if you lost your job, you could always dip into some of the retirement money you have in your regular taxable account.

96. INSURANCE

Insurance is a great way to cope with life's major financial risks—dangers such as getting sued, suffering a disability or dying prematurely and leaving your family in the lurch. It's far less appealing as a way of coping with lesser threats or when it's twinned with some sort of investment vehicle. We'll discuss this notion further in the pages ahead as we tackle the seven key types of insurance: health, life, disability, long-term care, auto, homeowner's and umbrella liability.

Any one of these policies might be affordable. But if you buy them all, you may find yourself blowing the family budget—unless you think carefully about how to tweak each policy. Those tweaks might include buying no more coverage than is really necessary, raising deductibles and opting for long elimination periods. The latter is the time you have to wait between making a claim and starting to receive benefits. The goal is to make sure you're covered for the major threats that could derail your financial future, while standing ready to pay smaller costs out of pocket.

One housekeeping tip: Make a point of keeping the latest copy of all insurance statements, and let family members know where they're located. Unless you have an outstanding claim or expect to make one, there's no need to keep old insurance policies.

97. HEALTH INSURANCE

The 2010 Patient Protection and Affordable Care Act, otherwise known as Obamacare, continued to dominate headlines in 2014. Yet most folks were unaffected because they receive health insurance through their employer or they're covered by Medicare. Still, however you get coverage, you are likely noticing two trends.

First, as health care costs rise, there's a push to get individuals to pick up more of the tab. This is showing up in higher premiums, deductibles and co-pays, plus certain medical costs are no longer getting covered. Partly, this is about employers, the government and insurance companies shifting more of the expense to individuals. But there's also an effort to get individuals to appreciate just how much health care costs, so they aren't quite so quick to seek medical help.

Second, individuals are being offered more health insurance choices, so they're compelled to consider how much coverage they want and whether they are willing to pay the associated price. Obamacare slots health plans into four categories, each with different levels of coverage and sometimes sharply different premiums. Those age 65 and up can choose from among ten Medigap plans that supplement the basic coverage offered by Medicare.

Alternatively, seniors can skip original Medicare and a companion Medigap policy, and instead go for a Medicare Advantage plan.

Meanwhile, many larger employers now offer two or more health plans, so employees have to decide whether, say, they want to pay more so they can see any doctor they wish, or whether they prefer to save money by sticking with a limited group of physicians and seeking authorization for some medical services.

98. EMPLOYER HEALTH PLANS

At most employers, gone are the days when you paid little for health insurance and you could see pretty much any doctor you wanted. You may still be able to pick a plan that gives you ample flexibility, but you'll likely pay a steep price for the privilege.

Fortunately, this is an area where you can legally trade on inside information. Do you or other family members go to the doctor frequently? How much do you value the ability to see any doctor you want? How many, if any, regular prescriptions do you have? Do you expect to need a particular procedure in the year ahead?

If you have a choice in health plans, you can take all this family information and weigh which plan makes most sense, given the deductibles, co-payments for each doctor's visit, prescription drug benefit and network of doctors available to plan participants.

Your employer may also offer a health care spending account, which you can fund out of pretax dollars and then use for medical costs not covered by the insurance company. When your employer's open enrollment period for benefits rolls around toward the end of the year, consider what health costs you might incur in the year ahead that won't be covered by the insurance company, and then use that to guide how much you contribute to the spending account. With these accounts, it's "use it or lose it," so be careful not to overfund your account.

Planning to change jobs? Until your new employer's coverage kicks in or until you purchase insurance through one of the health care exchanges, you may be able to continue your old employer's plan for a while, thanks to something called COBRA coverage.

99. COBRA

If you leave your job and your employer has 20 or more employees, you will likely be able to continue your employer's coverage for up to 18 months at your own expense. You will be sent a so-called COBRA notice, named after the Consolidated Omnibus Budget Reconciliation Act, giving you 60 days to decide whether you want the coverage.

Your employer can charge you 102 percent of the premium it currently pays. That might turn out to be a large sum. Still, you will be able to continue coverage for a while, without worrying about immediately finding a new health plan.

The 60-day decision period opens the door to a small potential cost savings. During those 60 days, you will have coverage if you have a medical issue—at which point, if you see a doctor, you would need to pay for COBRA coverage. But if you don't use any medical services during those 60 days, you might decide not to continue coverage and instead buy insurance elsewhere to cover you after the 60 days are up. In effect, that would give you 60 days of free coverage.

If you aren't getting coverage through a new employer, where should you turn for health insurance? That's where the 2010 Affordable Care Act comes in. A policy bought through your state's health care exchange will likely be cheaper than COBRA coverage. Nonetheless, it may be worth paying to keep your old employer's coverage through the end of the year if you have already met the policy's deductibles or out-of-pocket maximums for the year, or you're getting close. If you buy a new policy, you'll have new deductibles and out-of-pocket maximums to meet.

100. OBAMACARE

Here are the basics of the 2010 Affordable Care Act:

• Most U.S. citizens and legal residents are required to have health insurance. Tax penalties are levied on those who don't.

• If you don't have health insurance through your employer, you may receive a premium tax credit to help with insurance costs if your income is between 133 percent and 400 percent of the federal poverty level. To see whether you qualify, try the subsidy calculator offered by the Kaiser Family Foundation at KFF.org.

• If your income is below 133 percent of the federal poverty level, you may qualify for Medicaid, which has been expanded in many—but not all—states.

• You cannot be denied coverage because of preexisting conditions.

• Families can purchase coverage either through state-based insurance exchanges or directly from insurers. But to receive the premium tax credit, you have to use an exchange.

• All plans are categorized as bronze, silver, gold or platinum, depending on the level of coverage offered.

• Children can remain on their parents' plan through age 26.

To get a quick overview of what Obamacare means for your family, head to AARP's HealthLawAnswers.org.

101. HEALTH CARE EXCHANGES

As of late 2014, a third of states offered their own health care exchange. Residents of the other states can use the exchange set up by the federal government at HealthCare.gov. If you shop for health insurance on your own, you don't have to buy through the exchanges. In almost all states, you can also purchase policies directly from insurance companies or through an insurance agent.

Sidestepping the exchanges probably won't save you money. Indeed, if you purchase policies outside the exchanges, you won't receive the tax credit that you might be eligible for. Still, shopping outside the exchanges could give you a wider choice. You can find policies, including those not offered through the exchanges, at sites such as eHealthInsurance.com and GoHealth.com. According to eHealthInsurance's eHealth Price Index, the average monthly premium in late December 2014 for policies meeting the Affordable Care Act criteria was $285 for individuals and $715 for families.

Policies bought both inside and outside the exchanges must include the same essential benefits, and all must be categorized as bronze, silver, gold or platinum. Moreover, the same key principle applies: It's illegal for an insurer to deny you coverage because of preexisting conditions.

As you pick among policies, think carefully about the annual deductibles—which could be $2,000 or $3,000—and out-of-pocket maximums, and how you would meet that cost if you had a year with major medical expenses. For a health care policy to comply with the Affordable Care Act in 2015, the maximum out-of-pocket medical cost is $6,600 for individuals and $13,200 for families. This maximum, which doesn't include the monthly premiums paid to buy the policy, should help many folks avoid excessive medical debt—and it ought to be a factor when deciding how big an emergency fund you need.

102. MEDICARE

Approaching age 65, when you become eligible for Medicare? Spend some time perusing Medicare.gov, the federal government website. Here's what you'll discover:

• You typically aren't charged a premium for Medicare Part A, which helps cover hospital bills, a skilled nursing facility for a limited time, hospice care and some home health services.

• You are charged a premium for Part B, which covers doctor's visits, surgeries, lab tests and supplies such as walkers and wheelchairs. In 2015, most folks pay a monthly premium of $104.90, though you may pay as much as $335.70 if you have a high income. You also pay a monthly premium for Part D, the prescription drug program, with high-income folks again getting charged somewhat more.

• In addition to the monthly premiums, you may rack up substantial out-of-pocket medical costs. To cover some of those costs, you can buy a Medigap policy, for which you'll pay an additional premium.

• Instead of so-called original Medicare, with its Parts A and B, you can opt for a Medicare Advantage plan. Also known as Part C, Medicare Advantage plans are privately run health plans for retirees. Many of these plans operate like a health maintenance organization, or HMO, which means you have less choice in the doctors you can see.

• Original Medicare doesn't cover dental care, eyeglasses, long-term care, over-the-counter medicines and hearing aids. Some Medicare Advantage plans cover items like vision and dental care. But like original Medicare, they won't cover all medical services—especially the biggest potential expense, which is a long stay in a nursing home.

Even with Medicare, retirees face substantial out-of-pocket medical costs. AARP figures that Medicare only covers half of beneficiaries' total health care costs. The Kaiser Family Foundation calculates that households on Medicare spend an average $4,722 on health care expenses each year. That's equal to 14 percent of their total spending, versus 5 percent for other households. Fidelity Investments estimates that a 65-year-old couple retiring in 2014 will spend an average $220,000, in today's dollars, on their retirement medical costs—not including the cost of long-term care.

103. MEDICARE PART A

Medicare Part A covers in-patient hospital care and the services you might need immediately after, whether at home, at a hospice or at a skilled nursing facility. For instance, Medicare might cover costs for a nursing facility while, say, you're rehabilitating from an injury. It won't cover a nursing home if all you're receiving is custodial care, which involves help with daily living activities such as dressing, eating and bathing.

If you are already receiving Social Security retirement benefits, you will be automatically enrolled in Parts A and B at age 65. If not, you can sign up during a seven-month window that begins three months before you turn age 65. To enroll, visit your local Social Security office, apply online at SocialSecurity.gov or call 800-772-1213. To ensure that coverage for Parts A and B starts in the month you turn 65, you will want to sign up during the three months before your birthday.

Those who are eligible to receive any sort of monthly Social Security benefit, including spousal benefits, are also eligible to receive Part A for free, so there's usually no reason for Social Security recipients not to sign up. While you may not pay a premium for Part A, you will need to meet deductibles and make co-payments.

What if you are employed when you turn age 65? You can still sign up. If you don't, you can take advantage of a special eight-month enrollment period that typically starts when your employment ends. If you sign up during this period, you won't pay any penalty for signing up late. That penalty, in any case, is only an issue for those who aren't eligible to receive Part A for free.

104. MEDICARE PART B

While Part A covers in-patient hospital care and many expenses incurred during the aftermath, Part B covers outpatient care, including doctor's visits, diagnostic tests and medical equipment. A 20 percent co-insurance fee is charged for many services provided under Part B.

If you are receiving Social Security benefits, you will be contacted a few months before you turn age 65 with information about Medicare. You will then be automatically enrolled in Part B unless you opt out. Typically, you would want to opt out only if you're still working and covered by your employer's plan.

What if you aren't yet receiving Social Security? If you are retired, you should sign up for Medicare B by contacting Social Security during the seven-month initial enrollment period that starts three months before you turn 65. If you are retired and don't sign up during this initial enrollment period, your Medicare B premium may be permanently higher when you eventually enroll. That penalty is equal to 10 percent extra for every 12-month period that you could have been enrolled but weren't.

What if you are still employed? Signing up at age 65 and paying Part B's premium may not be necessary if you are covered by your employer's plan. Instead, you can take advantage of a special eight-month enrollment period that typically starts when your employment ends. If you sign up during this period, you won't pay a penalty for enrolling late.

Your premium for Part B will be deducted from your Social Security check. What if you aren't yet receiving Social Security because you're delaying benefits to get a larger monthly benefit? Instead of writing a check for your Part B premium every month, you can arrange to have the premium automatically deducted from your checking or savings account.

105. MEDICARE ADVANTAGE

Original Medicare is a traditional fee-for-service program that allows seniors to get treatment from any hospital or doctor that accepts Medicare patients. But in recent years, an alternative has sprung up: Medicare Advantage plans.

These plans grew out of the Medicare law passed by Congress in 2003, which also authorized the Part D drug benefit. That law established new rules for private insurers that want to offer plans that compete with original Medicare, with its Part A and B. Today, roughly 30 percent of Medicare beneficiaries are in Medicare Advantage plans.

Many of the plans are some form of managed care. You might be covered only if you use the plan's network of doctors or, alternatively, you could be covered if you go to an out-of-network doctor, but you will pay more.

Medicare Advantage plans combine almost everything offered in original Medicare's Part A and B, plus the plans often include Part D prescription drug coverage. In addition, you don't need to buy a Medigap policy (and, in fact, insurers are barred from selling Medigap policies to those enrolled in Medicare Advantage). You pay a monthly premium for all of this, though your premium will often be lower than the combined premiums for original Medicare Part B and D, plus a Medigap policy.

Intrigued? You can find plans in your area using the Medicare Plan Finder at Medicare.gov. Before you sign up for a Medicare Advantage plan, check to see which of your doctors are in the plan's network. Unhappy with your Medicare Advantage plan? It's possible to return to original Medicare, though you may not be able to get the Medigap policy you want.

106. MEDICARE'S PRESCRIPTION DRUG BENEFIT

Part D drug plans are offered through insurance companies. While most seniors will want to enroll, it isn't mandatory. You will pay a premium, plus there's an annual deductible and a co-payment on each prescription that's filled. The plans don't cover all drugs. Rather, they are required to cover at least two drugs in each therapeutic category.

If you wait beyond age 65 to enroll in Part D, you may pay a penalty unless you were, in the intervening period, receiving a prescription drug benefit from elsewhere that was equally good. The penalty is equal to a permanent 1 percent increase in the base premium for every month you delay, so 10 months of procrastination will cost you a 10 percent higher premium for the rest of your retirement. Result: Even if you don't currently have any prescription drug needs, you will likely want to enroll at age 65.

As you shop for a plan, see whether the drugs you take are covered by the plan and at what cost. The list of covered drugs is known as the "formulary." Need help choosing a Medicare drug plan? Check out the Medicare Plan Finder at Medicare.gov.

107. MEDIGAP INSURANCE

Once you enroll in Medicare Part B, you have six months to choose the Medigap policy you want. During this six-month window, you can't be denied coverage or charged a higher premium because of past or current health issues. If you wait until later, insurers can use medical underwriting, which means policies could cost significantly more, depending on the state of your health, and you may not be able to get the policy you want.

Medigap insurance—sometimes called Medicare supplement insurance—comes in 10 standardized policies, except in Massachusetts, Minnesota and Wisconsin, which have a different set of policies. Depending on the Medigap policy you choose, you will receive help with various deductibles, co-payments and other gaps in Medicare's coverage.

For instance, a Medigap policy might cover your Part A deductible, the co-insurance for a skilled nursing facility or your Part B deductible. It might also cover you while you are traveling outside the U.S. Be sure to shop around: Premiums for the same Medigap policy can vary widely. To search for Medigap policies offered in your state, try the Medigap Policy Search tool at Medicare.gov.

It's possible to change Medigap policies, but tread carefully. Depending on the circumstances, there could be medical underwriting involved, you might pay significantly more and you may not be covered for preexisting conditions for up to six months. Don't cancel your old policy until you receive written notification that you've been accepted for the new policy.

While Medigap policies can plug many of the holes in Medicare, none of them plugs the biggest hole—coverage for custodial stay at a nursing home. For that, folks will need to pay out of pocket, get long-term-care insurance or fall back on Medicaid, and sometimes a combination of all three.

108. MEDICAID

Medicaid is a means-tested program that provides hospital and medical coverage for those with low incomes and limited resources. It's funded by the federal and state governments, but the program is run by the states. Each state has its own rules about who is eligible and what is covered under Medicaid. The program provides comprehensive medical coverage—in some instances, more comprehensive than Medicare. Depending on the state, those who are eligible for Medicaid may be charged modest amounts for some services. A majority of Medicaid recipients are in managed-care programs run by private health plans.

While Medicaid is means-tested, income hasn't historically been the sole criteria for eligibility. You also needed to fall into certain categories, such as children in low-income families, the parents of these children, pregnant women, certain people with disabilities and low-income seniors.

Under the 2010 Affordable Care Act, Medicaid was greatly expanded so that states could offer coverage to those under age 65 with incomes of 133 percent or less of the federal poverty level. But fearful that the expansion would eventually be a burden on state budgets, almost half of all states have declined federal financing to expand Medicaid coverage.

In 2012, a quarter of Medicaid recipients were seniors or those with disabilities, but they accounted for nearly two-thirds of Medicaid spending, according to the Center on Budget and Policy Priorities. Indeed, Medicaid covers more than 60 percent of all nursing home residents. But qualifying for a Medicaid-paid nursing home involves meeting strict financial criteria—and will likely mean your heirs will receive little or nothing.

109. NURSING HOME COSTS

A majority of seniors will spend little or no time in a nursing home. But according to a study published in the Winter 2005/2006 edition of Inquiry, an estimated 16 percent will rack up six-figure costs, with government programs picking up much of the tab. It's easy to incur such hefty expenses: According to Genworth's 2014 Cost of Care Survey, the average annual cost of a semi-private nursing-home room is $77,000. Moreover, the cost varies widely. You might pay $237,000 in Alaska, $142,000 in Connecticut and $84,000 in Florida, but just $51,000 in Texas. Nursing homes in big cities tend to be especially pricey.

Ideally, you will have enough saved by retirement so you can pay nursing home costs out of pocket and skip long-term-care insurance (or "self-insure," as financial experts sometimes call it). But that option is probably only open to those with seven-figure portfolios. What about everybody else? You might plan on applying for Medicaid to pay any nursing home costs. Problem is, to qualify, you will first have to spend down most of your assets.

That might not seem so terrible if you have little money. But if you have done a moderately good job of saving for retirement and have, say, a $400,000 or $500,000 portfolio, it is hardly an attractive prospect. What's the alternative? You might look into long-term-care insurance, including hybrid policies that combine life and long-term-care insurance.

While both men and women need to consider how they will pay for long-term care, it's a particularly pressing issue for women. Because they typically live longer than men, they will often find themselves looking after an ailing husband. But when they need care, they're on their own—and a nursing home may be the only option.

110. LONG-TERM-CARE INSURANCE

Long-term-care insurance has proven to be a problematic product. Many insurers have dropped out of the market. Others have jacked up premiums, making coverage unaffordable for both potential and current policyholders. This is a shame, because long-term-care costs are a huge issue for retirees.

Thinking of buying a policy? The younger you are when you buy a policy, the less likely you are to be rejected for health reasons and the lower the annual premium. But you'll pay those premiums for more years, plus there's more time for the insurance company to drop out of the market or tinker with the policy.

Many folks purchase policies that will cover maybe three years of nursing home costs. Arguably, that's the wrong approach. Using savings, you might be able to afford a year or two in a nursing home. Instead, the big risk is spending five years or more in a nursing home. With that in mind, you might purchase a policy that will pay benefits for more years but hold down costs by opting for a long elimination period, such as six months or a year, which is the initial period when you have to cover costs before the insurance company starts paying.

You'll also need to decide what daily benefit you want, which is the maximum dollar amount the policy will pay each day you need care. To settle on the right number, think about how much you can afford out of pocket. For instance, between Social Security and portfolio income, you might be able to cover half the daily cost of a nursing home. You could then buy a policy that covers the rest. If married, consider a "shared benefit" rider that allows each spouse to use the other's benefit if one of you runs through the maximum benefit on your individual policy.

In addition, pay careful attention to the details. For a policy to start paying, what are the triggers? Usually, you have to display cognitive impairment or need help with at least two "activities of daily living," such as bathing and getting dressed. See if the daily benefit rises each year with inflation, and find out what's covered if you opt for in-home care.

What if you buy a policy and the premiums rise so much that it becomes unaffordable? Rather than dropping the policy, talk to the insurer about whether you can keep the premium the same by reducing the size of the benefit. That isn't ideal—but at least you'll have some coverage after all those years of premium payments.

111. HYBRID INSURANCE POLICIES

Instead of purchasing pure long-term-care insurance, you could buy cash-value life insurance with a long-term-care rider. We discuss cash-value policies later in this chapter. If you need to pay for a nursing home, you could tap into the policy's death benefit to cover your long-term-care costs. If not, the policy's proceeds can pass to your heirs.

That combination may appeal to folks who hate the idea of paying years of premiums for long-term-care insurance, but never getting anything back. It is, however, also a costly way to protect yourself. After all, you are buying life insurance at an advanced age, which is an expensive proposition, and yet you may not need life insurance at that juncture, because you don't have dependents who would suffer financially if you died suddenly.

You can also purchase tax-deferred fixed annuities that have a long-term-care rider. If you don't need long-term care, the money continues to collect interest. If care is needed, you can usually get access to a sum equal to some multiple of your original annuity investment. With the fixed annuity, you avoid buying life insurance you may not need—but you will likely be locking up a large sum that will then earn modest returns.

112. MEDICAID AND NURSING HOME COSTS

Medicaid eligibility rules vary from state to state. Still, before Medicaid starts paying your nursing home expenses, you will be expected to put much of your income and assets toward covering the cost, no matter which state you live in.

A major exception is your primary home. Depending on the state, between \$543,000 and \$814,000 in home equity may be protected in 2014. The house should also be exempt if your spouse, children under age 21, or a blind or disabled child of any age live there. If you are married, the at-home spouse can often keep all income that's solely in his or her name. The spouse who isn't in a nursing home may also be eligible to keep up to $117,240 of the couple's joint assets in 2014 and, depending on the financial circumstances, retain up to $2,931 of the institutionalized spouse's income.

To qualify for Medicaid, you might be tempted to transfer assets to family members. But those transfers need to occur more than five years before you apply for Medicaid or you could be penalized. Let's say you recently transferred $70,000 to your children and the monthly cost for a local nursing home is $7,000, so you effectively gifted 10 months' worth of nursing home expenses. Even if you are eligible for Medicaid based on your current financial situation, Medicaid won't pay your nursing home costs for 10 months after you apply for assistance.

After you die or, if married, after your spouse dies, federal law requires that your state try to recover your Medicaid-paid nursing home costs from your estate. States also have the option to try to recover other Medicaid costs. Want more information? Head to Medicaid.gov.

113. LIFE INSURANCE

Wealthy families sometimes purchase life insurance to save on estate taxes. We discuss that in Part XII. The chief reason to buy life insurance, however, is to provide for your family if you die prematurely.

With that goal in mind, think about who depends on you financially and how they would cope if you keeled over tomorrow. If you're single and don't support anybody, you probably don't need life insurance. Similarly, if you're married, the kids have left home, and you and your spouse are in good shape for retirement, you may not need coverage.

Instead, life insurance is crucial for those who have, say, young children, a stay-at-home spouse and few assets. If that describes you, you likely need a fair amount of life insurance. How much precisely? The suggested amounts are all over the map.

Experts sometimes advise buying enough insurance to cover your family's entire costs until the kids are through college, which is potentially a huge amount—and the insurance premiums may be unaffordable. Alternatively, one rule of thumb suggests you need coverage equal to five-to-seven times your income. That's more likely to fit within the budget, but it doesn't reflect your individual circumstances, including how old your children are, how much debt you have, the wealth you've accumulated and whether your spouse works.

What's the right answer? More than anything, it's important to have at least some coverage. If you're the main breadwinner and you die, your family will likely have to make big changes. You want them to have money to carry them through this transition period. That might mean enough insurance to pay off the mortgage, fund college accounts and cover a few years of living expenses. If you have very young children and your spouse stays home to look after them, you may also want insurance on your spouse's life, because you would face added expenses if he or she died.

Once you decide how much life insurance to buy, next comes a big issue: Should you buy term or permanent life insurance?

114. TERM LIFE INSURANCE

Looking for a low-cost policy that will deliver a big payout to your family if you die prematurely? Term insurance, which provides a death benefit and nothing more, will likely be your best bet.

When you first buy, you typically need to take a medical exam. Many term policies are convertible into permanent life insurance. Most are one of two types: annual renewable term or level-premium term.

Level-term policies are priced so you pay the same premium every year for, say, 10, 15 or 20 years. You may be able to continue coverage beyond the end of the policy's term, but another medical exam might be required. If your health has deteriorated, that could create serious problems. To sidestep this issue, before you first purchase a policy, think carefully about how long you'll need coverage for and don't skimp by buying insurance with a shorter term than you really need.

Meanwhile, with annual renewable term, the premium rises each year as you grow older. But these policies can give you more flexibility. They may be renewable up until age 95, with no further medical exam necessary.

Even if you can renew your term insurance late in life, you probably won't want to—because at that point the premiums can be exorbitant. But by then, you will likely no longer need coverage because your children will be out of the house, and you and your spouse should have enough socked away for retirement.

You might also hear about a third type of term policy: return-of-premium term life insurance. With these policies, if you live until the end of the term—which might be 20 or 30 years—some or all of your premiums are returned to you. That feature, however, means that the premiums on these policies are significantly higher than those on annual renewable term or level-premium term.

115. PERMANENT LIFE INSURANCE

While most folks don't continue term insurance into retirement, permanent insurance is designed to provide lifetime coverage. Also known as cash-value life insurance, a permanent policy involves far higher premiums, because part of each premium goes into an investment account. When you die, the investment account's cash value is used to pay the policy's stated death benefit. If the cash value is less than the death benefit, the difference is paid by the insurance company and represents pure insurance, just like a term policy.

In the early years of a cash-value policy, not much of your premium payment goes into the cash value, partly because the salesperson's commission comes out of those early payments and partly because so much pure insurance needs to be bought. But as time goes on, more and more of each premium payment gets put toward the cash value. This is reminiscent of a mortgage with its shifting mix of principal and interest, which we discuss in Part XI.

Thanks to the buildup in cash value, you don't have to buy so much pure insurance when you're older and life insurance becomes so much more costly. Result: Cash-value life insurance can be affordable in old age, while term insurance isn't.

The proceeds from a life insurance policy are income-tax-free to your beneficiaries. What if you need to tap into a cash-value policy during your lifetime? You may be able to withdraw a sum equal to the amount you put into the policy, with no taxes owed. Alternatively, you could take out a policy loan, though the loan will likely charge a higher interest rate than the return your cash value is earning. Both withdrawals and any loans outstanding at your death will reduce the policy's death benefit.

116. THREE TYPES OF PERMANENT INSURANCE

Intrigued by cash-value life insurance? There are three varieties to choose from:

Whole life. This is the most conservative type of cash-value life insurance, with the insurer guaranteeing that your premiums will remain the same and that the policy's cash value will earn a minimum rate of interest. A whole-life policy can also earn additional dividends that help your cash value grow faster, though these additional dividends aren't guaranteed.

Lately, whole life has received a big push from advisors who advocate BYOB, or "be your own banker," which involves building up a whole-life policy and then using it as a source of borrowed money. But the benefits claimed are inflated, and some of the advice offered, such as reducing your 401(k) contributions so you can put more into a whole-life policy, is dubious at best.

Universal life. While a whole-life policy has a fixed interest rate, the interest paid by a universal life policy varies over time. With indexed universal life, which has recently surged in popularity, the interest you receive can be linked to the returns of a stock market index, often the Standard & Poor's 500. Universal life policies give policyholders some flexibility to vary premium payments and raise or reduce the death benefit.

Variable life. Instead of earning interest, a variable life policy allows you to invest the policy's cash value in a series of subaccounts, which are similar to stock and bond mutual funds. Many variable life policies are actually variable universal life, meaning they offer flexibility to vary payments, like universal life. As stocks have rallied in recent years, sales of variable universal life have picked up.

If you aren't careful, cash-value life insurance's promise of lifetime coverage can break down. Suppose you take out a policy loan, cut back the premiums too much on a universal policy, make poor investment choices from among a variable policy's series of subaccounts or the interest rate drops sharply on a universal policy. In all of these situations, you may need to make big payments to keep the policy going—and without those big payments the policy could lapse or its death benefit could be sharply reduced.

117. INSURANCE COMPANIES

Insurance companies are either stock companies, meaning they are publicly traded and hence have outside shareholders, or they're mutual companies, which means they should be solely focused on helping policyholders. In practice, this oversimplifies the issue. Even a mutual company has multiple constituencies that it has to keep happy, notably its sales force and headquarter staff, including senior executives. Result: Just because you buy a cash-value policy from a mutual insurer doesn't mean the salesman isn't collecting a sizable commission or that the policy's ongoing costs will be low.

Still, it is worth keeping the distinction between stock and mutual insurers in mind if you're interested in buying a whole-life insurance policy. Many such policies are so-called participating policies. That means they are eligible to receive dividends from the insurer. While stock companies also sell participating whole-life policies, a mutual insurer has the potential to make more generous dividend payments because it doesn't also need to compensate public shareholders. The largest mutual insurers include Guardian Life, Massachusetts Mutual, New York Life and Northwestern Mutual.

The distinction between stock and mutual companies is less important when purchasing other types of cash-value life insurance or buying term insurance. With these other policies, you should probably be more focused on the policy's cost and on the insurer's financial strength.

For instance, it's easy enough to get a bunch of term-insurance quotes with a quick online search. But before buying the policy with the lowest premium, check the insurer's rating for financial strength. Favor insurers that are rated A or better by A.M. Best, AA or better by Fitch, Aa2 or better by Moody's, and AA or better by Standard & Poor's. What if you're looking for cash-value life insurance? Comparing costs is harder. But you might check out Ameritas Life Insurance and TIAA-CREF. Both are rated highly for financial strength and have a reputation for selling lower-cost policies.

118. TERM VS. PERMANENT

Life insurance offers one unbeatable advantage: The proceeds are income tax free to your beneficiaries. That's a key reason to buy a cash-value policy with the goal of having coverage at the end of your life, even if you die at a ripe old age. But set against that advantage are three drawbacks.

First, you probably don't need lifetime coverage. Instead, your need for life insurance will likely be over by your 50s or 60s because, by then, your kids will have left home and your spouse would have enough money if you died suddenly.

Second, because the premiums on a cash-value policy are so steep, you might skimp on the death benefit—and leave your family in the financial lurch if you die prematurely. In fact, because the premiums are so steep, many policyholders drop their policies. The Society of Actuaries estimates that 39 percent of whole-life policies are terminated within the first 10 years. These folks would have incurred the steep upfront commissions charged by cash-value policies, but managed to accrue precious little cash value.

Third, if you're looking to invest, there are lower-cost options with better return potential than building up an insurance policy's cash value. For instance, you could fund a 401(k), with its initial tax deduction, tax-deferred growth and possible matching employer contribution.

What about that income-tax-free legacy for your heirs? If that's your goal, you could fund a Roth 401(k) or Roth IRA. The bottom line: Instead of paying the large premiums on cash-value life insurance, most folks would likely get better returns by buying low-cost term insurance and investing the difference.

JONATHAN'S TAKE: As the saying goes, life insurance is sold, not bought. Unfortunately, the insurance that's sold most aggressively is cash-value life insurance. Meanwhile, term insurance could provide many families with great protection at relatively low cost, but it isn't nearly as lucrative for insurance agents to sell—and many customers, alas, don't seek it out on their own.

119. DISABILITY INSURANCE

Through their employer, many people have disability insurance, which provides them with income if they can't work. The term "disability" might suggest some sort of injury, but the vast majority of long-term work absences result from illnesses, such as heart disease or cancer. Don't have disability coverage through your employer? You might want to buy a policy on your own.

Think of it as protection for your human capital's income-earning ability. Disability insurance can be especially important for those who are single. While someone who is married can rely on the other spouse to keep bringing in a paycheck, you won't have that safety net if you're on your own.

Individual disability policies have elimination periods, such as 90 or 180 days, which is the time you have to wait for benefits to begin once you meet the policy's definition of being disabled. The longer the elimination period, the lower your premium will be. You can also hold down premiums by limiting the number of years that benefits are potentially paid and by reducing the monthly benefit amount. If you buy disability insurance on your own, using after-tax dollars, any benefits paid are tax-free. By contrast, if you have group coverage through your employer, any payout will be taxable.

Disability insurance is all about the details: You'll want to know whether you'll receive benefits if you can't do your current job or only if you can't do a similar job—or perhaps only if you can't work at all.

Disability benefits are also available from Social Security. But to receive them, your disability has to be sufficiently severe that it's expected to result in death or to prevent you from working for at least 12 months. Even then, once you're deemed eligible, you'll have to wait more than five months for payments to start.

120. AUTO INSURANCE

Many drivers view auto insurance as protection in case they wreck their car or the vehicle gets stolen. But the policies serve another, equally important purpose: They protect you in case you're sued. Here are the key elements of an auto policy:

Liability coverage. This tells you the maximum the policy will pay if you cause an accident in which somebody is hurt or which damages another vehicle or other property. Because of the risk of lawsuits, you may want to purchase an umbrella liability policy to provide additional protection. To qualify for umbrella coverage, the insurer may insist you raise the liability limits on your auto policy—which is probably a good idea.

Uninsured and underinsured driver coverage. This protects you if you're involved in an accident caused by another driver who either doesn't have insurance coverage or is underinsured. Even though you weren't responsible for the accident, your insurance company will often help pay your medical and auto repair bills if you have uninsured and underinsured driver coverage.

Collision and comprehensive. If you have an accident or your car is stolen, this covers the cost of repairing or replacing your own vehicle. Got a car that is only worth a few thousand dollars? You may want to drop collision and comprehensive coverage, because the financial loss would be modest if your car were totaled or stolen.

Deductibles. If you need collision and comprehensive coverage, consider raising the deductibles so you lower the premium. As always with insurance, the goal is to protect against big financial hits, not minor losses. You can also hold down your insurance costs by improving your credit score, maintaining a good driving record, claiming a low mileage discount if you drive relatively little and favoring cars that are cheaper to insure. A sports car often comes with a large insurance bill, while minivans and SUVs are relatively inexpensive to insure.

121. HOMEOWNER'S INSURANCE

Homeowner's insurance protects your house and personal belongings against risks such as fire, falling trees, theft and water damage from burst pipes, while also providing coverage if someone has an accident at your home and sues you. But are you fully protected?

Take a look at the policy's coverage limits. Would you be able to rebuild your house for the sum specified—or should you call your insurer and ask that it be increased? Homeowner's insurance typically caps how much it will pay out for specific items, such as jewelry, silverware, electronics, collectible coins, fine art and so on. If you have items that are especially valuable—meaning they're worth more than a few thousand dollars—you might talk to your insurance company about extra coverage.

In addition, standard homeowner's insurance typically doesn't cover earthquakes or flooding caused by, say, an overflowing river or an ocean surge. Instead, you'll need a separate policy or a special rider to cover those risks. In case you're sued, you may also want umbrella liability coverage to supplement your homeowner's policy.

All this extra coverage will boost your premium payments. To offset that hit, you might look for ways to trim your premiums. For instance, you could raise the deductible on the policy from, say, $500 to $2,000. You might also qualify for a discount if you have smoke detectors, a sprinkler system, or a fire and burglary alarm system that alerts an outside service. In addition, you may get a discount if you buy a variety of policies, such as auto, home and umbrella liability coverage, from the same insurance company. Maintaining a good credit score can also help hold down your insurance costs.

122. RENTER'S INSURANCE

If you rent a house or apartment, your landlord's insurance policy might cover the building, but it typically won't cover your possessions. That is where renter's insurance can come in handy.

The policies cover personal possessions, including furniture, computers, televisions and jewelry. If these items are stolen or damaged by a fire or broken water pipes, you should be reimbursed either for the current cash value or for the replacement cost. A policy might provide $50,000 in total protection, with caps on certain categories, such as limiting jewelry coverage to $1,000 unless a special rider is purchased. Renter's insurance doesn't cover damage from floods caused by, say, heavy rains, and it may not cover hurricanes.

Many policies provide liability coverage in the event someone is injured at your home. This typically covers claims of up to $100,000, including the related legal costs. You may also receive living expenses if you're unable to live in your home for a period of time.

What if you figure your personal possessions aren't worth that much or replacing them won't cause that much of a financial burden? If that's the case, you may want to skip renter's insurance—unless your landlord insists you get a policy as a condition of renting the apartment.

123. ASSET PROTECTION

What does "asset protection" mean? It's about fending off creditors who have a legal claim on your assets. That claim might arise because you took on too much debt or because you ended up on the wrong end of a lawsuit. While these might seem like two quite different problems, in both cases you could end up filing for bankruptcy.

By the time bankruptcy or litigation is threatened, however, there isn't much you can do. It's probably too late to rearrange your finances by, say, gifting assets to your children. Such gifts could be deemed a fraudulent transfer. Instead, your best bet is to take steps now, before there's any hint of a financial claim against you. That's especially true if you're in an occupation that tends to attract legal claims, such as working as an accountant, doctor or lawyer. Lawsuits are also a risk if you work in real estate, including as an architect, builder or developer. What to do?

• Find out which assets enjoy creditor protection in your state and consider making the most of those assets. Your retirement accounts, and possibly your home, may be protected. A few minutes with an Internet search engine will likely turn up key details about the law in your state.

• Look into buying umbrella liability insurance to supplement whatever liability coverage you have through your auto, homeowner's or renter's policies.

• Think about whether your business life puts your investment accounts and other personal assets at risk and, if necessary, take steps to limit that risk.

• If you're wealthy, you might talk to an attorney about trust arrangements that can help protect your assets. Different trust arrangements are discussed in Part XII.

What if you have already been slapped with a lawsuit or you're considering bankruptcy? You will need to hire a qualified attorney. Ask which assets enjoy creditor protection in your state. It might be ill-advised to move money into these assets now, but you also shouldn't pull money out. For instance, given the creditor protection enjoyed by retirement accounts, you don't want to use those accounts to pay legal bills and other expenses. If you fear a lawsuit, you should also immediately contact your insurance company to see if your various policies will provide liability coverage.

124. RETIREMENT ACCOUNTS

If you file for bankruptcy, the money in your retirement accounts should be protected from creditors. For employer-sponsored plans, such as 401(k) or 403(b) plans, the amount is unlimited. For IRAs, the protected sum is increased periodically and currently stands at $1,245,475. If you roll over money from an employer's plan into an IRA, this money should remain fully protected and not count toward the $1,245,475. But as a precaution, keep your rollover IRA in a separate account from your regular IRA.

What if somebody slips on your sidewalk and successfully sues you? Again, employer-sponsored plans should be protected. But solo 401(k) plans and IRAs, including rollover IRAs, are at risk under federal law. There's a good chance, however, that your state's law may provide protection.

There are a few caveats to bear in mind. First, your retirement accounts aren't protected from the IRS if you owe federal taxes. Second, any money you withdraw from retirement accounts will no longer be protected, and creditors could seize it. Third, the Supreme Court ruled in 2014 that, if you file for bankruptcy, an inherited IRA isn't protected from creditors, unless you inherited the money from your spouse.

Retirement accounts aren't the only type of tax-sheltered account that's potentially off-limits to creditors. In some states, money in cash-value life insurance, annuities and 529 college plans also enjoys creditor protection.

125. HOMESTEAD EXEMPTION

The phrase "homestead exemption" occasionally refers to a break on property taxes that's available in some states. But at issue here is something quite different: In some states, you can't be forced to sell your home to satisfy the demands of creditors.

In states such as Alaska, California, Colorado and New Mexico, the amount of protection is capped at a relatively modest level. But in other states, such as Florida, Iowa, Kansas, South Dakota and Texas, the protection is quite broad.

A homestead exemption may help if you lose a lawsuit, have nonmortgage debt or file for bankruptcy. But it only applies to your primary residence, not a second home. Moreover, it probably won't help you if you default on your mortgage or owe taxes.

Don't live in a state with a robust homestead exemption? You might see if you and your spouse can title your home and other assets as "tenancy by the entirety." This form of ownership is only available to married couples and only in some states. What's the advantage of tenancy by the entirety? You can't transfer your ownership stake without the consent of your spouse. That could prevent a forced sale of your home if one of you loses a lawsuit. It won't, however, help if you are both sued.

126. UMBRELLA LIABILITY INSURANCE

Got money in a regular taxable account? If you lose a lawsuit, the plaintiff won't have much trouble claiming that money—which is why you might want umbrella liability insurance, sometimes known as excess liability insurance.

With homeowner's and auto policies, a big chunk of your premium payment goes toward buying liability coverage. If somebody sues you because they're hurt at your home or because you cause an auto accident, your homeowner's and auto policies will cover your attorney's fees and any judgment against you. But the liability coverage may be capped at $250,000 or $300,000, and it could be significantly lower.

Plaintiffs might settle for that, rather than coming after your personal assets. But what if they demand more? That's where umbrella liability insurance comes in. It provides additional protection, perhaps $1 million or more, that's over and above what your homeowner's and auto policies provide. Umbrella liability insurance is typically purchased from the same insurer that covers your home and car.

In addition to providing protection if you're sued for damaging property or causing bodily injury, an umbrella policy can also cover other situations, such as if you're sued for slander or libel. Pay attention to the exclusions. For instance, the policies typically won't protect you if there's a legal claim resulting from your business or professional life, or if you deliberately damage somebody else's property.

Premiums seem to have increased a fair amount in recent years, but the policies remain relatively inexpensive compared to the potential payout. Got assets you're aiming to protect? It's worth looking into an umbrella policy.

127. BUSINESS LIABILITY

Just as you can purchase umbrella liability insurance to protect your personal life, there are policies that cover business liability. These might be part of a business owner's policy that also provides property coverage, or they can be bought separately.

General liability insurance typically covers bodily harm and property damage. But what about the risk that someone sues you for, say, behaving negligently or making a damaging mistake? For that, you might take out professional liability insurance such as the malpractice insurance purchased by doctors or the errors-and-omissions policies bought by lawyers, real estate brokers, consultants and others.

If you're self-employed or run a small business, you might also want to organize the business as a limited liability company or an S corporation, rather than operating it as a sole proprietorship. Why take that added step? If you run the business as a sole proprietorship, you could be personally liable if the business gets sued, while an LLC or S corporation can protect your personal finances from claims by creditors against the business. Typically, with an LLC or S corporation, you can't lose more than the money you put into the business.

While an LLC or S corporation can provide additional protection against creditors, it shouldn't make any difference from a tax point of view. If you operate a business as a sole proprietorship, you include the income and expenses of the business on your personal tax return, with the details listed on Schedule C. Similarly, both an LLC and S corporation are so-called pass-through entities, which means gains and losses pass directly through to the owners, who then include them on their personal tax returns.

Which is better, an LLC or S corporation? An LLC offers substantially more flexibility, involves less paperwork and may provide better protection if someone tries to seize your business stake to satisfy a personal debt. But if you envisage your business attracting venture capital funding and maybe even issuing shares to the public, you might use the S corporation structure because it's easier to turn an S corporation into a C corporation, the structure used by larger companies. Before making a decision, consider consulting a knowledgeable attorney, in part because there are differences in state law that could sway your decision.

PART VI

SPENDING
NO, THIS ISN'T SOME BORING
CHAPTER ABOUT BUDGETING

I f you come across a chapter on spending in a personal-finance book, you should immediately be on high alert. There's a good chance the author is about to berate you for spending too much and—horror of horrors—insist that you create and follow a written budget.

So let's start with a basic truth: After exhaustive research, it's been scientifically established that there are only three people in America who draw up and follow detailed monthly budgets and, no, you wouldn't want to go out for a drink with any of them.

What's the alternative? Consider a much simpler approach: Make sure you save enough every month toward your various goals. If you do that, there's no need to budget. Instead, you should feel free to spend your remaining money on whatever takes your fancy. We'll tackle saving money in Part VII.

That said, here are two suggestions: First, make sure you have some sense for how much of your monthly spending goes toward fixed costs and how much is discretionary. This can be crucial information if you find yourself out of work, you get hit with large unexpected expenses or you're figuring out how to generate enough retirement income. Second, think hard about how you spend your money and what financial goals you pursue— and make sure you're squeezing plenty of happiness from your hard-earned dollars.

128. MAJOR EXPENSES

Some monthly expenses are pretty much unavoidable—and the two biggest are typically housing and transportation. On average, American families spend more than $17,100 a year on housing, according to the Bureau of Labor Statistics' Consumer Expenditure Survey that was released in September 2014. That's equal to a third of the average American household's $51,100 in spending during 2013. Included in that figure are not just mortgage or rent, but also utilities, property taxes, furniture and appliances.

Don't forget that this is an average, one that's dragged down by those retirees who are living mortgage-free. For folks who just bought a house, often they'll be spending close to a third of their pretax income just on mortgage payments, homeowner's insurance and property taxes.

The BLS survey found that transportation eats up another $9,000 a year, or almost 18 percent of spending. This number takes into account vehicle purchases, gas, repairs and auto insurance, among other items. Add it up, and half our monthly spending is getting swallowed up by our cars and our homes.

We all need somewhere to live. Most of us need a car. The Federal Reserve's 2013 Survey of Consumer Finances found that 86.3 percent of families own a car or other vehicle. The question is, are you spending more on your home and transportation than is really sensible? You don't want to box yourself in financially by committing to fixed monthly costs that are too high. Indeed, if you find yourself living paycheck to paycheck, consider taking a close look at your fixed monthly expenses.

129. HOW OUR SPENDING HAS CHANGED

Over the past 50 years, we've seen two key changes in the way America spends, according to a June 2011 study by the Commerce Department's Bureau of Economic Analysis. First, we're devoting far less of our income to life's basics. Clothing, footwear, food and beverages accounted for just 11 percent of spending in 2009, down from 27.4 percent in 1959. This excludes restaurant meals, which have held fairly constant at around 6 percent of total expenditures.

Second, spending on health care, financial services and insurance has soared. For instance, health care rose from 5.9 percent of total spending in 1959 to an astonishing 19.7 percent in 2009. This includes hospital costs, doctor visits, prescription drugs and eyeglasses. Much of this cost wasn't paid directly by consumers, but rather by private insurers, Medicare and Medicaid.

Looking to spend less and save more? You should have plenty of leeway. Less of our income is needed to cover life's basics. Meanwhile, there are plenty of ways to cut your insurance costs, as you can learn in Part V, and also money-management costs, as you will discover in Part VIII. Health care is another area where you could potentially save money by exercising regularly, eating sensibly, not smoking, wearing a seat belt and taking other steps to look after your health.

130. SPENDING FOR FUN

How much do we spend on fun, broadly defined? Based on 2013 figures from the Commerce Department's Bureau of Economic Analysis, it's a hefty sum.

U.S. households spent an average $4,300 on eating out and $1,400 on concerts, gym memberships, amusement parks, sports events, museums and movie theaters. We spent another $800 on cable and satellite television, $900 on tobacco, $1,000 on gambling, $1,100 on beer, wine and spirits, another $700 on alcohol when eating out, $700 on hotels and motels, and $1,100 on foreign travel.

Keep in mind that these are averages. For instance, the $900 average for tobacco lumps together both smokers and nonsmokers, so presumably the smokers are spending significantly more than $900 a year.

The Commerce Department looks at personal consumption using top-down economic data, while the Bureau of Labor Statistics' Consumer Expenditure Survey relies on individuals to report their own spending. How truthful are survey participants? It seems they aren't so truthful when it comes to spending on things like cigarettes and booze. According to the BLS survey for 2013, households reported spending $330 on tobacco and $445 on alcohol, far less than the Commerce Department's top-down data indicate.

It's important to spend money on things you enjoy—but it's also important to save enough for retirement and other goals. Saving enough? Keep spending as you are. Not saving enough? Maybe it's time to look closely not only at your fixed costs, but also at discretionary "fun money" spending.

131. FIVE STEPS FOR 2015

Want to get a handle on your monthly expenditures and whether all those dollars are being spent wisely? To kick things off, try these five steps:

• Think back to 2014 and all the things you spent money on, whether it was clothes, dinners out, a vacation or a hobby. Which expenditures brought you the most pleasure? Use that to guide your spending in 2015. Next, repeat the exercise—but this time think about expenditures that brought you little or no happiness and which you might even regret. Some of these expenses might have been unavoidable, but others were likely discretionary—and maybe you should skip this discretionary spending in future.

• Suppose you were hit with the financial equivalent of the plague of locusts. Maybe you'll lose your job, the roof needs replacing, the car needs major repairs and you need to provide financial help to your favorite relative. What's the minimum dollar amount you would need each month to keep your household running?

• If you're struggling to save money on a regular basis, get a notebook and make a point of writing down every dollar you spend during the course of a month. This won't just give you insights into where your money goes. Along the way, you may also find your spending starts to drop. Why? Because you're writing down what you spend, you will likely think harder before opening your wallet, and that alone may prompt you to spend less.

• Look back and pinpoint the times in your life when you were happiest. What made these times so happy? What part did money play? Money supposedly buys happiness. But often, the happiest times in our lives are when we have relatively little money, and instead our happiness has more to do with what we are doing and who we are with.

• Think about what career you would pursue if money weren't an issue. Many folks in middle age grow weary of their current jobs and think of changing. What would it take financially to make a big career shift?

132. FIXED VS. DISCRETIONARY EXPENSES

While it probably isn't necessary to track every dollar you spend, there is value in knowing one key number: How much of your monthly spending goes toward fixed costs.

We're talking here about the total monthly amount devoted to items such as mortgage or rent, property taxes, car payments, insurance premiums, student-loan payments, utilities, Internet access, phone and groceries. Given enough time, you could probably trim these fixed costs and, indeed, you might need to do that if you find you simply can't save enough for your various goals. Still, fixed costs are tough to reduce in the short term. By contrast, discretionary expenses—like vacations, entertainment and eating out—can be quickly eliminated if the need arises.

That need might arise if you find yourself out of work or you suddenly need to pay for, say, a major home or car repair. Until you find work or pay the repair bills, you might cut out discretionary expenses and instead limit your monthly spending to fixed costs. The amount of your fixed monthly costs might also help determine the size of your emergency fund, a topic we tackle in Part V.

In addition, knowing your monthly fixed costs is useful as you develop your retirement-income strategy. As discussed in Part II, you might endeavor to have enough regular monthly income from Social Security, any employer pensions, income annuities, dividends and interest to cover your fixed costs. That way, you can be reasonably confident you can pay the bills if there's a major slump in stock and bond prices.

133. KEEPING FIXED COSTS LOW

If you find it tough to save, the reason may not be lavish spending. Instead, there could be another explanation: Maybe your fixed monthly costs are too high, leaving you with little financial breathing room.

The biggest culprit is likely to be your mortgage or rent payment. For instance, if you live in a major city, it can be hard to find reasonably priced housing, even if you opt for a small place or a less desirable neighborhood. Alternatively, maybe you have boxed yourself in by committing to a slew of monthly payments, everything from car-lease payments to cell-phone plans to cable television.

Taken together, these fixed monthly costs can take a big chunk out of your income, especially if you're early in your career and not yet making decent money. What to do? You might aim to keep your fixed monthly costs at 50 percent or less of your gross (meaning pretax) income—and the lower, the better.

JONATHAN'S TAKE: I have come to believe that holding down fixed monthly living costs is perhaps the key contributor to financial success. If your fixed costs are low relative to your income, you will find it easier to save, you will be in better shape if you get laid off, you will need a smaller nest egg to retire in comfort and, if you become discontented with your current career, you'll have the financial flexibility to take a job that's less lucrative but perhaps more fulfilling.

134. RUNNING FAST ON THE HEDONIC TREADMILL

Money may buy happiness—but not nearly as much as we imagine. For proof, think about the major purchases you've made over the past five years. You might have bought a new house or car, purchased furniture for the living room or remodeled the kitchen.

In all likelihood, you contemplated these expenditures for months. You imagined how great it would be to take delivery of the new car or to have a spanking new kitchen. You thought about how these purchases would make your life so much better. And sure enough, you were happy at first. But within a few weeks or months, you likely found yourself barely noticing the new car and the new kitchen. Instead, you were increasingly preoccupied and excited about something else—your next big expenditure and how that new purchase would somehow transform your life.

What's going on here? At issue is a psychological phenomenon known as the hedonic treadmill. We spend our lives lusting after the next promotion, the next pay raise or the next major purchase, only to find we quickly become dissatisfied and start hankering after something else.

This is another trait we can blame on our hunter-gatherer ancestors: They survived in a hostile world because they were never satisfied with what they had and strove constantly to get ahead—and we still carry those instincts within us. So how can we get more happiness out of our dollars? Academic research offers some intriguing insights, as you'll learn in the next section.

Our tendency to adapt to material improvements in our lives may thwart the pursuit of greater happiness. But adaptation can also save us from everlasting misery. Just as we grow accustomed to good things in our lives, we also adapt to terrible developments. Getting laid off, suffering a disability or a family member's death can all seem like events from which we'll never recover. And yet we do.

135. GETTING MORE HAPPINESS FROM YOUR DOLLARS

How can we get off the hedonic treadmill—and squeeze more satisfaction out of our time and money? Here are some insights from the academic literature:

• Spend time with friends and family. Throw a party. Go out to dinner with friends. Fly across the country to see your children or grandchildren. Happiness research suggests a robust network of friends and family can be a huge source of happiness.

• Devote yourself to work and hobbies that you find challenging, you're passionate about, you think are important and you feel you're good at. While achieving our goals often isn't as satisfying as we imagine, making progress toward these goals can give us great satisfaction. Think about those moments when you're engaged in activities you love, you're completely absorbed and time just whizzes by. Those can be among our happiest times.

• Buy experiences, not things. The new car will likely go from a source of happiness to a source of unhappiness as it gets dinged up and breaks down. By contrast, a vacation can provide not just a wonderful week or two with family, but also many months of eager anticipation and many years of fond memories.

• Move closer to work. Research suggests a long commute can be terrible for happiness. We like to feel in control, and that's tough to do when you're dealing with traffic or public transportation.

• Don't move to a ritzier neighborhood than you can truly afford. Your wealthy neighbors will be a constant reminder that you aren't so fortunate.

• Give a little. Volunteering doesn't just help others. It can also make us feel good about ourselves. Ditto for buying gifts.

• Count your blessings. Okay, maybe the new car doesn't give you the same thrill it once did. But you might be able to squeeze a little more happiness from the vehicle if you pause for a moment, admire it and think how lucky you are.

136. WOULD MORE MONEY MAKE YOU HAPPIER?

Ask folks the above question and they almost always answer with a robust "yes." And they're right—but not to the degree they imagine.

If you lift people out of poverty, you can greatly improve their level of happiness. But from there, gains come more slowly, and it can take large sums of money to make someone measurably happier. A big reason is the hedonic treadmill: We quickly adapt to material improvements in our lives.

Still, those with higher incomes and greater wealth tend to report that they're happier. That suggests that more income and wealth do help. But this could also be the result of a so-called focusing illusion. In other words, when you ask those who are better off about their level of happiness, they may think about how fortunate they are and that prompts them to say that yes, of course they're happy.

But are they? It isn't clear. For instance, those with higher incomes also typically report that they suffer more stress and anger during the day—hardly hallmarks of happiness.

Moreover, while more money may help happiness, many other factors are also at work. We all seem to have a happiness "set point"—a predisposition to be more or less happy—and that's tough to change. In addition, happiness seems to be related to age.

137. MIDDLE-AGED AND MISERABLE

Yes, the midlife crisis is a real phenomenon. Happiness through life tends to be U-shaped. Most of us start our adult lives feeling pretty happy. But things deteriorate through our 30s, we often hit bottom in our 40s and then our happiness rebounds from there. In fact, our later years can be among the happiest times in our life.

What's going on here? It may be that our 40s are relatively unhappy because we're under substantial stress as we juggle children and work responsibilities, while perhaps also helping elderly parents. As we get into our 50s, the pressure starts to subside.

Alternatively, maybe our deteriorating happiness through our 30s and 40s reflects a realization that we won't fulfill our youthful ambitions, our accomplishments won't be all that notable and we won't make much of a mark on the world. We eventually come to terms with this, and that's when our happiness rebounds.

Whatever the reason for this phenomenon, it has practical implications. To make sure you don't reach your 40s feeling financially trapped, try to save diligently as soon as you enter the workforce. That will get you on track for retirement, because you'll enjoy decades of investment compounding, and you may be able to avoid some of the financial anxiety that consumes others throughout their adult lives.

By starting to save early, you might also give yourself options that can ease any midlife unhappiness, such as changing careers. We are often happiest when we're engaged in activities that we're passionate about and that we think are important. If you save diligently, while also keeping your fixed living costs low, you may have the freedom later in life to work for a smaller paycheck but greater satisfaction.

138. JONATHAN'S TAKE: MONEY AND HAPPINESS

I think money is sort of like health. It's only when you're sick that you realize how great it is to feel healthy. Similarly, it's only when you don't have enough money that you realize how great it is to be on a solid financial footing. More money may not make you happier—but not having money could make you extremely unhappy.

What does this mean for your personal finances? You want to get to the point where money isn't something you worry about. And the way you do that is to live beneath your means, save like crazy and try to accumulate a decent-size investment portfolio.

At first blush, this may not sound like a whole lot of fun. But the truth is, if you're like most people, the dollars you spend aren't buying you a whole lot of happiness. All those cars and houses and toys you want? They will likely bring you surprisingly little pleasure.

Instead, research suggests there are two keys to happiness. First, we need to spend our days striving after things we think are important. Second, we need to be surrounded by friends and family. We need fulfilling work—and we need community. If you manage your finances carefully and don't get sidetracked by excessive spending, you should be able to build a life where both are possible.

PART VII

SAVING

IT'S THE WAY EVERYDAY AMERICANS GET RICH

B y definition, the money we don't spend is saved. So why bother with a separate chapter on saving? There are two reasons.

First, saving deserves its own chapter because there simply isn't enough of it going on. In 2014, the monthly savings rate ran at around 5 percent, far below the 9 to 13 percent we saw from 1950 through the mid-1980s. Yes, some people inherit fortunes or build successful small businesses. But for most of us, if we're to grow rich, we need to save diligently month after month.

Second, while saving money sounds simple, it sure doesn't come naturally to us. Like dieting and exercising regularly, it takes a lot of self-control to save money every month. Think about our hunter-gatherer ancestors. They didn't worry about stashing part of their paycheck in a 401(k) plan to pay for a retirement that might be decades away. Their focus was on surviving until tomorrow, and that meant consuming whenever they got the chance.

Today, we have constant chances to consume and, thanks to our ancient instincts, we're often tempted to seize those opportunities. But if we're to avoid a life of financial stress and eventually retire in comfort, we need to beat back our desires and save perhaps 12 to 15 percent of every paycheck for retirement, and even more if we have other goals. How can you get yourself on the right track? You might consider the many advantages of saving a healthy sum on a regular basis, and then nudge yourself to save more by employing a host of tricks.

JONATHAN'S TAKE: For ordinary Americans, what's the secret to getting rich? It's no secret at all: You need to live beneath your means and save a healthy sum. Without that discipline, your chances of amassing significant wealth are slim. The good news: It doesn't take much to become a great saver. Suppose you're currently spending 95 cents out of every $1 you earn, while saving the other 5 cents. To increase your monthly savings rate by 100 percent, all you need to do is to trim your spending to 90 cents out of every $1 earned, a mere 5 percent decline.

139. AMERICA'S SAVINGS HABITS

In the 11 months through November 2014, Americans saved between 4.4 and 5.1 percent of their disposable personal income each month, calculates the Commerce Department's Bureau of Economic Analysis. This is savings as a percentage of after-tax income. Why is that important? The 10 percent-plus savings rates suggested by many financial experts are typically couched in terms of pretax income. Those suggested savings rates would be even higher if they were expressed as a percentage of after-tax income. In other words, the official savings rate is even more disappointing than it seems.

It wasn't always this way. During the 35 years through 1984, the annual savings rate averaged 11.1 percent and never fell below 9 percent, according to Commerce Department figures. Since then, the annual savings rate has never been as high as 9 percent. From 1985 to 1998, it averaged just 7.3 percent. From 1999 to 2013, it was even worse, averaging a meager 4.7 percent, despite a modest improvement since the Great Recession of 2008.

In short, what we've seen is a gradual collapse in our savings habits in the years since the Second World War. As memories of the Great Depression of the 1930s have faded and life in the U.S. has grown more comfortable and stable, it seems Americans have felt less urgency to save. By contrast, the savings rate in China is three times higher than in the U.S., according to World Bank figures for 2012. Clearly, the Chinese aren't quite so confident about their financial future.

Increasing income inequality may also lie behind America's lowly savings rate, as well as our high household debt. As those lower down the income spectrum worry less about their financial future and more about keeping up with rising living standards, they have ended up spending more than is prudent.

In the late 1990s, some argued that America's collapsing savings rate shouldn't concern us, because it failed to take into account rising stock prices, which were more than compensating for our dismal savings habits. The same argument was made in the early 2000s about rising home values.

Problem was, these exceptionally good stock and housing returns effectively borrowed from the future. Sure enough, the good times were followed by stretches of truly wretched performance—and those who hadn't saved were left shaking their heads at the sorry state of their finances.

140. FIVE STEPS FOR 2015

If you aren't a diligent saver, you are highly unlikely to amass a decent-size investment portfolio. Time to make amends? Here are five steps that can help get your finances pointed in the right direction:

• Add up how much you saved for retirement in 2014, both in your employer's plan and elsewhere. Include any matching employer contribution you received. Did you manage to save at least 12 percent of your pretax income? If not, you may want to crank up your savings rate in 2015.

• Make sure you're investing at least enough in your employer's 401(k) or similar retirement plan to get the full matching employer contribution.

• Set up mutual fund automatic investment plans. Don't have enough to open a fund account? Artisan Funds, Buffalo Funds and Scout Investments will waive their required minimums if you commit to investing $50 or $100 every month. Meanwhile, at Charles Schwab, the regular mutual fund minimum is just $100. You can find further low-minimum ideas in Part XIII.

• Commit to stepping up your savings rate if the stock market drops 10 percent or more in 2015. This will give you the sort of performance boost promised by a strategy known as value averaging.

• Talk to your children about your own financial struggles when you were younger. These sorts of family stories are much more powerful than any lecture you can deliver on the importance of financial prudence—and you may inspire not only your children, but also yourself.

141. HOW MUCH SHOULD YOU SAVE?

One rule of thumb says that, if you're in the workforce, you should save 10 percent of your pretax income every year toward retirement.

But with both future investment returns and future employment uncertain, it's probably wiser to save 12 to 15 percent and to start socking away money as soon as you enter the workforce. By starting in your 20s, you will have a cushion if you later find yourself out of work, and you'll get greater potential benefit from investment growth.

What if you will receive a traditional employer pension or your employer matches part of your contribution to your 401(k) or similar plan? You might save somewhat less than 12 to 15 percent. On the other hand, if you don't start saving for retirement until your 30s or 40s, you will likely need to save far more. In addition, you probably have other goals, such as buying a home or putting the kids through college, and those goals will necessitate additional savings.

Add it all up and you might find you ought to save 20 percent of your income every year and possibly more. That, alas, is a target few people will hit. But even if your neighbors don't save that much, maybe you can. In all likelihood, you will never regret the sacrifice and you'll be thrilled with the results. As you'll learn in the pages ahead, by saving regularly starting early in your adult life, you can enjoy a host of advantages—including getting time on your side, saving a bundle in taxes, avoiding all kinds of costs and sharply reducing the nest egg you need to support a similar spending level once retired.

142. THE EARLIER, THE BETTER

The sooner you start setting aside money for retirement and other goals, the easier it will be to amass the necessary sums, partly because you will have more months when you're saving and partly because you should benefit more from investment compounding.

Compounding is the process by which money grows over time. Imagine you started with $1,000 and earned 6 percent a year. During the first year, your $1,000 would earn $60, turning your $1,000 into $1,060. If that $1,060 again earns 6 percent during the second year, you'd be up to $1,124, as you notch gains not only on your original $1,000, but also on the $60 reinvested from the prior year. And so it goes on, with your $1,000 growing to $1,191 after three years, $1,338 after five years, $1,791 after 10 years, $3,207 after 20 years and $10,286 after 40 years.

The miraculous way that money compounds, which we discuss further in Part VIII, is captured by the rule of 72. If you take your expected rate of return and divide it into 72, you can find out how long it will take to double your money. For instance, at 6 percent a year, it takes 12 years to double your money.

The numbers are even more impressive if you combine investment compounding with regular saving. Suppose you earn 6 percent annually and also save $1,000 a year. At that rate, you would have $5,975 after five years, $13,972 after 10 years, $38,993 after 20 years and $164,048 after 40 years.

Problem is, the benefits of both compounding and regular saving can seem meager in the early years. But if you keep at it for maybe a dozen or 15 years, you should reach a tipping point, where your annual investment gains start to surpass the annual amount you save. Suddenly, your portfolio will be hitting on both cylinders—and you may find your portfolio growing by leaps and bounds.

143. WHY SAVING IS A BARGAIN

There are all kinds of good reasons to save regularly. Here's another to add to the list: Saving is a bargain—and spending is mighty expensive.

How expensive? Let's say you earn an extra $1,000 and you're in the 25 percent federal income tax bracket. After deducting federal income taxes, Social Security and Medicare payroll taxes, and state income taxes, you might be left with $650 to spend. When you spend that $650, you might end up with barely $600 of merchandise, because in most places you'll also need to pay sales taxes.

By contrast, if you put the $1,000 in your employer's 401(k) or similar retirement plan, you get to keep the entire $1,000. As an added bonus, if your employer matches your 401(k) contributions at 50 cents on the dollar, your $1,000 would become $1,500.

That's pretty enticing. Instead of $600 of spending, you might have $1,500 for retirement—and that $1,500 could double or triple in value, and perhaps more, by the time you quit the workforce. True, you'll need to pay income taxes when you withdraw the money in retirement. But all the intervening years of tax-deferred growth should go a long way toward offsetting that eventual financial pain.

144. HOW MONEY SAVES YOU MONEY

Life is cheaper when you have some savings. How so? Think of all the extra costs you incur when your finances are tight—and how you can sidestep those costs as you build up your retirement and taxable accounts.

For instance, as your savings grow, your need to borrow fades. Initially, that might mean never carrying a credit card balance and incurring finance charges. Later, you may have enough to pay cash when you buy a car. You might also put down 20 percent or more when you buy a home, thus avoiding the need for private mortgage insurance. Perhaps you'll even get to the point where you don't need a mortgage to purchase a house.

Your burgeoning wealth should also allow you to avoid fees for bouncing checks, having financial account balances below the required minimum, and paying bills late. Your lower debt and history of on-time payments should boost your credit score, which ought to trim your borrowing costs when you next need a loan.

Similarly, as your wealth increases, you may be comfortable raising the deductibles on your health, homeowner's and auto insurance and extending the elimination period on your disability and long-term-care insurance. You might even self-insure for nursing home costs, so you don't need a long-term-care policy. You might also decide your family would be fine financially if you died or suffered a disability, prompting you to drop your life and disability insurance.

All this can lead to a virtuous cycle. As your savings balloon, you can shave your cost of living further, giving you yet more money to save. There is, as they say, a reason the rich get richer.

145. DILIGENT SAVERS NEED LESS FOR RETIREMENT

One rule of thumb says that, for a comfortable retirement, you need to have enough savings and other sources of retirement income to replicate 80 percent of what you earned while you were in the workforce. But few retirees hit this lofty goal and, for those with good savings habits, it may not make sense to try.

To understand what's at issue, consider two examples. First, imagine that, while you were working, you saved around 10 percent of your income each year and you lost another 7.65 percent to Social Security and Medicare payroll taxes. Both those drains on your income would be gone once you retire, so aiming to have retirement income equal to 80 percent of your working income would likely give you a similar amount of disposable income.

Next, imagine that you were a great saver who socked away 25 percent, rather than 10 percent. Clearly, you're used to living on a relatively small portion of your paycheck. Result? To maintain your standard of living after quitting the workforce, you might need a nest egg and other sources of retirement income that together will give you not 80 percent of what you used to earn when working, but perhaps just 65 percent.

146. NUDGING YOURSELF TO SAVE MORE

How can you get yourself to sock away more money? Try these strategies:

• Automate your savings. Sign up for payroll deduction into your 401(k) plan. Also set up automatic investment plans, where money is plucked from your checking account every month and invested in a savings account or the mutual funds you choose. Once you have automated your regular savings, inertia kicks in and you're likely to stick with it. Got a pay raise? Make sure you save part of your increased income by upping the sum you save automatically every month.

• Save all windfalls. Think about the extra money you sometimes receive, such as overtime pay, income from a second job, tax refunds, a year-end bonus and the occasional inheritance. These sums aren't part of your regular paycheck, so you're probably used to living without this money and thus it can be a painless source of extra savings.

• Round up the mortgage check. Do you usually pay $1,422 every month? Instead, make out the check for $1,500. Extra principal payments can allow you to pay off your mortgage years earlier.

• Write down everything you spend. This can make you more careful about your spending. Also pay cash, rather than using a credit card. Spending seems more real when you have to hand over dollar bills.

• Stash savings in accounts you consider off-limits. While folks will let themselves spend money that's in their checking account, they are often reluctant to tap their savings and investment accounts. To take advantage of this mental accounting, get extra money out of your checking account and into an account you consider untouchable, like your brokerage account or your individual retirement account.

• Set a savings target for the months ahead—and then tell others about your goal. That may make you more tenacious. You might also think harder about why you're investing and try to visualize how great it will be to realize your financial dreams. That may give you additional motivation.

• Turn debt payments into savings. Just finished paying off a student or car loan? Let's say it was costing you $300 a month. Keep writing that check every month—but instead send it to your favorite mutual fund. You are used to living without the money, so this shouldn't be any great sacrifice.

147. WHERE TO STASH YOUR SAVINGS

Where should you stash your savings? You might take the opportunities available to you and array them from most to least attractive based on their tax advantages, investment costs and potential return.

For many of us, the most attractive place for our savings will be our employer's 401(k) or similar retirement plan, which can offer the investor's triple play: an initial tax deduction, tax-deferred growth and possibly a matching employer contribution. Depending on the size of that employer match, you might effectively receive an immediate 50 or 100 percent return on the money you contributed.

Your next most attractive opportunity will likely be paying off high-cost debt, notably credit card debt. Don't have any? You might stash additional savings in a tax-deductible or Roth IRA, assuming you're eligible. You won't get an employer match, like you can with a 401(k), but the tax advantages are comparable.

After that, the decision is less clear-cut. If you aren't eligible for a tax-deductible or Roth IRA, you might fund a nondeductible IRA and possibly look to convert it to a Roth. Alternatively, if you're an aggressive investor, you could purchase stocks or stock funds in your regular taxable account and aim to invest in the most tax-smart way possible. What if you're more conservative? Look into paying down your mortgage and other debt.

Have yet more money to save? If you want additional tax-deferral, consider a tax-deferred fixed or variable annuity. But you should also carefully consider the drawbacks. You can learn more about these various savings vehicles in Part X, the chapter on taxes.

148. PRAY FOR LOUSY RETURNS

In Part II, we discussed how sequence-of-return risk can derail a retirement. But what's bad news for retirees can be good news for retirement savers. While a stock market plunge can cause folks to freeze and stop adding fresh money to their retirement stash, this is the time when you should continue to sock away money regularly and even step up your savings rate.

Imagine your goal is to amass the maximum sum for retirement. What sequence of returns would you want? Sure, it's gratifying when a market rally bloats your portfolio's value. But what you really want are lousy returns throughout your working years, followed by a world-class rally right before you retire. That way, you would buy investments at rock-bottom prices and cash out at nosebleed valuations.

The importance of the sequence of returns, and how you react to good and rotten markets, is captured by the difference between time-weighted and dollar-weighted returns. Examples of time-weighted returns include the results you see published by mutual funds and exchange-traded index funds. They would accurately reflect your performance if you had invested, say, five years ago and never subsequently added or withdrew money.

But such time-weighted returns may be misleading if, for instance, the market had dropped sharply during the five years and then rebounded, and you continued to save regularly throughout this period, possibly using a strategy known as dollar-cost averaging. In that case, your personal performance would be higher than the time-weighted return, because some of your purchases would have occurred at the lower prices. To gauge your performance accurately, you would want to calculate a dollar-weighted return, which reflects when you bought and sold. Fortunately, some mutual fund companies do this calculation for their investors. This performance number is often labeled your "personal rate of return."

149. DOLLAR-COST AVERAGING

Suppose you contribute $400 each paycheck to your employer's 401(k) plan. Whether you know it or not, you're engaging in dollar-cost averaging. A good idea? Saving on a regular basis is a great habit to get into. But despite what some folks suggest, it's neither magical nor a sure way to make money in the markets.

To understand the purported magic, imagine your regular $400 investment goes into a stock mutual fund. Your first investment is at $10 a share, which means your $400 buys 40 shares. The market promptly plunges 20 percent, so your next $400 investment buys 50 shares at $8 apiece. You now own a total of 90 shares.

Over the weeks that follow, the market partially recovers, so your stock fund's share price rises to $9, halfway between your two purchase prices. But at $9 a share, your 90 shares—for which you paid $800—are now worth $810. There is, however, nothing magical about this. You ended up with a profit simply because you invested a constant dollar amount, so you bought more shares when the price went down.

Suppose, instead, that you focused on regularly buying 40 shares. You would have invested $400 when the share price was $10 and $320 when the price was $8, for a total of $720. What happens when the share price bounces back to $9? Your 80 shares would be worth $720, the same as the amount you paid.

In other words, dollar-cost averaging works because it's a slightly contrarian strategy, where you're buying more shares when the market goes down. For the strategy to work, the investment needs to recover from any price decline. That's a reasonable bet with a diversified stock mutual fund, but it may never happen with an individual stock.

If a slightly contrarian strategy pays off, what if you were even more contrarian? That's the thinking behind value averaging.

150. VALUE AVERAGING

As an alternative to dollar-cost averaging, consider value averaging, a strategy developed by a former Harvard Business School professor, Michael Edleson, and described in his 1993 book, "Value Averaging."

The math involved is fairly complicated. But the idea is simple enough: You set a target growth rate for your stock portfolio and then vary your regular investment, depending on how your stocks perform. Let's say you want your portfolio to grow $500 a month. A month after you make your first $500 investment, your stock portfolio is worth $526. That means that, in the second month, you would need to invest $474 to hit your target portfolio value of $1,000. You might stash the other $26 in a money-market fund.

That cash in a money-market fund could come in handy if there's a spell when the market performs poorly and you need to invest substantially more than $500 each month. On the other hand, if the market enjoys a strong run, you could find yourself selling stocks to keep your stock portfolio on that $500-a-month growth path. That selling could trigger capital gains taxes and some messy tax accounting, but you can sidestep those problems by value averaging within your retirement accounts.

Like dollar-cost averaging, value averaging compels you to buy more shares when the market is depressed and fewer shares when it's buoyant. But with value averaging, the effect is even stronger. Indeed, value averaging can be seen as a cross between dollar-cost averaging and rebalancing, a concept we tackle in Part VIII.

151. TURNING YOUR CHILDREN INTO SAVERS

If there's one financial skill you should teach your children, it's the ability to delay gratification. This isn't just good for them. It's also good for you. After all, if your kids grow up to be financially irresponsible adults, there is a fair chance you will ride to the rescue. Want to teach younger children to be smart about money? Here are five strategies:

• Values are passed down through the generations in the stories that we tell. Talk about how you made ends meet when you first entered the workforce. Tell your kids how your parents or grandparents struggled financially.

• Encourage your children to save part of their allowance for larger purchases. You might have your children save a few dollars every week for a month or two, and then arrange a special trip to the mall so they can buy the toy of their dreams.

• Teaching your kids to delay gratification doesn't have to involve money. When you tell your children they can't have dessert until they eat their main course, or they can't play until they finish their homework, you are also teaching an important lesson about the need for self-discipline.

• Have your youngsters create a wish list of gifts they want for their birthday or the holidays, or items they want to save up for. Every month, go over the wish list with your children. Point out how much the list changes from month to month, so they start to see how quickly their desires pass.

• Your children may grow up spending your money, but you want them to feel like it's their own money that they're spending. To that end, push them to make financial choices. For instance, if they go on the school field trip, give them $5 for the museum gift shop—but tell them that, if they don't spend the money, they can keep it and spend it on something else. Similarly, when you go to restaurants, offer them a choice: They can order a soda—or they can drink tap water and have a dollar.

152. TEACHING TEENS AND ADULT CHILDREN ABOUT MONEY

As your children grow older, you will want to give them more financial responsibility, talk about money in depth and prod them to make smarter decisions. These strategies might help:

• As with younger children, you want your teenagers to feel like they're spending their own money, even if it's your money that they are spending. For instance, you might deposit their allowance in a bank account that comes with a cash-machine card. That way, when they want money, they'll no longer ask you. Instead, they will have to ask themselves and then head down to the ATM.

• You might give your teenagers a larger allowance but less often, such as once a month or once every three months. That will compel them to budget. You might also increase their allowance to include a clothing budget, so they have a growing sense of responsibility and they have to make more financial choices.

• Once your children are in the workforce, encourage them to save for retirement by, say, offering to give them 50 cents for every dollar they put into their 401(k) plan. Similarly, to encourage them to save for that first home, you might offer to contribute to a savings account intended to pay for a house down payment—but only if your children also contribute to the account.

• Set a good example. If you're obviously thoughtful and prudent in the way you handle money, your kids are more likely to follow your example. Consider showing them your account statements when they arrive in the mail. Discuss how you paid for their college education. Talk about what you've done to prepare for retirement. Any one of these discussions may have limited impact. But over time, your children will likely learn a lot.

PART VIII

INVESTING
A SIMPLE TASK
WITH A MISERABLY LOW SUCCESS RATE

his is a golden age for investors, who can take advantage of wonderful tax breaks, rock-bottom investment costs and a dazzling array of investment choices. All of which means there are more ways to shoot yourself in the foot than ever before.

Think of investing as a triangle with return, risk and costs forming the three sides. There are the raw returns we earn, the risks we take to earn those returns and the costs we incur along the way. Most investors focus heavily on returns. Wall Street does everything possible to fan this interest, because investors' relentless pursuit of market-beating returns is a great moneymaker for brokers, fund companies and money managers. But that typically doesn't turn out so well for investors, as we discovered again in 2014, with many small-company growth stock funds stalling out and many funds that employ hedge-fund-like strategies notching mediocre returns.

What's the alternative? You might focus less on returns and more on building a portfolio that avoids unnecessary risks and minimizes investment costs, including tax costs. Unlike returns, risk and costs are two aspects of investing over which you have a lot of control and where a little effort can pay big dividends.

To be sure, there are all kinds of strategies that will supposedly allow you to beat the market. For those who want to delve more deeply into the topic, some of those strategies are described in Part IX. Even this chapter, where we'll look at the basics of portfolio building, has the potential to overwhelm and befuddle the novice. But, as you'll discover in the pages ahead, you can keep yourself on track if you think of portfolio building as a simple four-step process.

153. FINANCIAL MARKETS 2014

At the start of 2014, many pundits were predicting another rough year for bonds and another good year for stocks. "In the many years I've been surveying experts for their predictions for the coming year, I cannot recall another time when optimism about the stock market, the economy and corporate profits was so widespread," wrote James Stewart in the New York Times on Jan. 3, 2014. "As is pessimism about the bond market," he added.

That isn't exactly how things panned out. Yes, the Standard & Poor's 500-stock index was up 11.4 percent in 2014, excluding dividends. But other parts of the global stock market had a tougher time. The Russell 2000 index of U.S. small-company stocks finished the year up 3.5 percent, MSCI's emerging-markets index was off 4.6 percent and MSCI's Europe, Australasia and Far East index was down 7.3 percent. Developed foreign markets have also trailed U.S. shares over the past five and 10 years, suggesting they could be better value.

At year-end 2014, the stocks in the S&P 500 were yielding 1.9 percent and trading at close to 20 times trailing 12-month reported earning, making them expensive by historical standards. Since the market bottomed on March 9, 2009, the shares in the S&P 500 have climbed 204 percent, though they remain just 35 percent above their March 24, 2000, peak.

But bonds and oil prices were 2014's biggest surprises. Despite a near consensus that interest rates were headed higher, the benchmark 10-year Treasury note finished 2014 yielding 2.17 percent, versus 3.04 percent at year-end 2013. As yields fell, bond prices—which move in the opposite direction—posted gains. Meanwhile, short-term interest rates remained miserably low, with money-market mutual funds yielding little or nothing.

An oversupply of oil drove prices down to $54 a barrel at year-end 2014, compared to $99 a year earlier. That sharp decline rattled global financial markets. Gold rallied and then fell back, finishing 2014 at $1,184 an ounce, versus $1,205 at year-end 2013. The dollar strengthened against major currencies, which trimmed the value of foreign investments held by U.S. investors.

154. FIVE STEPS FOR 2015

Reviewing your investment strategy? Start with these five steps:

- Calculate your portfolio's current split across stocks, bonds, cash investments and alternative investments. Many of the big mutual fund companies and brokerage firms have account aggregation software that allows you to pull in information from outside accounts, making it easy to figure out your overall investment mix. This basic asset allocation is the key driver of your portfolio's risk and potential return.

- See if any individual stock positions account for more than 5 percent of your stock portfolio's value. It's dangerous to bet too heavily on any individual stock—and that's doubly true if it is your employer's stock. Instead, most folks should probably stick with funds, either mutual funds or exchange-traded index funds.

- Find out the annual expenses for all your funds. If any charge more than 1 percent of assets per year, look for lower-cost alternatives—and seriously consider market-tracking index funds.

- Look up how your stock funds performed in 2008 and how your bond funds performed in 2013. Are you mentally prepared for losses like that? If not, you might adjust your portfolio now, before you find yourself panicking and selling in the midst of a market decline.

- Figure out how much cash you will need from your portfolio over the next five years—and make sure that money isn't in stocks or riskier bonds.

155. BUILDING A SMARTER PORTFOLIO

As you make your way through this chapter, you may find it helpful to think of portfolio building as a four-step process. First, consider why you're investing. That will give you a sense for your time horizon and hence how much risk you can take. Keep in mind that some goals have a harsh deadline, such as the day you make the house down payment, while other goals involve spending your savings over time, as happens with retirement.

From there, proceed to the second step: settling on your asset allocation, which is your portfolio's basic mix of stocks, bonds and other investments. Stocks get all the media attention, but just over half of American families don't have any stock exposure, according to the Federal Reserve's 2013 Survey of Consumer Finances. Your asset allocation will be driven heavily by your time horizon, though you will also want to consider other factors, such as your job security and how comfortable you are taking risk.

After you have settled on your asset allocation, it's time for the third step: figuring out how you'll diversify your stock market money, your bond market money and so on. This means deciding what percentage of your portfolio you want in, say, U.S. smaller-company stocks, foreign-government bonds or U.S. high-yield junk bonds.

Suppose you opt to invest 5 percent of your stock portfolio in emerging-market stocks. Now, you can proceed to the fourth and final task: selecting investments to build your desired portfolio. You will likely want to favor funds, especially those that will allow you to capture the market's performance at low cost.

Successful investing, however, isn't just about knowing the basics. It's also about attitude. To succeed as an investor, you need to avoid mental mistakes and approach the markets with the mindset of a seasoned investor.

156. MENTAL MISTAKES

Think back to late 2008 and early 2009, when the stock market offered investors one of the great buying opportunities. Did you take advantage— or did you simply sit tight or perhaps even panic and sell? We like to believe we're clearheaded and rational. But when it comes to managing money, we tend to be all too human. Here are three mental mistakes many of us make:

Excessive self-confidence. We tend to attribute our investment winners to our own brilliance, while blaming our losers on others. In fact, during rising stock markets, our self-confidence can balloon, leading us to take more risk and trade excessively. But all that trading is costly, while the greater risk can come back to haunt us when the market next turns down.

Extrapolation. The stock market's daily performance may be unpredictable, but we often think we see patterns. For instance, we tend to extrapolate returns, prompting us to assume that a rising market will keep on rising—and that tumbling shares will continue to fall.

Loss aversion. Most of us are deeply reluctant to sell stocks at a loss, because it means admitting we made a mistake and giving up all chance of recouping the loss. The desire to "get even, then get out" can be a helpful trait during broad market declines, because it may stop us from selling at the worst possible time. But our reluctance to sell losers isn't so helpful with individual investments. If we own a badly run mutual fund or a stock that's in financial trouble, we might be better off selling, taking the tax loss and reinvesting the money elsewhere.

JONATHAN'S TAKE: I believe investing is sufficiently simple that most folks can learn the basics. But just because investing is simple doesn't mean it's easy. Saving for retirement, college and other goals is so important that you need to minimize self-inflicted investment wounds. Find it hard to keep your emotions in check? Can't think like a seasoned investor? That's a key reason to hire a financial advisor—though, as we'll discuss later in this chapter, that also can be risky.

157. THE SEASONED INVESTOR

How do you know you're a seasoned investor? Here are some signposts:

• You have mixed feelings about rising markets. Yes, it's great that your portfolio has grown fatter. But it also means future returns will be lower. By contrast, tumbling markets excite you, because you could get the chance to scoop up investments at bargain prices.

• You select stock and bond funds that you would be happy to hold for a decade or longer—and you do indeed hold them for that long.

• When you make investment decisions, you think not only about the potential return, but also about risk, investment costs, taxes, why you're investing and your broader financial picture.

• You can succinctly explain why you own the portfolio that you do, including the reason for each investment.

• When your investments lose value, you're never surprised, because you have a good handle on the likely risk and reward for every investment you own.

• You realize that markets are unpredictable and that it's extremely difficult to earn market-beating returns, so you always have some money in bonds and some money in stocks, and you avoid overly large bets on individual investments and narrow market sectors.

• You can coolly decide whether to buy or sell, without getting fixated on what's happened in the market recently or what price you paid for a particular investment.

158. WHY WE INVEST

Often, we set ourselves up for trouble before we even buy our first investment—by failing to consider why we're investing. No, we shouldn't invest to earn the highest possible returns, amass as much money as possible or prove how clever we are. Instead, we invest now so we can spend later on goals such as retirement, the kids' college or a house down payment.

As you pursue these goals, the amount of investment risk you take should hinge on three factors. The most important of the three: How far off do your goals lie? If you have five years or less to invest, the biggest risk is short-term market declines, so you should probably focus on cash investments and shorter-term high-quality bonds. Cash investments include things like savings accounts, money-market funds and short-term certificates of deposit, where returns are modest but you can be confident you won't lose money.

What if you have more than five years to invest? You're likely more concerned with making your money grow, especially after taking into account inflation and taxes. In pursuit of higher investment returns, you might buy riskier bonds, stocks and possibly alternative investments. Alternative investments include a grab-bag of stuff, including real estate, private-equity investments, timber, gold, commodities and hedge funds. Stocks, riskier bonds and alternative investments can suffer severe short-term losses. But if your time horizon is more than five years, you should have time to ride out any market dips.

Time horizon, however, shouldn't be the only driver of your asset allocation, which is your basic mix of stocks, bonds, cash investments and alternative investments. You also need to give some thought to two other factors: your human capital and your stomach for risk.

159. SHORT-TERM THREATS

If your time horizon is five years or less, the big threat can be summarized in two words: losing money.

To get a sense for the range of potentially rotten returns, consider the worst annual returns for some of Vanguard Group's mutual funds. In 2008, when the financial crisis hit with full fury, Vanguard's Standard & Poor's 500-stock index fund declined 37 percent, its small-company index fund fell 36.1 percent and its total international-stock fund tumbled 44.1 percent. And these numbers don't fully reflect the punishment suffered: The market's slide started in late 2007 and continued into early 2009, before global stock markets bounced back beginning in March. The S&P 500's peak-to-trough price decline was a staggering 57 percent.

For bonds, 2013 was a rough year. How rough? Vanguard's long-term Treasury fund fell 13 percent that year, its inflation-indexed bond fund slumped 8.9 percent and its long-term corporate bond fund slid 5.9 percent. Vanguard's high-yield corporate bond fund, which invests in low-quality "junk" bonds, made money in 2013, returning 4.5 percent. Instead, its rough year was 2008, when it fell 21.3 percent, reflecting junk bonds' tendency to trade more like stocks than bonds.

Want to see how the funds you own performed? You might check the website for the fund company involved or head to Morningstar.com and look up your funds.

The bottom line: If you have money that you will need to spend in the next five years, you probably shouldn't own anything riskier than short-term bonds. The worst annual performance of Vanguard's short-term corporate bond fund was a 4.7 percent loss in 2008—and it easily recouped that loss the following year. Vanguard's short-term Treasury fund has given shareholders an even smoother ride, including notching a 6.7 percent gain in 2008's turbulent market.

For greater safety, you might go for money-market mutual funds, which strive to maintain a stable $1 share price, or even an FDIC-insured savings account or certificate of deposit. One tip: You may find you can come out ahead by buying longer-term CDs, with their higher yields, even if you have to cash out before maturity and pay an early-withdrawal penalty.

160. LONG-TERM THREATS

If you're a long-term investor, the biggest risk isn't short-term market declines—unless you panic and sell during those declines. Instead, the big risk is failing to beat back the twin threats of inflation and taxes.

Suppose that, after investment costs, you earn 4 percent a year. If you lose 25 percent of that gain to taxes, you'll be left with 3 percent. But if annual inflation is also 3 percent, you are—in financial terms—just running in place. How can you earn returns that outpace taxes and inflation? Smart tax management, especially the use of retirement accounts, can greatly reduce the threat from taxes. We tackle that topic in Part X.

Even with smart tax management, you'll find it tough to fend off inflation with Treasury bills, money-market funds, savings accounts and other cash investments. With these, the best you can hope for are returns that approach the inflation rate—and you may earn substantially less, as investors have in recent years, thanks to the artificially low short-term yields engineered by the Federal Reserve and other central banks around the world.

Instead, to outpace inflation, you'll need to look to bonds and especially stocks. With bonds, you might earn 0 to 2 percentage points a year more than inflation, depending on how much risk you take. The potential return from stocks is even greater, though so too is the risk. Over the long run, U.S. stocks have delivered close to 7 percentage points a year more than inflation. But given today's rich valuations and relatively sluggish economic growth, you probably shouldn't expect long-run returns on a globally diversified portfolio that are more than 3 to 4 percentage points a year above inflation.

161. YOUR HUMAN CAPITAL

If you are still in the workforce, give some thought to your paycheck as you design your portfolio. Let's say you are a university professor with a steady income and a traditional pension awaiting you upon retirement. Both your paycheck and your future pension are akin to collecting interest from a huge position in bonds. You may want to diversify that big bond position by investing heavily in stocks.

By contrast, if you're a contract worker or a commission salesperson whose income can vary sharply from month to month, your human capital looks more like a stock than a bond. To compensate, you may want to tilt your portfolio toward bonds.

As you settle on an investment mix, also think about the industry where you work. Often, realtors own rental real estate, Silicon Valley employees dabble in technology stocks and doctors buy medical shares. These folks may think they have an edge because of their intimate knowledge of their own business. But from a risk perspective, they're effectively doubling down, betting both their paycheck and their portfolio on the same sector of the economy.

The most egregious example: Employees will often invest heavily in their own employer's stock. But if the company gets into financial trouble, they could end up both out of work and also holding a fistful of worthless shares.

162. PERSONAL RISK TOLERANCE

Your time horizon and human capital may suggest that you ought to invest heavily in stocks. These aren't the only factors to consider, however. Suppose you're a unionized government worker with 25 years to retirement. At first blush, it seems like you ought to invest heavily in stocks.

But before you dive into the market, give some thought to how much risk you need to take to reach your goals—and how much risk you can stomach. Even if your job situation suggests you can take a lot of investment risk, you might hold a more conservative portfolio if you're already well on track to meet your various goals. More important, you shouldn't take a lot of risk if you are uncomfortable with wild fluctuations in your portfolio's value. The danger: Stocks dive, you sell in a panic and you end up locking in your losses at the worst possible time.

Personal risk tolerance is tricky to assess because it changes over time. When markets rise, we often grow more bullish as we extrapolate those gains into the future and we attribute our fattened portfolio to our own brilliance. We may also feel we can take extra risk because financially we're ahead of where we expected to be. But when markets dive, these good feelings can evaporate, and we often grow less risk tolerant. To get a sense for how risk tolerant you really are, try to recall how you felt and how you behaved in late 2008 and early 2009. Did you sell stocks in a panic, sit tight or buy more? To refresh your memory, you might pull out your account statements from those years and look at the trades you made.

Even if you have been a nervous investor in the past, you may discover you grow more comfortable as you become accustomed to the market's craziness. While 20-year-olds should supposedly have a healthy appetite for risk because they won't need income from their portfolio for many decades, often the investors who are bravely buying at market bottoms are wizened market veterans in their 50s and 60s.

163. ASSET ALLOCATION

Your asset allocation is the key driver of your portfolio's risk and return. The more you have in stocks, the higher your potential long-run return, but the rougher the ride will be. You're fine with that? In theory, buying a 100 percent stock portfolio will give you the highest return.

Still, there are good reasons to hold other assets. For starters, there's no guarantee stocks will win, even over the long run. During the 10 years through year-end 2008, the Standard & Poor's 500-stock index lost 1.4 percent a year, including reinvested dividends, while the broad bond market returned 6.2 percent.

Moreover, a portfolio that includes some combination of the four major assets—stocks, bonds, cash investments and alternative investments—offers three benefits that you can't get by owning just one of these four assets.

First, by holding multiple assets, you can get the same reward with less dramatic day-to-day and month-to-month swings in your portfolio's value, thanks to the lack of correlation among these assets. This is the magic of smart portfolio building, and it can make investing far more pleasant.

Second, by owning assets that aren't perfectly correlated with one another, you can reduce the chance that you'll suffer big losses. Those losses can wreak havoc with your portfolio's long-run return, while steadier performance can help your nest egg compound at a faster rate.

Finally, you can turn this lack of correlation into additional portfolio gains—by engaging in regular rebalancing.

164. CORRELATIONS

Stocks fluctuate more in value than bonds, so you can calm down a stock portfolio by adding a small position in bonds. The calming effect may be greater than you imagine. Bonds don't just bounce around less than stocks. They could climb in value when stock prices are tumbling, especially if you own government bonds.

At issue here is the crucial concept of correlation. Most parts of the global stock market are highly correlated. In other words, when U.S. large-company stocks are slumping, there's a good chance U.S. small-company shares, developed foreign markets and emerging markets are also getting hammered.

By contrast, stocks and bonds aren't closely correlated. It's quite possible that bonds will tread water and perhaps post gains when stocks fall in value, thus helping to offset your stock market losses and prop up your overall portfolio's value. Similarly, you can be pretty confident that your cash investments (which are, in effect, just very short-term bonds) won't fall in value, so they too can stem your portfolio's loss.

This is also the promise held out by alternative investments. The hope is that, when stocks are getting trounced, perhaps your gold shares, real estate investment trusts or market-neutral mutual fund will head in the other direction.

But noncorrelated assets, whether you own bonds, cash, alternative investments or all three, aren't just a potential source of solace during turbulent stock markets. By helping you avoid large short-term losses, they could also boost your long-run return.

165. COMPOUNDING AND VOLATILITY

Owning a mix of stocks, bonds, cash and alternative investments can reduce the chances of a huge short-term decline in your portfolio's value. That's crucially important, because the math of investment losses is brutal. If you lose 10 percent, you need to make 11 percent to get back to even. If you're down 20 percent, you need a 25 percent gain to recover the money lost. What if you lose 50 percent? Now, it'll take a 100 percent gain to make you whole.

Imagine two portfolios. Over the next five years, the first portfolio notches annual returns of 15 percent, -10 percent, 25 percent, -15 percent and 10 percent. The second portfolio has annual returns of 5 percent, 10 percent, 5 percent, -5 percent and 10 percent. If you add up the annual returns for each portfolio and divide by 5, you get a simple average of 5 for both portfolios.

In fact, the cumulative return for the second portfolio was 27 percent, while the first portfolio earned just 21 percent. What explains the difference? The first portfolio had a couple of bad down years, which it struggled to recover from.

To reflect this, mutual funds report their performance using compound average annual returns. This annualized return is the return they would need to earn each year to produce the cumulative amount made for shareholders over, say, the past five or 10 years. For instance, our first portfolio had a five-year compound annual return of 3.9 percent, while our second portfolio had an annualized gain of 4.9 percent.

Clearly, avoiding big portfolio declines can help your portfolio's performance. But to get the full benefit, you need to layer on an additional strategy: rebalancing.

166. REBALANCING

Once you settle on target portfolio percentages for stocks, bonds, cash investments and alternative investments, you'll want to check where you stand at least once a year and also after major market moves. Why? You may find you have drifted far from your target percentages.

Let's say you earmarked 50 percent of your money for stocks and 50 percent for bonds. Stocks then plunge 20 percent, while bonds climb 10 percent. Result? Your 50-50 mix would now be 42 percent stocks and 58 percent bonds. To get back on target, you should rebalance. If you're dealing with a tax-sheltered retirement account, you might sell some bonds and purchase stocks. But with a taxable account, any selling could trigger capital gains taxes, messy tax accounting and possibly trading costs. Instead, you might try to rebalance within your taxable account by directing new savings, as well as any dividend and interest payments, to the stock side of your portfolio.

This rebalancing will keep your portfolio's risk level in line with your targets. If stocks have declined, it can also set you up nicely for any market rebound by ensuring you have a full position in stocks.

But much of the time, you will probably find yourself cutting back on stocks. This will ensure you aren't hurt excessively by the next market downturn, but it will likely also crimp your long-run return, because you are selling what should be your best-performing investment. That said, rebalancing can enhance returns—especially if you're rebalancing among stock market sectors or among bond market sectors. We'll discuss this later in the chapter.

167. HOW OFTEN SHOULD YOU REBALANCE?

Investors take all kinds of approaches toward rebalancing: Some rebalance every quarter, some every year and some only after major market moves. What's the right strategy? Rebalancing every year has the virtue of simplicity and it introduces a healthy dose of self-discipline. But there are five reasons to be a little more flexible.

First, you should pay attention to the investment costs involved. This shouldn't be an issue if, say, you own no-commission mutual funds bought directly from the fund companies involved. If there's any sort of trading cost involved, however, you should factor that into your decision.

Second, you need to consider the tax consequences. That isn't a worry if you are rebalancing within a retirement account. But if you are handling a taxable account, any selling could trigger capital gains taxes. That may prompt you to rebalance less often.

Third, a sharp rise or fall in the stock market may push you far off your target percentages. Your portfolio might suddenly be substantially more aggressive or conservative than you intended, and you might want to rebalance right away.

Fourth, because stocks tend to fare better over time, there's a decent chance you will earn better long-run returns if you rebalance, say, every two years. The reason: You will give your stocks longer to earn returns before you cut them back. This, of course, means you will have more in stocks, on average, and thus it's a riskier strategy.

Finally, in the stock market, there is evidence of momentum, the tendency for shares to continue performing well if they've recently had strong returns. That also might lead you to rebalance less often, especially if stocks are recovering from a bear market and are in the early stages of a rebound. There's a chance that the upward share-price momentum from the initial recovery will carry over into the year ahead.

168. JONATHAN'S TAKE: ASSET ALLOCATION GUIDELINES

Your mix of stocks, bonds, cash and alternative investments will be driven by your goals and individual circumstances. Still, it's helpful to have some guidelines. For retirement savings, one rule of thumb suggests that you take 100 and subtract your age. Whatever the result, that's the percentage of your investment portfolio that you should put in stocks. For instance, the rule suggests a 30-year-old should have 70 percent in stocks.

As rules of thumb go, it isn't bad. But I would tweak it. I think those in their 20s and 30s could have as much as 90 percent in stocks, though I wouldn't go any higher. I believe everybody should keep a minimum 10 percent in bonds, because it notably reduces risk without putting much of a dent in returns. Among retirees, I would peg stocks at a minimum 30 percent. If you have less than that, you leave yourself vulnerable to long-run inflation. Indeed, with the right portfolio design, I think a 50 percent stock allocation may make more sense for retirees.

What about alternative investments? I don't think they're a necessary part of a portfolio. But if you want a position in a mix of, say, gold stocks and real estate investment trusts, I would probably cap that position at 10 percent of your portfolio, no matter what your age.

Finally, cash investments make sense for money you plan to spend in the near future, such as savings earmarked for a house down payment or spending money for the next five years of your retirement. But I don't see cash as a necessary part of a long-term investment portfolio. If you are inclined to hold cash for the long haul, consider instead a high-quality short-term bond fund or your 401(k) plan's stable-value fund. Both should offer somewhat higher yields than a savings account or a money-market mutual fund.

Settled on your portfolio's target asset allocation? It's time for the next step: deciding how you will diversify within these asset classes.

169. DIVERSIFICATION

The key driver of your portfolio's risk and return is your asset allocation between stocks and more conservative investments. The more you invest in stocks, the greater the swings in your portfolio's value—but the higher your potential return.

How can you improve the odds of getting that richer reward? What can you do to lessen those wild price swings? That's where diversification comes in. Put simply, diversification involves buying lots and lots of individual securities from all over the globe.

For instance, you can damp down your portfolio's volatility if you diversify across U.S. stocks and foreign shares, including emerging markets. As mentioned earlier, different stock market sectors tend to be highly correlated. Still, when U.S. stocks tumble, maybe foreign markets won't fall as much and perhaps a declining dollar might boost the value of foreign stocks for U.S. holders, thus helping to trim your portfolio's overall loss.

Diversification also increases the chances you'll be rewarded for the risk you are taking. If you purchase just a handful of stocks, it's entirely possible you could earn wretched returns in a year when the overall stock market generates dazzling performance. In fact, if a company you own gets into financial trouble, you could lose everything you invested in the stock.

As you increase the number of stocks you hold, the potential damage done by a few troubled companies becomes less and less. You also reduce your portfolio's "tracking error": It becomes more likely that your returns will approximate those of the broad market averages—and thus there is a greater likelihood you'll get rewarded for the risk you are taking.

170. DIVERSIFYING STOCKS

As you consider how to diversify your stock portfolio, you might look at the world of stocks through three prisms:

By geography. You will likely want exposure to U.S. shares, developed foreign stock markets such as Japan, Germany and the U.K., and also emerging markets like Brazil, China and India. Based on the allocations in the FTSE Global All Cap Index, roughly 50 percent of the world's stock market value is accounted for by U.S. shares, 40 percent by developed foreign markets and 10 percent by emerging markets.

You shouldn't necessarily replicate those percentages, however. If you plan to retire in the U.S. and send your children to U.S. colleges, your future spending will be in U.S. dollars, so you should probably be leery of taking too much currency risk and instead tilt your portfolio toward U.S. investments, especially as you approach the time when you will start drawing down your portfolio.

By company size. Stocks are often categorized as small, midsize and large (or "blue chip") based on their total stock market value (otherwise known as their "capitalization" or "cap"). You will likely want exposure to all three categories, whether you're buying U.S. stocks or investing in developed foreign markets.

By whether a company is considered a growth or value stock. Growth stocks are typically more expensive based on market yardsticks like dividend yield and price-earnings ratios, but they offer the prospect of rapidly growing revenues and profits. Value stocks aren't growing so quickly, but they have the advantage of being less richly priced.

You should probably have exposure to all the different stock market segments described above. Fortunately, you can get that exposure with a relatively modest number of investments—thanks to mutual funds and exchange-traded index funds.

171. DIVERSIFYING BONDS

How should you diversify your bond portfolio? You can slice up the world of bonds in six ways:

By geography. As with stocks, you can divide the world of bonds between U.S., developed foreign and emerging markets. But the case for buying foreign bonds isn't as compelling. The investment costs can be high, and you could be introducing the wild card of currency swings into what's supposedly the conservative part of your portfolio.

By maturity. Bonds have maturities of up to 30 years and occasionally longer. But the longer the maturity, the more a bond will fluctuate in price in response to interest-rate changes. Historically, you have earned much of the yield of longer-term bonds by purchasing securities with five years or less to maturity.

By how interest payments are calculated. While most bonds make fixed interest payments, some offer interest payments that "float" with the overall change in interest rates or that increase along with inflation.

By whether the interest is taxed. Interest from corporate bonds is fully taxable. Interest from Treasury and some government agency bonds isn't taxable at the state level. Municipal bonds are exempt from federal taxes and, if you own bonds from your own state, possibly also state and local taxes.

By whether the issuer is part of the public or private sector. Corporate bonds are riskier than government bonds, but offer higher yields.

By the quality of the issuer. While bond investors can usually expect to get both the promised interest payments and their principal back at maturity, that isn't a sure thing with so-called junk bonds, which are issued by companies with shaky finances. To compensate investors for the greater risk of default, junk bonds offer higher yields.

Sound overwhelming? It'll seem less baffling if we look at some sample portfolios.

172. SAMPLE PORTFOLIO: SIMPLE

Suppose you have settled on a basic mix of 60 percent stocks and 40 percent bonds. This 60-40 mix is often referred to as a balanced portfolio. You can find mutual funds that offer this combination in a single fund, thus giving you one-stop shopping.

For instance, you could buy a traditional balanced fund, though you might find the stock portion is invested largely or entirely in U.S. shares, with no foreign exposure. Alternatively, you could purchase a target-date retirement fund that has a 60-40 mix. Target-date funds often have more diverse portfolios than traditional balanced funds. But you'll also find these funds become more conservative as they approach their target date. Target-date funds, which are found in many 401(k) plans, are geared to folks retiring in the year specified in the fund's name or within a few years of that date. Both balanced funds and target-date funds might appeal to those who find investing nerve-racking, because all you see is one share price, which will move relatively sedately compared to those of more narrowly focused funds.

What if you want to build your own balanced portfolio? You could do it with as few as three mutual funds.

- U.S. stocks: 40 percent
- Foreign stocks: 20 percent
- U.S. bonds: 40 percent

Because you're buying a single fund for each of three key market sectors, you'd want to avoid funds that are too specialized in their focus. For instance, for your U.S. stock fund, you might look for a fund that buys large and small companies and doesn't tilt strongly toward growth or value stocks. Similarly, you might favor a foreign-stock fund that invests in both developed and emerging markets and a bond fund that focuses on higher-quality bonds with short or intermediate maturities. A popular strategy: Play it safe with bonds, by sticking exclusively with short-term securities, and compensate for the lost yield by investing somewhat more heavily in stocks.

173. SAMPLE PORTFOLIO: MODERATELY COMPLICATED

As your wealth grows, you might venture beyond a one-fund or three-fund portfolio and get a little more sophisticated. Here's what an eight-fund balanced portfolio might look like:

- U.S. large-cap stocks: 27 percent
- U.S. small-cap stocks: 9 percent
- Real estate investment trusts: 3 percent
- Developed foreign stock markets: 14 percent
- Emerging stock markets: 4 percent
- Gold stocks: 3 percent
- Short-term corporate bonds: 25 percent
- Inflation-indexed Treasury bonds: 15 percent

What do these extra funds get you? You gain greater control over your diversification, with dedicated exposure to, say, emerging markets and U.S. small-cap (or "capitalization") stocks. You add alternative investments through real estate investment trusts and gold stocks.

You also improve the diversification of your bond allocation with the addition of inflation-indexed Treasury bonds, an intriguing diversifier thanks to the guaranteed inflation protection, though less intriguing at today's modest yields. On top of all this, you introduce the chance to goose returns by rebalancing within asset classes.

174. SAMPLE PORTFOLIO: COMPLICATED

Consider yourself an investment junkie? Here's what a balanced portfolio might look like if you were willing to buy a dozen funds:

- U.S. large-cap value stocks: 13 percent
- U.S. large-cap growth stocks: 13 percent
- U.S. small-cap value stocks: 5 percent
- U.S. small-cap growth stocks: 5 percent
- Real estate investment trusts: 3 percent
- Developed foreign markets large-cap stocks: 10 percent
- Developed foreign markets small-cap stocks: 4 percent
- Emerging stock markets: 4 percent
- Gold stocks: 3 percent
- Short-term corporate bonds: 22 percent
- Inflation-indexed Treasury bonds: 14 percent
- High-yield junk bonds: 4 percent

This portfolio is probably most notable for what it doesn't include. There are no bonds from developed foreign markets. This avoids inserting currency risk into the conservative portion of a portfolio. Similarly, there's no emerging-market debt, which is now mostly denominated in local currencies, not U.S. dollars. In addition, there's no dedicated U.S. mid-cap exposure, in large part to hold down the number of funds.

Academic research suggests you can boost performance by tilting a portfolio toward value and small stocks. We'll discuss that further in Part IX. You could easily adapt the above portfolio to that strategy by upping the allocation to U.S. large- and small-cap value funds, while shrinking the stake in the two growth funds.

Beyond the chance to tilt toward value or growth, what's the advantage of this more complicated portfolio? As with the moderately complicated portfolio, you gain greater control over your diversification and get the opportunity to bolster returns through rebalancing, but to an even greater degree.

175. REBALANCING WITHIN ASSET CLASSES

Earlier, we discussed rebalancing between stocks, bonds and other asset classes. This might boost returns over the short run by forcing you to buy stocks during a market decline, which then sets you up nicely for the market rebound. But over the long run, this rebalancing will likely crimp your returns because you'll often be cutting back on stocks. Instead, the main reason to rebalance between asset classes is to control risk by keeping your portfolio's asset allocation in line with your target portfolio percentages.

By contrast, rebalancing within asset classes has the potential to boost returns. Suppose you own the moderately complicated portfolio described earlier, which includes 27 percent in U.S. large-cap stocks, 9 percent in U.S. small-cap shares, 14 percent in developed foreign stock markets and 4 percent in emerging stock markets. Let's also assume that these different parts of the global stock market generate similar long-run returns.

As long as these various investments don't notch the same return every year, you should bolster your long-run returns if you follow a strategy of regularly rebalancing back to your target percentages. Let's say U.S. large-cap stocks outperform U.S. small-cap shares this year, but next year U.S. small-cap stocks make up the ground lost. If you rebalanced at the end of this year, you should boost returns next year by making sure you have a healthy weighting when small-cap stocks outperform.

This comes with a few caveats. You need to make sure that any performance advantage isn't eroded by investment costs and taxes. In addition, while rebalancing sounds simple, it can be tough in practice. It means bucking the crowd and buying into parts of the market that others currently loathe.

176. SELECTING INVESTMENTS

Once you've settled on your target mix of stocks, bonds, cash investments and alternative investments and then decided how you'll diversify within these categories, you have your portfolio's framework. The next step: Decide which investments you'll buy for each slot in your portfolio, such as the 15 percent you plan to invest in large-cap value stocks, the 5 percent you have earmarked for emerging stock markets or the 10 percent for short-term bonds.

For the vast majority of investors, the right choice will be funds, whether it's actively managed mutual funds, index mutual funds or exchange-traded index funds. If you're investing through your employer's 401(k) or similar retirement plan, mutual funds may be your only choice.

What about buying individual stocks and bonds? Unless you have a multi-million-dollar portfolio, it's hard to purchase enough individual investments to get broad diversification. One rule of thumb suggests you need at least 20 individual stocks to be diversified. While that might be enough to reduce the risk that you'll be seriously hurt by a single rotten stock, you still run the risk that your stock portfolio's performance will lag far behind the market averages.

Moreover, when investing in foreign securities, funds are the only practical choice for the typical investor. An additional reason to favor funds: You'll likely find it less nerve-racking than owning individual securities, because the diversification offered by funds should make for a smoother ride.

Any exceptions? You might avoid fund expenses by purchasing individual Treasury bonds, where there's scant risk of default and hence diversification isn't that important. That's discussed in Part IX. If you have the speculative urge, you might also set aside 3 to 5 percent of your portfolio for a "fun money" account and use that to purchase individual securities.

177. MUTUAL FUNDS

Looking to buy funds to build your desired portfolio? You'll be immediately confronted with a crucial choice: Should you buy actively managed funds, market-tracking index funds or some combination of the two?

Most funds are actively managed, meaning they try to pick securities that will outpace some market index. This has proven tough to do, with the vast majority of active funds generating market-lagging results.

For proof, check out the regularly updated study from S&P Dow Jones Indices, part of McGraw Hill Financial. The so-called SPIVA study (short for Standard & Poor's Indices Versus Active) can be found at us.spindices.com. It compares the performance of actively managed stock and bond funds to appropriate benchmark indexes. The results are not encouraging for active funds, with most funds trailing behind the market.

Why have actively managed funds struggled? You can blame it on two issues: The cost of active management and the efficiency of the markets. We take a closer look at investment costs in the sections that follow, including the cost of using a financial advisor, and then turn to the issue of market efficiency.

The poor performance of actively managed funds has driven many investors to dump active funds and instead buy index funds, which simply seek to replicate the performance of a benchmark index. According to the Investment Company Institute, stock index mutual funds accounted for 18.4 percent of stock mutual fund assets at year-end 2013, up from 11.4 percent a decade earlier.

Moreover, mutual funds aren't the only way to index. If you go the indexing route, you'll need to choose between index mutual funds and exchange-traded index funds. Over the past decade, ETFs have exploded in popularity, and their total assets now rival those of index mutual funds.

178. WHY COSTS MATTER

When the stock market can soar 30 percent in a year and individual stocks double in value, investment costs might seem like a minor issue. But the market doesn't soar 30 percent every year, and most of your stocks, if they double in value, will likely take many years to do so.

Indeed, in a lower-returning market, costs can loom large. Suppose the stock market notches 6 percent a year. If you lose 1.5 percentage points to mutual fund expenses and other costs, you would be left with 4.5 percent. Trade frequently? You could surrender 25 percent of your annual gain to taxes, which means your 4.5 percent would become less than 3.4 percent. That might not seem so bad—unless inflation is running at 3 percent, in which case you're making almost nothing.

You can't do anything about inflation. But you can do your best to hold down investment costs and minimize taxes. Let's say you bought a mutual fund that charges 0.5 percent in annual expenses and held it inside a Roth IRA. Even if the fund's manager picks stocks that perform no better than the market, you would earn a 5.5 percent annual return, leaving you comfortably ahead of the 3 percent inflation rate.

So which costs should you watch out for? Try to keep a close eye on trading costs, fund expenses and the amount you pay for financial advice.

179. TRADING COSTS

You're highly unlikely to earn market-beating returns either by picking individual securities on your own or hiring a fund manager to do so on your behalf. That doesn't mean your stocks and bonds won't enjoy occasional market-beating years. But long term, even if your investment picks are better than average, any edge will likely be more than offset by the trading costs you incur:

Brokerage commissions. These get all the advertising attention, but don't let those $5 trades fool you. Brokerage commissions are often the least important cost when buying and selling stocks.

Bid-ask spreads. Every stock has two prices, the price at which you can buy (the ask) and the lower price at which you can sell (the bid). Result: If you bought and immediately resold a stock, you would lose money, perhaps as much as 5 percent with a thinly traded small-cap stock.

Markups. If you buy a bond that has been issued and is now trading in the secondary market, the brokerage firm involved will take the current asking price and add a markup. The markup on bonds sold to individual investors might be 2 or 3 percent of the price.

Sound grim? The good news is, if you invest through mutual funds, you should enjoy lower trading costs because funds can use their buying power to demand tiny commissions, markups and bid-ask spreads.

There are, alas, also two pieces of bad news for mutual fund investors. First, funds suffer market-impact costs. Their own buying can drive up the price of a security, making it more expensive to accumulate a position, and their selling can drive down a security's price, so they end up with less money when they sell. Second, if you invest in mutual funds, you have to pay all the fees charged by the funds themselves.

180. MUTUAL FUND COSTS

As a fund investor, you incur the fund's trading costs—but you also have the costs associated with buying, owning and selling the fund itself.

Mutual fund commissions. Broker-sold funds, sometimes referred to as load funds, might charge a commission when you buy, an ongoing commission that's levied every year (known as a 12b-1 fee) and a commission when you sell.

Investing on your own? You can buy no-load funds, which don't charge any sort of commission. What if, instead of buying your no-load funds directly from the mutual fund company involved, you invest through one of the fund marketplaces operated by a discount brokerage firm? You may pay a transaction fee when you buy or you could find that the funds levy somewhat higher annual expenses.

Annual fund expenses. All funds charge annual expenses to cover the cost of managing the fund and handling administrative tasks. In addition, the annual expenses may include a 12b-1 fee to cover marketing and distribution. This fee is often used to compensate brokers. A fund's trading costs aren't included in its published annual expenses.

Fund expenses are expressed as a percentage of fund assets, so a fund with a 1.5 percent expense ratio is charging you $1.50 a year for every $100 you have invested. You can also think of this as the breakeven hurdle rate. If a fund charges 1.5 percent a year, it has to pick securities that beat the market by 1.5 percentage points just to match the performance of the fund's benchmark index.

Account maintenance fees. You might be charged an annual fee if you hold your funds in a brokerage account or in an IRA.

On top of all this, there's the biggest investment cost of all: taxes. We tackle that topic in Part X.

181. LOAD FUNDS

Many load mutual funds have a bewildering array of share classes, each typically designated by a letter. Working with a financial advisor who is compensated through commissions? The broker will likely suggest one of three share classes:

A shares. These charge a significant upfront commission, often 5.75 percent for stock funds, and a modest ongoing 12b-1 fee, typically 0.25 percent per year. Despite the upfront cost, A shares are often the best choice for longer-term investors and those with large sums to invest. If you invest a significant sum with one mutual fund company, or once your account has grown large enough, the upfront purchase commission can be sharply reduced. Ask your broker about so-called rights of accumulation.

B shares. These funds charge a hefty annual 12b-1 fee, usually 1 percent, and a back-end commission if you sell in the first five or six years. That so-called contingent deferred sales charge might scale down from 5 to 1 percent as you hold the fund for longer. If you have a modest sum to invest and, say, an eight-year time horizon, these can occasionally be the best share class to buy. But most of the time, you would fare better with another share class, given the sizable 12b-1 fee on B shares and the fact that the back-end commission isn't reduced if you invest large sums.

To curb abuses, fund companies sometimes cap the amount that can be invested in B shares at $100,000. Dishonest brokers may try to sidestep this restriction and earn larger commissions by spreading an investor's money around multiple fund companies. Dishonest brokers may also pitch B shares as having "no initial commission," while neglecting to mention the back-end charge.

C shares. These shares might charge a 1 percent commission if you sell in the first year. After that, there's no back-end commission. You will, however, incur a large annual 12b-1 fee that's often 1 percent, similar to B shares. But while B shares can convert to A shares after perhaps seven years, at which point the 1 percent 12b-1 often drops to 0.25, this never happens with C shares. The upshot: C shares make most sense for those who are investing for only a few years.

182. FEE-BASED ACCOUNTS

Historically, brokers have been paid through the commissions they charge every time you buy and sell. But spurred by the example of fee-only financial planners, even the major brokerage firms are now looking to reduce the emphasis on commissions and instead charge a percentage fee based on an account's size. For instance, a financial advisor might charge 1 percent annually on a $1 million account, equal to $10,000 a year.

This eliminates many of the conflicts-of-interest that come with paying commissions. Still, fee-based arrangements can be expensive—and perhaps so expensive that good investment performance is unlikely.

For a $250,000 or $500,000 account, the advisor's fee might be 1.5 percent. Add that to the annual expenses of the mutual funds that are bought, which could be 1 percent, and clients might find themselves paying 2.5 percent a year. It is extremely unlikely that the funds involved will perform well enough to compensate for those costs and keep up with the market averages over the long haul. What if you have less than $250,000 to invest? You'll struggle to find a traditional advisor who will manage your account on a fee basis. Instead, check out the burgeoning group of online advisors.

JONATHAN'S TAKE: Despite the drawbacks, paying fees is preferable to paying commissions. But here are three pieces of advice: First, try to limit the fee to 1 percent—and even less if you have a seven-figure portfolio. Second, push your advisor to find you funds with low annual expenses, preferably below 0.5 percent, on average. Third, make sure that, in return for your annual fee, you get more than just investment management. Your advisor should meet with you regularly, help you develop a financial plan and offer advice beyond investments, including suggestions on estate planning, insurance, and handling debt and real estate.

183. CONFLICTS OF INTEREST

A financial advisor can potentially offer three key benefits: expertise in personal finance, access to investment products you couldn't get on your own and a steadying hand that prevents you from making crucial mistakes. Set against these potential benefits are two drawbacks: the cost involved and the risk that the advisor is either incompetent or puts his or her interests ahead of yours.

With any luck, after reading this guide, you will know what prudent investment advice looks like, so you can tell if an advisor is pushing some dubious strategy. Still, you should be alert to the potential conflicts of interest that come with the four different methods of compensating an advisor:

Commissions. If advisors are paid through commissions, they have an incentive to get you to trade more frequently and to buy higher-commission products.

Percent of assets. If an advisor is compensated by charging, say, 1 percent of the assets that you have invested, that helps to align your advisor's interests with yours because you both benefit if the account grows in value.

Nonetheless, it does create subtle conflicts. For instance, advisors might dissuade clients from taking money from their investment account to pay down debt because the shrunken account would generate less in fees. Advisors might also push clients to claim Social Security early, so the investment account shrinks more slowly in the early years of retirement and hence generates larger fees.

Hourly fee. Only a small number of advisors work on an hourly basis. There is a risk they will drag out the work, costing clients more than is necessary. But the potential financial loss would be relatively modest.

Flat monthly or annual fee. Again, only a small number of advisors charge flat monthly or annual fees, though this includes some of the fast-growing online advisors. The risk is that, even if you get a lot of value in the initial months, your need for help diminishes over time and yet you keep paying that regular fee. But as with the hourly arrangement, the risk seems modest and is more than offset by knowing precisely what you're paying.

The method of compensation and the total cost are crucial. But price isn't the only consideration. You also need to ask tough questions, so you're confident an advisor is likely to provide good advice.

184. INTERVIEWING ADVISORS

If you need a financial advisor, by all means ask the neighbors for recommendations. But keep in mind that a lot of folks are good friends with their advisors. What they pay in fees, and the quality of the advisor's recommendations, are secondary considerations. Want to hire a top-notch advisor? Forget friendship—and focus on asking the right questions:

• How are you compensated and what's the total cost I can expect to pay each year? Ask for a dollar amount, not just percentages. What other expenses will I incur, such as fund expenses and account fees?

• Are you held to a suitability or a fiduciary standard? An advisor who is held to a fiduciary standard must act in your best interest. Those held to a suitability standard, which is what happens when a broker is paid commissions, must merely recommend investments that are suitable.

• What credentials do you hold? There's a maddening array of credentials held by advisors, some of them meaningless. You should be comforted if an advisor is a Chartered Financial Analyst (CFA), Certified Financial Planner (CFP) or Chartered Financial Consultant (ChFC). If they have a business, accounting or law degree, that's all the better. While brokers will trumpet that they've passed, say, the Series 7 or the Series 6, those are technically licenses that allow them to do business, not credentials that prove they're knowledgeable about the finer details of personal finance.

• Where have you worked and how long have you been in the investment business? While everybody needs to start somewhere, there's no need to let an advisor learn the ropes with your money.

• How would you describe your investment philosophy? Here, you're looking for some intelligent summary of how they navigate the financial markets, not a series of clichés or hollow boasts about beating the market.

• What complaints have been lodged against you by customers? While there might have been legal claims, most formal complaints result in arbitration proceedings. If advisors are licensed with FINRA, you can see whether there are any "disclosure events" by going to FINRA.org and using the site's BrokerCheck database.

• Beyond putting together a portfolio, what other aspects of my financial life will you help with? Some advisors assist with tax returns, estate planning, insurance and when to claim Social Security. Will they charge extra for these services—and do they outsource them to another firm?

185. ONLINE ADVISORS

Looking for a low-cost advisory service? It may be no farther away than your computer keyboard.

In recent years, there's been a proliferation of online advisors, including firms such as Betterment.com, FutureAdvisor.com, Jemstep.com, LearnVest.com, PersonalCapital.com, Rebalance-IRA.com, SigFig.com, Wealthfront.com and WiseBanyan.com. These firms typically either charge a percentage fee, based on the assets you invest, or they levy a monthly charge. Either way, you'll likely pay far less than the 1 percent of assets or more charged by many traditional advisors. Many of the online advisors further trim your costs by recommending low-cost exchange-traded index funds.

Some big financial firms are also muscling into the low-cost advice business. Vanguard Group's Personal Advisor Services costs just 0.3 percent a year. Charles Schwab plans to launch a free advisory service, using its own and other firms' exchange-traded index funds, in early 2015.

The downside is that you typically lose the face-to-face contact you enjoy with a traditional advisor. Still, these computer-driven services can offer a more rigorous approach than you get with many traditional advisors, who may be basing decisions more on gut instinct and an occasional review of your portfolio. In addition, if you have less than $250,000 to invest, it's hard to find an advisor who will manage your account on a fee basis and give your finances the attention they deserve, so an online advisor may be your best bet for low-cost, high-quality advice.

186. MARKET EFFICIENCY

You come across a company with a great product that's growing like a weed, you buy the stock—and the shares go nowhere. The Commerce Department announces robust economic growth for the latest quarter—and stocks tumble.

What's going on here? Stock and bond prices reflect both currently available information and also investors' collective expectations about future developments. When that new information becomes available, investors quickly buy and sell securities based on whether the news was better or worse than expected. Suppose a company reports a 25 percent increase in earnings. Impressive? If analysts were forecasting 29 percent growth, the stock could get pummeled.

This puts ordinary investors in a tough spot. No matter how much research you do, you're highly unlikely to know something that other investors don't know (unless you are trading on insider information, which is not advised). True, you could prove better at interpreting this information by, say, predicting correctly that a company's new product will be more successful than other investors imagine. But how likely is this, especially when you're competing against professional investors with business degrees, great analytical tools and access to the latest market research?

Alternatively, you could hire some of these professionals to pick investments for you, which is what you do when you purchase actively managed mutual funds. But history tells us most active funds lag behind the market. It isn't that these managers are dummies. The problem is that they and other professional investors are super-smart. If there are investment bargains to be had, they don't stay that way for long.

The markets aren't perfectly efficient. But they are efficient enough that, once you figure in investment costs, it's unlikely you will earn market-beating returns, whether you invest on your own or hire a professional money manager. The upshot: In growing numbers, investors are opting to index.

187. INDEXING

The math of investing is brutally simple: Before costs, investors collectively earn the market's performance. After costs, they must earn less. In fact, investors collectively trail the market averages by an amount equal to the investment costs they incur. Some folks may get lucky and beat the averages. But the vast majority won't.

What to do? You might focus on capturing the market's return at the lowest possible cost—by purchasing market-tracking index funds. Index funds buy many or all of the securities that make up a market index in an effort to match that index's performance. The funds almost always fall short of their goal, because they charge annual expenses and incur trading costs. Result: If a market index is up 8 percent in a year, the corresponding index funds might earn 7.8 or 7.9.

That might not sound great. But it's a lot better than most actively managed funds, which might earn just 6.5 or 7 percent, on average, because of their higher costs. Admittedly, by purchasing index funds, you give up all chance of beating the market. But you also eliminate the risk that you'll fall far behind. As an added bonus, index funds tend to be highly tax-efficient, because they don't actively trade their portfolio and thus they're slow to realize capital gains. That means they can be an especially good choice if you are investing taxable account money, as we'll discuss in Part X.

Convinced? You still have a key choice: Should you buy index mutual funds or purchase exchange-traded index funds?

JONATHAN'S TAKE: I'm a huge fan of indexing, whether with index mutual funds or ETFs. Extraordinarily few investors manage to beat the market over the long term, so why try? With index funds, you may not beat the market—but you'll beat most other investors.

188. INDEX MUTUAL FUNDS VS. ETFs

Index funds come in two flavors. The pioneers were of the mutual fund variety. With a mutual fund, you can buy and sell just once a day, with the share price established as of the 4 pm ET market close. If you purchase no-load index funds, typically your only cost is the fund's annual expenses.

The upstart competitors are exchange-traded index funds, or ETFs, which are listed on the stock market. You can trade them throughout the day, just like any other stock. ETFs have exploded in popularity over the past decade. They usually have lower annual expenses than comparable index mutual funds—but they ought to, because they don't have the administrative costs associated with shareholders' buying and redeeming shares. Instead, those costs are borne directly by the shareholders themselves. If you want in or out of an ETF, you have to go through a brokerage firm and trade the exchange-listed shares. That will mean paying the bid-ask spread, typically a brokerage commission and maybe also an annual brokerage-account maintenance fee.

Which are better, index mutual funds or ETFs? Many folks end up with ETFs because they're looking to trade frequently in and out of the market, a costly strategy that can quickly wipe out indexing's low-cost advantage. ETFs also come in more varieties, so they may be your only choice if you want a more specialized index fund, and you can buy them in any brokerage account. In addition, ETFs have the potential to be more tax-efficient than index mutual funds, thanks to a peculiarity related to the way ETF shares are created.

ETFs will often be the better choice if you plan to invest a large sum and leave it there for many years. But that doesn't describe the behavior of many ordinary investors, who might invest a modest sum initially and then add to their holdings frequently thereafter. If that describes you, you will likely find that index mutual funds make more sense, because you'll avoid the trading costs involved with frequent ETF purchases.

189. PICKING ACTIVE FUNDS

You've heard all the arguments in favor of indexing—but you still want to try your hand at picking actively managed funds. What should you look for as you seek market-beating funds for each slot in your target portfolio?

• You want fund managers with great performance over five years and preferably longer. If a mutual fund has notched market-beating returns but the manager responsible has since moved on, the record is meaningless.

• You want managers with strong records relative to an appropriate benchmark index. If we've had a period when small-company growth stocks have sparkled, small-company growth-stock managers will have good absolute performance. But how do these managers compare to an index of small-company growth stocks?

• You want to see consistency. If a manager has a great five-year record but it's built on one spectacular year, you may be looking at a fluke performance.

• You want low annual expenses. An actively managed fund will charge more than an index fund. Still, if the expenses are too high, the manager will find it awfully tough to beat the market.

• You should be leery of funds with high portfolio turnover. Like high expenses, high turnover means high costs—and it'll be that much harder for the manager to beat the market. High turnover also usually means big annual taxable distributions.

• You should favor smaller funds. If a fund's dazzling record has attracted billions of new dollars from investors, the manager could struggle to invest the money involved and may be forced to buy less attractive investment ideas.

As you search for actively managed funds, be sure to spend some time on Morningstar.com, where you can find the data you need to analyze funds.

190. CORE AND EXPLORE

Actively managed funds or index funds? Many investors opt for "all of the above." They build a core position in index funds, thus ensuring that part of their money captures the market's return, and then enhance it with actively managed funds in hopes of goosing performance.

For instance, once you've settled on your target investment mix, you might build two parallel portfolios, one entirely of index funds and the other with active funds. Alternatively, you might use, say, 80 percent of your savings to build your target portfolio using index funds and then invest the other 20 percent in actively managed funds that seem promising, without worrying too much about which market sectors these managers focus on.

Some investors take a third approach: They view the market for blue-chip U.S. stocks as highly efficient, so they index that portion of their portfolio using, say, a Standard & Poor's 500-index fund. Meanwhile, they figure smaller U.S. stocks and foreign markets are less efficiently priced, so an active manager has a better shot at generating market-beating returns.

The latter argument is a little dubious: The reason small stocks and foreign markets may be less efficiently priced is because it's more expensive to trade these shares—and thus trying to exploit the inefficiencies may not be worth the trading costs involved. Moreover, actively managed funds that focus on smaller U.S. shares and foreign markets tend to charge higher annual expenses. Those high expenses also make it harder to earn market-beating returns.

191. INDEX MUTUAL FUND MANAGERS

Led by founder John C. Bogle, Vanguard Group introduced the first index mutual fund for ordinary investors in 1976. The fund, which tracks the Standard & Poor's 500-stock index, was slow to attract investors. But as it took hold through the 1980s and 1990s, Vanguard introduced additional index funds that tracked other parts of the market. By the late 1980s, other major fund companies were also trying to get into the market.

Still, for ordinary investors, Vanguard remains the leading provider of index mutual funds, in part because of its unusual ownership structure. Vanguard is effectively owned by the shareholders of its mutual funds, who are rewarded for their ownership through lower annual expenses. This allows Vanguard to offer index funds with rock-bottom annual expenses.

Other lower-cost providers of index funds include Fidelity Investments and Charles Schwab. Schwab's index funds have a minimum initial investment of just $100, making them an intriguing choice for investors with limited means. To keep up with the world of indexing, visit Bogleheads.org and check out the latest conversations.

While Vanguard dominates the market for index mutual funds geared to ordinary investors, Dimensional Fund Advisors has carved out a niche among financial advisors, who are drawn to DFA's unique collection of index funds. The strategies employed by DFA funds are heavily influenced by academic research.

192. EXCHANGE-TRADED FUND MANAGERS

State Street Global Advisors launched the first exchange-traded index fund in 1993 with the introduction of SPDR S&P 500 ETF. The fund now has almost $190 billion in assets and is easily the largest ETF.

Still, if anything, State Street's SPDR family of ETFs has been playing catch-up in recent years. In 2000, the iShares group of ETFs, then owned by Barclays Global Investors and now part of BlackRock, was launched. Thanks to an aggressive marketing campaign that saw a slew of new funds introduced, iShares quickly grabbed significant market share and today ranks as the largest manager of ETFs.

Reluctantly, Vanguard followed suit in 2001 with its own lineup of ETFs, which were based on the firm's existing collection of index mutual funds. BlackRock's iShares, State Street's SPDR ETFs and Vanguard are now the three largest managers of ETFs, though a host of smaller players have also entered the market. WisdomTree has a broad selection of funds that weight stocks by their earnings and dividends. PowerShares offers a slew of ETFs focused on narrow industry sectors. Charles Schwab has a relatively small collection of stock and bond funds, most of which have rock-bottom annual expenses.

193. ACTIVE FUND MANAGERS

Want to put together a portfolio of actively managed mutual funds? Your first hurdle: the overwhelming number of funds to choose from.

You could narrow your focus by sticking with one of the big three no-load mutual fund companies—Fidelity Investments, T. Rowe Price Group and Vanguard Group—and then picking among their funds. But you may be shortchanging yourself.

Other fund families worth checking out include American Century Investments, Artisan Funds, Charles Schwab, Dodge & Cox, Janus, Loomis Sayles, Nicholas Funds, Pimco Funds, Oakmark Funds and TIAA-CREF. Also spend some time investigating fund companies that have a distinctive investment approach, like Conestoga Small Cap Fund, Fairholme Fund, FPA Funds, Longleaf Partners Funds, Mairs & Power, Royce Funds, Selected American Shares, Sound Shore Fund and Tweedy, Browne. These funds all specialize in a single part of the market or are renowned for a particular stock-picking style, and perhaps that focused effort will pay off.

To find actively managed funds that hold promise, you'll need to play detective. Head to the library and leaf through back copies of Forbes, Kiplinger's Personal Finance and Money magazines. Check out the Wall Street Journal's regular section devoted to mutual funds. Spend some time on Morningstar.com. Soon enough, you'll have a list of funds that have decent returns for the past three or five years. But will that market-beating performance continue? That's the big question with actively managed funds—and much of the time, the gamble doesn't pay off.

PART IX

FINANCIAL MARKETS
WHERE WE DISCUSS NERDY STUFF YOU PROBABLY OUGHT TO IGNORE

In the last chapter, I encouraged you to keep things simple and not be too clever with your investing. Here, we'll discuss some of the ways that folks try to be clever.

We'll talk about what drives stock and bond returns, including the connection to economic growth and the importance of valuations. This is the basic return you should capture if you buy index mutual funds or exchanged-traded index funds.

We will also discuss various ways folks try to improve upon this return. They might do so by guessing the overall market's direction, overweighting particular sectors or picking investments that perform better than average. In particular, we'll discuss factors associated with superior stock market returns. We'll look at various bond market categories, everything from Treasury notes to junk bonds to emerging-market debt. We'll wrap up the chapter with an overview of different alternative investments.

Inevitably, this survey will be less than comprehensive. In their hunger for higher returns, investors employ an astonishing array of strategies—and only a smattering are covered here. This chapter's goal: Offer some thoughts that might make you a better judge of markets and asset classes, and perhaps allow you to earn somewhat better returns.

194. WHAT'S HOT

Every year, particular investment products enjoy a certain buzz—and 2014 was no exception. Hot topics included low-volatility stock funds, floating rate bank loan funds, liquid alternatives (often referred to as "liquid alts"), global unconstrained stock and bond funds, active exchange-traded index funds, smart beta funds and bitcoins.

These aren't new financial products. Smart beta funds, for instance, are an attempt to improve on the basic index fund, which simply weights stocks by their total market value. That attempt has been going on for years, though it's picked up speed since the idea of fundamental indexing was first advanced. Similarly, liquid alternatives take strategies popularized by hedge funds and aim to make them available as mutual funds or ETFs. What about bitcoins? In many ways, they're the 21st century version of gold.

What's driving all the buzz? Think about recent market history. Stocks had wretched performance from early 2000 through early 2009, including back-to-back bear markets. Bond returns were substantially better, but it's hard to get excited about fixed-income performance given today's low yields. That has prompted a hunt for higher returns, coupled with some nervousness about the short-term outlook for stocks and bonds. Result: Investors today are more willing than usual to consider exotic strategies and exotic investments.

195. FIVE STEPS FOR 2015

This chapter is designed to get you to think—but not necessarily to act. In fact, the strategies discussed here should probably be pursued only by a relatively small number of investors with many years of market experience and a healthy appetite for risk. Still, even if you don't tweak your investment strategy after reading this chapter, maybe you'll look at your portfolio a little differently.

• Think about what stock and bond returns you might earn over the next 10 years. Given the risk of modest returns, are you sure you're saving enough each month for your various goals?

• Check whether your portfolio is tilted toward growth or value. Growth stocks come with compelling stories. But academic research suggests that prosaic value stocks win over the long haul.

• Find out the duration for the bonds and bond funds you own, so you know how much rising interest rates could potentially hurt you.

• Look up the expense ratio for every bond fund you own. What's the sign of a brilliant bond-fund manager? He or she was smart enough to get hired by a fund with rock-bottom annual expenses. Low expenses—more than anything—determine which funds perform best within any particular bond-fund category.

• Calculate how much of your portfolio is in alternative investments. Allocating 10 percent of your total portfolio might be reasonable, but you probably shouldn't go much above that. Make sure you truly understand the strategies employed by the funds you own.

196. WHY STOCKS SHOULD BEAT BONDS

Stocks have been a miserable investment over the past 15 years, but a great investment over the past century. What can we expect in future? Nobody knows, of course. But for stock investors, there's reason for both optimism and caution.

Depending on which indexes you look at, stocks have lagged behind bonds over the past 15 years. But that shouldn't persist. Stocks are riskier than bonds, so they should be priced to deliver higher returns. When you buy a stock, you become an owner, with the prospect of endless gains if things go well and the possibility of losing everything if they don't. Meanwhile, as a bond investor, you are merely a lender, with limited upside—represented by the yield—but also less risk. If a company gets into difficulty, its bondholders will be paid off before stock investors receive anything. The bottom line: If stocks didn't hold out the prospect of higher returns, people would be crazy to buy them (which, in retrospect, was true in early 2000).

But it isn't just that investors demand a higher return when they buy a risky asset like stocks. Corporations should also supply it. As the economy grows, corporate earnings ought to climb, and shareholders may also collect dividends. By contrast, with bonds, overall yields shouldn't be greater than the rate of nominal gross domestic product growth—and right now they're below the GDP growth rate. That suggests bond investors will earn modest returns, and they could see bond prices tumble as interest rates rise.

While the long-term outlook may be brighter for stocks than for bonds, there's one caveat and one wildcard. The caveat: The full benefits of economic growth don't necessarily flow through to shareholders. Earnings per share likely won't match the economic growth rate, which means share price gains will probably lag behind GDP. And then there's the wildcard: What value will investors put on corporate earnings and dividends? The fact is, as of early 2015, U.S. stocks aren't cheap.

197. WHAT DRIVES ECONOMIC GROWTH

Real economic growth—meaning growth over and above inflation—is driven by increasing the number of workers and by raising their productivity. The latter is the reason innovation is so important. If productivity rises, we increase GDP per capita, which means the standard of living for the average American ought to rise.

As both the number of workers and their productivity rises, GDP should grow. Over the past 50 years, the U.S. has enjoyed 3 percent annual growth in real GDP, with roughly half coming from productivity gains and half from increases in the working population.

That real GDP growth should, in turn, propel corporate earnings higher. As corporate profits rise, share prices will also tend to climb. The two, however, don't move together in lockstep, and there's a decent chance that, in future, shares will lag behind economic growth.

Still, if you're a stock market investor and hence hoping for higher corporate earnings, you might cheer for greater immigration, while also being concerned about the aging population and the falling birth rate. Greater immigration should mean more workers and hence faster economic growth. But fewer babies and lots of workers reaching retirement age isn't so good, because that means fewer workers and potentially higher taxes to pay for retirees' Medicare and Social Security benefits.

Over the 10 years through 2022, the Bureau of Labor Statistics projects that the civilian workforce will grow at just 0.5 percent a year, versus 1.2 percent for 1992-2002 and 0.7 percent for 2002-12. That slowing growth is one reason some observers argue we'll see disappointing GDP growth in the years ahead—and possibly modest stock returns.

JONATHAN'S TAKE: While the U.S. and other developed nations could grow more slowly as their populations age, this isn't yet an issue for emerging markets like India, Malaysia and Mexico. The implication: You may want to include a healthy exposure to emerging markets in your portfolio.

198. STOCK RETURNS AND ECONOMIC GROWTH

Day to day, stock prices are driven by the latest news—government data, corporate announcements, political developments, you name it—which is why it's so hard to forecast short-term returns. But in theory, over the long term, the key driver of stock returns should be economic growth.

That certainly appears to have been the case over the 50 years through year-end 2013. During that stretch, nominal U.S. economic growth (which includes inflation) averaged 6.8 percent a year, per-share profits for the companies in the Standard & Poor's 500-stock index rose 6.6 percent and, lo and behold, the S&P 500-index climbed at 6.6 percent. Meanwhile, annual inflation ran at 4.1 percent.

In other words, the growing economy drove up corporate profits and that, in turn, propelled share prices higher. On top of that, investors also collected dividends. Fifty years ago, the S&P 500 companies collectively generated a yield of 3.1 percent. As of year-end 2013, the yield was 1.9 percent. The stock market's share price-to-earnings multiple at both the beginning and end of the 50 years was somewhat above 18.

Problem is, this 50-year stretch is a little misleading, as you'll learn in the next section. Yes, there may be a long-term relationship between economic growth and stock returns. But stock investors likely won't reap the full benefits of economic growth.

Moreover, economic growth and stock returns seem barely related in the short term. Why not? Investors don't care whether the economy is booming or suffering right now. They're focused on what might happen next year or the year after that. This is the reason savvy investors will often buy stocks in the midst of a recession, anticipating that the economy will soon recover.

199. WHY HIGH GROWTH DOESN'T MEAN HIGH RETURNS

Based on the U.S. experience of the past 50 years, there appears to be a tight connection between economic growth and stock returns. But the story is messier than it seems.

While economic growth and per-share profits for the S&P 500 companies grew at almost exactly the same pace over the past 50 years, earnings per share were only able to keep up with economic growth because of falling corporate tax rates and rising corporate profitability. After-tax corporate profits grew from 6.9 percent of GDP at year-end 1963 to 10.2 percent at year-end 2013. This growth in profits, which comes at the expense of salaries and wages, can't go on forever—and it could reverse.

That would be grim news for stock market investors. Over the past 50 years, the combination of falling taxes and rising profitability helped offset one of the most insidious threats to stock market investors: dilution. As corporations issue more shares and as new companies emerge, existing shareholders see their claim on the economy's profits diluted. Indeed, the economy's fastest growth often occurs among privately held companies. Ordinary stock market investors can't buy into these private companies until they have grown large enough to be taken public in an IPO, or initial public offering.

The historical dilution suffered by existing shareholders has been estimated at around two percentage points a year by money managers Robert Arnott and William Bernstein in a September/October 2003 article for the Financial Analysts Journal. In other words, if the economy grows at a nominal 5 percent a year, earnings per share might grow at only 3 percent. If earnings per share trail the economy's growth rate, share-price appreciation is also likely to lag, unless there's an offsetting rise in the stock market's price-earnings ratio.

Could you compensate by investing in faster-growing companies? For instance, would it make sense to invest in IPOs? Even though companies sold through IPOs are often growing fast, they typically prove to be disappointing investments. Why? Fast growth alone doesn't make for a good investment. It also matters what price you pay for that growth.

That brings us to one of investing's most counterintuitive notions: Often, slower-growing companies and slower-growing countries turn out to be better stock market investments—because they can be bought at more reasonable valuations.

200. PRICE-EARNINGS RATIOS

How much you make as a stock market investor depends on how fast earnings per share grow at the companies you own and on how much you collect in dividends. But it also depends on the price you pay. How can you gauge how expensive stocks are? Probably the most popular measure is the price-earnings ratio, which is a company's stock price divided by its earnings per share. Suppose you have a $34 stock with earnings per share of $2 for the past 12 months. The stock would have a P/E of 17.

P/E ratios can be tricky to analyze. For starters, make sure you understand what earnings are being used. Some P/Es are calculated using the last 12 months' reported earnings. Based on that measure, the U.S. market's average P/E multiple was 16 over the past 100 years and 18.9 over the past 50 years. As of year-end 2014, it stood at almost 20, close to the 50-year average.

Some investors prefer instead to use expected operating earnings for the next 12 months. This has the benefit of looking to the future, which is what investors care about. It also ignores the onetime writedown of assets, which can distort reported earnings, and instead focuses on underlying corporate profitability.

Using expected operating earnings has its own problems, however. You are relying on analysts' forecasts, which are notoriously rosy. Moreover, while writedowns may be onetime, they do reflect an admission of management error (yes, money was lost), and those onetime writedowns seem to occur all too often.

Whether you are looking at trailing or expected earnings, those numbers are captive to the business cycle. During economic booms, robust earnings can make the market's P/E ratio appear more reasonable than it is—which could be the case right now. Conversely, during recessions, companies may lose money, driving up the market's P/E ratio and scaring off investors, when in truth it may be a great time to buy. To address this issue, some investors have turned to cyclically adjusted P/E ratios or they look at other popular measures of the market's value, such as dividend yields and price-to-book value.

201. CYCLICALLY ADJUSTED PRICE-EARNINGS RATIOS

Because standard price-earnings ratios can be misleading, some investors rely on cyclically adjusted price-earnings ratios, or CAPE, a measure developed by Yale University professor Robert Shiller and fellow economist John Y. Campbell. CAPE is often referred to as the Shiller P/E.

The Shiller P/E is based on an average of reported earnings for the past 10 years, with earnings from earlier years adjusted upward to reflect inflation. This averaging has the benefit of smoothing out earnings, which can fluctuate widely from year to year. The average Shiller P/E was 19.6 over the past 50 years and 16.6 over the past 100 years. But the average since 1990 has been 25.2, suggesting that the CAPE multiple may have moved into a permanently higher range. As of year-end 2014, it was at 27.2.

If the Shiller P/E has moved permanently higher, that's both good news and bad news. The good news is, we may not see a reversion back to the 50-year average P/E of 19.6, which would knock 28 percent off current share prices. The bad news is, with valuations so elevated, returns are likely to be modest because we probably won't see valuations climb much higher. Those rising valuations have helped to contribute to the stock market's impressive long-run return.

If you want to dig deeper into the data on market valuations, do an Internet search for Robert Shiller's home page and then click on the "Online Data" tab. You can also find thought-provoking commentary on P/Es at CrestmontResearch.com.

202. DIVIDEND YIELDS

Many companies don't pay dividends, so looking at dividend yields won't necessarily tell you whether one stock is better value than another.

But it can be useful in gauging how expensive the overall market is. At year-end 2014, the S&P 500 companies were yielding 1.9 percent. That's an improvement over the 1.2 percent at year-end 1999, but well below the level of earlier decades. Yields stood at 3.5 percent at year-end 1969, 5.2 percent at year-end 1979 and 3.2 percent at year-end 1989, and have averaged 3 percent over the past 50 years and 4.1 percent over the past 100 years.

The market's dividend yield has trended down partly because stocks have become more expensive over time and partly because companies have instead used their spare cash to buy back their own shares. Historically, total shares outstanding have grown almost every year, as employees exercise stock options and companies issue new shares to raise cash or finance acquisitions. But that's changed over the past decade: Corporations have been big buyers of their own stock, and these share buybacks have roughly offset new issuance. Buybacks are seen as a more tax-efficient way to return money to shareholders, because the money is used to cash out investors who want to depart without saddling the remaining shareholders with taxable dividends.

Trouble is, companies appear to be terrible market timers. They aggressively bought back their own shares ahead of the 2007 stock market peak, slashed their buying during the market slump that followed and now, with stock prices up sharply, they're once again aggressively buying back shares. One explanation: Buybacks are driven less by companies' belief that their shares are undervalued and more by a desire to offset the dilution caused by employees exercising stock options. The latter is more likely to happen in buoyant markets.

Will the craze for buybacks continue? It's hard to know. Buyback programs are often quietly abandoned. Meanwhile, dividends seem like a surer thing. Companies are loath to cut their dividend. Indeed, knowing they have to pay a regular dividend can be a healthy discipline for management, forcing them to be more careful in how they handle the company's cash.

203. PRICE-TO-BOOK VALUE

If you open a company's annual report and turn to the page showing its balance sheet, you'll see something called stockholder's equity, which is the value of the company's assets minus its liabilities. Stockholder's equity reflects the amount investors have put into the company through stock offerings and reinvested earnings—and how much they might receive if the company were liquidated and all liabilities paid off.

Investors will sometimes take stockholder's equity, figure out this "book value" on a per-share basis, and then compare it to the current stock price. A stock might be considered undervalued if it trades below book value and overvalued if it trades well above.

But this can be overly simplistic. For instance, if a company has to write down the value of some of its assets, that can take a big chunk out of book value—and make its shares seem overvalued based on price-to-book value. Similarly, if a company has intangible assets such as brand names and patents, these may not be listed at full value on the asset side of the ledger, and thus won't be fully reflected in stockholder's equity. Based on price-to-book value, certain companies—such as banks and insurers—look consistently cheap, while technology companies often appear expensive.

Despite its flaws, price-to-book value remains a popular yardstick, especially among value investors. While price-earnings ratios based on recent or expected earnings can sometimes be misleading, book value often provides a steadier gauge of a company's value.

204. HISTORICAL VALUATIONS

If you had bought U.S. stocks a century ago, at year-end 1914, you would have paid 14 times trailing 12-month reported earnings and earned an initial dividend yield of 5.7 percent.

In the years that followed, the market and valuations fluctuated widely, with shares posting healthy gains in the 1920s, suffering mightily in the 1930s, bouncing back in the 1940s, roaring in the 1950s, losing steam in the 1960s and struggling through the 1970s.

By July 1982, after more than 16 years of often wretched stock returns, investors had scant appetite for stocks. Shares traded at less than eight times earnings and yielded 6.2 percent in dividends. A spectacular two-decade bull market followed, interrupted only briefly by the 1987 market crash and the 1990 market decline. By early 2000, U.S. stocks were trading at a flabbergasting 29 times earnings and yielded just 1.2 percent.

There followed not one but two huge bear markets, both of which saw the value of U.S. stocks roughly cut in half. By the end of the second bear market, in early 2009, stocks were at a statistically meaningless 110 times earnings. That price-earnings multiple resulted from severely depressed corporate profits at many corporations and huge losses at a few companies.

A truer gauge of stocks' value was the dividend yield, which stood at 3.6 percent, though even that was a little misleading because many companies were slashing their dividends at the time. Still, by the 2009 stock market bottom, stocks were yielding more than 10-year Treasury notes. That had been typical up until 1958, but many market participants never thought they'd see it again.

Since the 2009 market bottom, shares have tripled in price. Today, after that long rally, U.S. stocks are at 20 times trailing earnings, with a dividend yield of 1.9 percent. That's not cheap by historical standards, which raises a key question: What return can investors expect from here?

205. WHITHER STOCKS?

Predicting short-term stock market returns is impossible. Even forecasting long-run returns is tough to do with any precision. Still, it's important to have some sense for what you might earn over the next 10 years, so you don't save too little or spend too much.

Where to begin? Don't simply extrapolate recent returns or rely on long-run historical averages. Instead, consider stock market returns in terms of three components: the dividend yield, earnings growth and the price put on those earnings, in the form of the price-earnings ratio.

If you buy the stocks in the S&P 500 today, you'll get a dividend yield of close to 2 percent. You might assume that the economy—and hence corporate profits—will grow at a nominal 5 percent a year, comprised of perhaps 2½ percent inflation and 2½ percent real economic growth. Combining the 2 percent dividend yield and 5 percent nominal growth would give you a 7 percent return.

But what about the market's P/E? It's higher than the long-run historical average based on cyclically adjusted 10-year earnings, so the odds suggest P/Es are more likely to fall over the next 10 years than climb.

Even if the market can maintain its current P/E, there are three added risks to consider. First, profit margins may shrink. Second, earnings per share may lag behind economic growth because of share dilution. Third, economic growth may disappoint. Result? Over the next 10 years, stocks might have a total return—share-price gain plus dividends—of 6 percent and quite possibly less, while inflation runs at between 2 and 3 percent. This 6 percent doesn't reflect the hit from investment costs and taxes.

What if the stars align, the bad stuff doesn't happen and the market's P/E climbs from current levels? While that might seem like a happy prospect, don't be too quick to cheer: You may discover that you're effectively borrowing from the future.

206. BORROWING FROM THE FUTURE

Stock prices should rise with per-share earnings growth. What if we do better than that in 2015, thanks to rising P/E multiples? Given that the stock market has rebounded nicely from the 2007–2009 bear market, we wouldn't be playing catch-up after a period of depressed valuations. Instead, we would likely be borrowing from the future.

As our portfolios grow fatter, that might not seem so bad. But remember, richer valuations mean future returns will likely be lower, and any new dollars invested will buy shares at those higher valuations. In fact, as discussed in Part VII, those still saving for retirement should probably pray for lousy returns.

This same phenomenon occurs with other investments. Remember the housing boom during the initial years of this century? Annual price increases raced far ahead of inflation. But those gains effectively borrowed from the future, resulting in wretched returns from mid-2006 onward.

Similarly, bond investors notched handsome returns as the 10-year Treasury yield plunged to record lows in 2012. But from there, bond returns have been relatively weak, and any new dollars invested have bought bonds at extremely modest yields.

207. MARKET TIMING

When you look at charts of long-run stock returns, the road to wealth seems obvious: You want to own shares during bull markets and sidestep those nasty market declines. Yet that has proven extraordinarily difficult to do. Stock market gains and losses tend to occur in short bursts, so it's all too easy for market timers to be caught flat-footed. While market-timing was popular decades ago, today money managers typically stay fully invested in the market, and instead try to add value through stock-picking.

But doesn't it make sense to steer clear of stocks when they are well above their historical valuations? Problem is, stocks can stay overvalued for many years and may never revert to the low valuations we've seen in the past. Shares have, by historical standards, been expensive for much of the past 25 years. Those who took that as a sell signal would have missed the 2000–02 and 2007–09 bear markets—but they would also have missed the huge gains of the 1990s, when U.S. stocks returned more than 400 percent, including dividends.

Instead of focusing on valuations, some investors try to divine the market's direction by studying stock-price movements and looking for patterns. This search for pattern drives so-called technical analysis, which is the study of past security-price movements in order to predict what will happen next.

For instance, among market timers, a popular strategy is to track the stock market's 200-day moving average. If the stock market moves above the average closing price for the past 200 trading days, this is taken as a buy signal, while falling below is seen as a signal to sell.

Does this work? For a February 2013 article for MarketWatch.com, Mark Hulbert, founder of the newsletter Hulbert Financial Digest, looked at how you would have fared historically if you had used the 200-day moving average to time the market. He found that, since 1990, your annualized return would have been just 3.8 percent, compared with 7.3 percent if you had simply bought and held stocks.

208. FAT TAILS

Extreme events happen more frequently than we imagine. Think back over the past two decades in the financial world. We had the extraordinary stock market rally of the late 1990s and the subsequent extraordinary decline, especially among technology stocks. We had the housing mania that peaked in mid-2006 and the grueling bust that followed. We had the financial crisis of 2008, with reverberations still felt today. In his 2007 book "The Black Swan," Nassim Nicholas Taleb highlighted how the supposedly improbable occurs with surprising frequency—and yet folks are shocked every time.

Such extreme events suggest that, instead of market returns being normally distributed, with most years seeing middling performance, the tails of this humped-back distribution curve tend to be fat because of the surprising number of extreme events, hence the term "fat tails." This can be seen as evidence of market inefficiency: Far from being rational, investors tend to be a little manic, becoming both overly exuberant and excessively pessimistic in response to economic and political developments. For those looking to time the market, this might make their venture seem more promising.

But fat-tail events might also be viewed as another reason for humility. Few people forecasted the extreme events that we have seen in recent decades. Given that these extreme events seem to be relatively commonplace, we should probably avoid making overly large bets on any one investment, so we don't miss out on the next surprising market surge or run the risk of seeing our portfolio hurt by the next unforeseen disaster.

209. STOCK PICKING

While market timing has fallen from favor, many investors still have an enduring belief in good old-fashioned stock-picking. The hope: If they invest with a collection of skilled mutual fund managers who each have a laser-like focus on one part of the market, they can earn above-average returns.

This approach has led to "style box" investing. Investors might buy a selection of U.S. stock funds that focus on large-capitalization, mid-cap and small-cap stocks. Within these three size ranges, they might purchase a top-rated growth fund, value fund and blended-style fund. That means they end up with nine different U.S. stock funds. They might then purchase a similar collection of mutual funds to give them exposure to foreign markets.

A recipe for success? It seems not. S&P Dow Jones Indices, part of McGraw Hill Financial, puts out a regularly updated study comparing actively managed funds to appropriate market indices. Over the five years through midyear 2014, the vast majority of funds in the nine U.S. style boxes underperformed their benchmark index. The failure rate ranged from 78 percent for small-cap value funds to 93 percent for mid-cap growth funds. You can find the study at us.spindices.com.

This market-lagging performance should be no great surprise. It isn't easy to find market-beating stocks. Every trading day, investors pore over the market, hunting for bargains. If a stock is undervalued, it's unlikely to stay that way for long. But while the search for winning stocks is often fruitless, it isn't cheap. Many stock funds charge 1 percent or so in annual expenses and might incur another 0.5 percent in transaction costs. Sure enough, that's the sort of shortfall you typically see each year when you compare funds to their benchmark index.

210. HIGHER STOCK RETURNS THROUGH HIGHER RISK?

The efficient market hypothesis suggests that investments are properly priced most of the time, so you're unlikely to earn superior long-run returns by trying to identify market-beating stocks. This insight, coupled with ample evidence that most professional money managers don't beat the market, has led many investors to give up on actively managed funds. Instead, these investors have sought to capture the market's return at the lowest possible cost by buying market-tracking index funds.

What if you want to earn more than the market is delivering? The capital asset pricing model, which assumes efficient markets and which was developed during the 1960s, offered its answer: You need to take greater risk. We're talking here not about crazy risk, such as betting everything on one stock, but rather risk that can't be eliminated through broad diversification.

How do you measure this risk? Initially, it was assumed to be captured by a single factor, volatility, which was measured using something called beta. The overall stock market has a beta of 1, but you could potentially raise your portfolio's beta to, say, 1.1 by favoring more volatile stocks or using leverage.

Problem is, beta proved to be a poor predictor of returns. Research found that low-volatility stock portfolios generated higher risk-adjusted returns than high-volatility portfolios. In fact, in recent years, there's been a surge of interest in low-volatility portfolios, prompting the launch of exchange-traded index funds such as iShares MSCI USA Minimum Volatility ETF and PowerShares S&P 500 Low Volatility Portfolio.

With beta failing as a predictor of stock returns, academics started casting around for other factors that might explain why some groups of stocks perform better than others. Over the past three decades, a slew of research has been conducted on the topic, which has turned up four factors that appear to be associated with superior returns—and, no surprise here, Wall Street has been quick to capitalize.

211. ENHANCED INDEXING

In recent years, Wall Street has been abuzz with terms like smart beta, factor investing and fundamental indexing. What's this all about? Think about the money-management business from Wall Street's perspective.

Actively managing portfolios is lucrative for financial firms. But many investors have wised up to their poor performance, prompting them to buy index funds instead. Problem is, index funds aren't nearly as profitable for Wall Street. What to do? Wall Street's answer: Find a way to make more money off indexing by offering index-like funds that hold out the promise of market-beating returns.

Welcome to the world of enhanced indexing, where the goal is to capture the performance of those parts of the market that tend to outperform. Enhanced indexing has two strands.

The first strand focuses on factor investing, which involves overweighting stocks with certain attributes. Academics have long contended that, if you want higher returns, you need to take greater risk. That greater risk comes partly from favoring stocks over more conservative investments. But even within the stock market, academic research suggests you can enhance returns by taking the risk of overweighting four types of stocks: smaller companies, value stocks, those displaying price momentum and those with greater gross profitability.

The second strand involves a push to adopt alternative systems for weighting the stocks held within an index fund. Known as fundamental indexing, the idea is to own companies based on their economic importance, rather than their value as judged by the market. That economic importance is assessed using measures such as a company's total earnings, dividends or sales.

You can now buy mutual funds and exchange-traded index funds that seek to take advantage of factor investing and fundamental indexing. ETFs, in particular, have been launched thick and fast, as Wall Street firms vie to get their slice of the market for enhanced indexing.

JONATHAN'S TAKE: With my own portfolio, I tilt toward value stocks and small-company stocks. But I am not entirely convinced that these two sectors will continue to outperform, which is why it's just a tilt—and I make sure my portfolio also includes funds that give me exposure to the broad stock market, both in the U.S. and overseas.

212. SMALL-STOCK EFFECT

Historically, small-company stocks have outperformed shares of larger corporations. For academics, this outperformance wasn't, by itself, surprising. Small stocks are more volatile than large stocks, so theory suggests they ought to compensate investors with higher returns. Instead, academics were intrigued because this outperformance was greater than could be explained by small stocks' higher volatility, as measured by beta.

The small-cap effect was detailed in a 1981 academic paper by Rolf Banz, then at Northwestern University. If greater volatility didn't fully explain small stocks' outperformance, what else was going on? It seems small-stock investors were getting rewarded for taking a risk that wasn't reflected in volatility.

This extra reward might be compensation for the higher trading costs involved with small-company stocks or the greater risk that these companies will end up in bankruptcy, because small stocks aren't as financially strong as large-cap stocks. Alternatively, it might be explained by the relative dearth of information available on smaller companies, in part because they aren't widely followed by analysts.

Why does it matter whether the small-stock effect, as well as other market anomalies, can be attributed to greater risk? If there is greater risk involved, such as the chance that you'll lose far more than the broad stock market during the next market slump and perhaps even see some of your holdings go bankrupt, the superior performance will likely continue. But if the extra return isn't a reward for taking extra risk, there's a good chance it will disappear as investors flock to take advantage of this "free lunch."

The discovery of the small-stock effect spurred the 1981 launch of an index fund devoted to U.S. microcap stocks. It was the first mutual fund offered by Dimensional Fund Advisors, which sells its funds through independent financial advisors. Since then, DFA has been at the forefront in creating funds based on the latest academic research. Many other fund companies now also offer small-cap index funds.

213. VALUE EFFECT

Like small-company stocks, value stocks have outperformed historically. Value investing is often associated with legendary investor Benjamin Graham, co-author of "Security Analysis," the classic investment tome first published in 1934. But the value effect received its most famous academic endorsement in a 1992 paper by finance professors Eugene Fama and Kenneth French, who defined value stocks as those whose shares trade at a low price relative to their book value.

The following year, the two professors proposed their three-factor model. That model argued that a portfolio's return could be largely explained by its exposure to the overall stock market, to small-cap stocks and to value stocks.

Value's outperformance, which has occurred historically in both the U.S. and foreign markets, has been attributed to the greater risk involved. The companies involved often have shaky finances. That means there's a danger they could get into serious difficulty, especially during an economic downturn, and shareholders might lose everything.

Still, not everybody has been convinced by the risk argument. Before academics documented value's outperformance and attributed it to risk, these stocks were typically viewed as less risky than growth stocks, because their share prices were less volatile. An alternative explanation: It could be that the value effect is a behavioral phenomenon. Perhaps investors become overly enamored of growth companies and pay too much for their shares, while mistakenly shunning value companies, where growth prospects often appear grim. If that's the case, it could be that the value effect will disappear as investors adjust their behavior.

Intrigued by the value effect? There are plenty of index funds available that allow you to tap into large-cap and small-cap value stocks. Vanguard Group offers four value-tilted index mutual funds that are available directly to investors, while Dimensional Fund Advisors offer a variety of value funds through its network of independent advisors. There are also a slew of ETFs available, including those from BlackRock's iShares unit, State Street's SPDR ETFs and Vanguard.

214. MOMENTUM EFFECT

What goes up, it seems, keeps going up. Numerous academic papers have documented momentum in stock prices, notably the 1993 paper by Narasimham Jegadeesh and Sheridan Titman. Many quantitatively driven money managers follow a value strategy, but also look for upward price momentum, with a view to buying beaten-down value stocks that are just beginning to bounce back.

Researchers have found that stocks with strong short-term performance, typically over 12 months or less, often continue to perform well during the 12 months that followed. What's behind this share-price momentum? It seems difficult to explain the rewards of momentum investing in terms of increased risk (though that argument has been made).

Instead, it could be that, when good news emerges about a company, investors bid up the share price. But the initial share-price increase doesn't fully reflect the good news, perhaps because some potential buyers are concerned the improvement may be a flash-in-the-pan. Gradually, investors shed their concerns and purchase the stock, causing the shares to continue climbing.

PowerShares offers a series of ETFs that use momentum strategies, including funds focused on U.S. stocks, international shares and industry sectors. Other offerings include iShares MSCI USA Momentum Factor ETF and SPDR S&P 1500 Momentum Tilt ETF.

215. PROFITABILITY EFFECT

The latest contribution to factor investing comes from Robert Novy-Marx, a finance professor at the University of Rochester. He examined the stock market performance of companies based on their profitability, as measured by the ratio of gross profits to assets. Gross profits are a company's revenues minus what it cost the company to make the goods that were sold.

Don't confuse gross profits with net income, which is the earnings number that investors typically look at. Novy-Marx notes that net income isn't necessarily a good indicator of profitability because it can be depressed by, say, spending on research and development or an aggressive advertising campaign. That spending can mean greater profits down the road, yet it takes a short-term toll on reported earnings and thus can make companies look less profitable than they really are.

Novy-Marx found that buying companies with high gross profits, which is a form of growth investing, generates higher stock market returns. He also found that the strategy is especially effective if you buy more profitable companies, but focus on those with lower share prices relative to book value. In other words, by combining Novy-Marx's profitability criteria with French and Fama's value criteria, you should be able to identify stocks that are profitable but undervalued.

It would be hard to argue that buying more profitable companies is a riskier strategy, so there's a greater danger that the premium offered by the profitability effect will disappear relatively quickly. Both Dimensional Fund

Advisors and AQR Capital Management have introduced funds designed to take advantage of the profitability effect. As they and others seek to exploit Novy-Marx's insight, the stocks involved could see their prices bid up—and future returns will be lower.

216. FUNDAMENTAL INDEXING

Historically, index funds have weighted stocks based on their total stock market value. But critics claim this overweights expensive stocks, because a stock's importance in an index climbs as its share price climbs. One solution: Change the way you weight stocks.

That's the idea behind fundamental indexing, which was developed by Research Affiliates, a Newport Beach, Calif., money manager headed by Robert Arnott. In 2005, the firm launched its Research Affiliates Fundamental Index, or RAFI, which weights companies by fundamental measures of size, rather than by each company's market value.

Those fundamental measures of size include sales, cash flow, dividends and book value. By weighting stocks in an index fund using these measures of a company's fundamental value, the hope is to underweight stocks that are currently overvalued, while overweighting those stocks that are undervalued. This results in portfolios that look similar to those created by fans of factor investing, with tilts toward value stocks and small-cap shares.

Both PowerShares and WisdomTree offer a huge array of ETFs that are fundamentally weighted, while Charles Schwab offers six mutual funds and six ETFs that use fundamental weightings.

217. WHAT DETERMINES BOND RETURNS?

On Sept. 30, 1981, the yield on the benchmark 10-year Treasury note hit a high of 15.84 percent. More than three decades later, on July 25, 2012, the yield touched bottom at a slim 1.43 percent. And that, in many ways, was the big financial story of the past three decades. As interest rates fell, bond prices rose. That enriched existing bondholders, while also sparking interest in stocks, which appeared more attractive as bond yields declined. The fall in interest rates also made it cheaper for almost everybody to borrow, including corporations, governments and homebuyers.

But the big decline in interest rates is over. With the 10-year Treasury note finishing 2014 at a yield of 2.17 percent, there's precious little room for interest rates to fall further—and ample room for them to rise. That means that, from here, all bond investors can reasonably expect to earn is the yield on the bonds they buy. Just purchased a 10-year Treasury yielding

2.17 percent? You shouldn't expect to collect anything more than that.

That 2.17 percent is barely above the 1.7 percent inflation rate (excluding food and energy) for the 12 months through November 2014. Moreover, the ride in the years ahead could be rough. In recent years, the Federal Reserve's bond-buying program has artificially depressed interest rates in an effort to spur the economy's growth. But with the bond-buying program wrapping up at the end of 2014, interest rates could climb, driving down the price of existing bonds.

How high could rates climb? Historically, bond yields have closely tracked nominal economic growth. For instance, if GDP grows at 5 percent (including inflation) over the next few years, the yield on the 10-year Treasury note could rise to that level. What to do? You might start by looking at your bond portfolio, considering the risks you're exposed to—and asking how you would react if the worst came to pass.

JONATHAN'S TAKE: While a globally diversified stock portfolio might return 6 percent a year over the next decade, bond investors probably shouldn't expect to earn much above 3 percent—and that assumes you lean toward corporate bonds and hence take a moderate amount of credit risk. That 3 percent or so may barely outpace the inflation rate.

218. RISK AND BOND RETURNS

Bond investors face a number of risks, such as inflation eroding the spending power of their interest payments and the possibility that the issuer of their bonds might default. But with interest rates so low, the big concern today is that rates will rise sharply. That will drive down the price of existing bonds, which will appear less attractive compared to newer bonds with their higher interest payments.

For an individual bond or bond fund, this risk is captured by a measure known as duration. For instance, if a bond has a duration of seven years, its price will likely climb 7 percent if interest rates fall by one percentage point and lose 7 percent if rates rise by a full point. If interest rates climb by one percentage point, bond investors today could easily lose more to price losses than they'll collect in interest over the course of a year. And it's entirely conceivable that rates could climb more than one point. On their websites, many mutual fund companies report the average duration of the bonds in their funds. You can also find duration information for funds at Morningstar.com.

Looking at big potential losses? That doesn't necessarily mean you should sell. There's no guarantee interest rates will rise. If you sell and buy short-term bonds or cash investments, you will give up income. Still, you should be aware of the risk you face, so you aren't unpleasantly surprised and panicked into selling. You might also focus on the silver lining. If rates rise, that will ultimately help your bond portfolio, as you invest new savings—and reinvest interest payments and the proceeds from maturing bonds—at the higher yields.

What if you'd rather not see your bond portfolio roughed up by rising rates? Instead of a portfolio with, say, 60 percent stocks and 40 percent bonds, you might opt for 75 percent stocks and 25 percent cash investments—or, alternatively, close-to-cash investments, in the guise of short-term bonds and certificates of deposit. The expected long-run return of those two portfolios should be similar. Indeed, historically, shorter-term bonds have delivered much of the yield of longer-term bonds, but with significantly less risk.

219. COSTS AND BOND RETURNS

In today's low-yield world, it's more crucial than ever to hold down investment costs. Suppose a bond fund charges 1 percent in annual expenses. If the fund owns bonds yielding 10 percent, the after-cost yield collected by the fund's investors would be 9 percent. That means investors are losing a tenth of their investment income to expenses. But if the fund's bonds are yielding 3 percent and the fund charges 1 percent, investors will collect just 2 percent, as expenses snag a third of their potential yield.

Moreover, what counts is your return after inflation and taxes. You can fend off taxes by holding your bonds in a retirement account or buying municipal bonds. But inflation is harder to combat—and high expenses, whether they're charged by a fund or you incur them trading individual bonds, could leave you earning a yield that's below the inflation rate.

None of this would matter if bond-fund managers or individual investors were skilled enough to earn back their expenses and post market-beating results. But there's scant evidence of that. Instead, over five-year periods, the top performers in any particular bond-fund category will usually be those funds with the lowest annual expenses.

There's also a danger that higher-cost funds will prove riskier than their low-cost competitors. Managers of higher-cost funds may be especially aggressive as they strive to overcome their costs and thereby keep up with lower-expense funds. That extra risk could come back to haunt these fund managers—and their shareholders.

Costs can also be a big issue when buying and selling individual bonds, thanks to the large markups that retail investors often pay. Check out the Market Data page offered by FINRA.org, where you can get details on individual bond issues. (From the home page, click on the link labeled "Become a Smarter Investor" and then look for the "Market Data" tab.) If you plan to buy or sell an individual bond in the secondary market, it's helpful to review recent trade data to see whether you're being offered a fair price. Better still, if you want to buy individual bonds, consider purchasing new issues and then holding the bonds to maturity.

220. BONDS VS. BOND FUNDS

Investors will often tout the benefits of individual bonds, while disparaging bond funds. Why? Owners of individual bonds not only avoid fund expenses, but also enjoy a comforting degree of certainty. If you buy a seven-year bond, you know how much interest you will receive each year and what sum you'll get back when the bond matures in seven years. By contrast, if you own a fund that focuses on bonds with an average maturity of seven years, you can't be sure how much interest you'll collect each year or what your fund shares will be worth seven years from now.

But in reality, the performance difference between the individual bond and the fund likely won't be that great—and the individual bond comes with greater risk. If you purchase an individual bond, you're making a big bet on a single issuer, while a fund offers broader diversification.

Moreover, when ordinary investors buy individual bonds, they're often charged huge markups, though you can sidestep this problem by purchasing new issues. A bond fund, meanwhile, should get the benefit of institutional pricing. Funds are also easier to buy and sell, plus you can reinvest your fund distributions in additional fund shares, no matter how small those distributions are.

That ability to reinvest is a key advantage, especially when interest rates are rising. Yes, rising interest rates will depress the price of both individual bonds and bond funds. But with a fund, you can easily take advantage of those higher rates by reinvesting your distributions in additional fund shares.

221. NEW BOND ISSUES

The case for low-cost funds, including index funds, is especially compelling when it comes to bonds. But you might do even better—by buying newly issued Treasury, municipal and corporate bonds, and then holding them to maturity.

That way, there's typically no commission involved, you pay the same offering price as everybody else, including institutional investors, and you don't have to worry that the dealer has marked up a bond's price excessively. In the secondary market, where already issued bonds are traded, individuals often pay 2 or 3 percent more for bonds than institutional investors, and the markup (or markdown if you're selling) could be as much as 5 percent. The secondary market can be an especially rough place for retail investors in municipal bonds.

To purchase new Treasury bond issues, check out the website TreasuryDirect.gov. Most new municipal bond issues have a so-called retail order period, which allows individuals to place orders ahead of institutional investors. One problem: Your brokerage firm may not have access to the muni issues you're interested in. Similarly, it can be difficult to get your hands on new corporate bond issues. It may pay to work with a broker or brokerage firm that specializes in these bonds.

But the biggest drawback with purchasing individual bonds is the lack of diversification. This isn't an issue with Treasurys, where a default is highly unlikely (though it may not seem that way amid all the political wrangling in Washington). But with munis and corporates, the risk of default is real. Unless you have huge sums to invest, you may not be able to buy enough issues to protect yourself against the financial impact of one or two rotten bonds.

222. TEN-YEAR TREASURYS

As of June 30, 2014, the total value of all U.S. bonds was $38.1 trillion, according to the Securities Industry and Financial Markets Association. Treasury bonds were the biggest component, accounting for 31.7 percent, followed by mortgage bonds at 22.8 percent, corporate bonds at 20.1 percent and municipals at 9.6 percent.

But the Treasury market isn't important simply because of its size. It also provides investors with a crucial number: the yield on the 10-year Treasury note. This benchmark rate is used for all kinds of purposes, including figuring out a fair price for corporate bonds, valuing stocks, forecasting inflation and pricing mortgages.

Why is the 10-year Treasury so important? Many investors view it as the risk-free rate. In other words, if no other investment seems compelling, you could always buy 10-year Treasurys and collect the stated interest rate for the next decade, confident that there's little risk that you won't get your regular interest payments and that you won't get your principal back upon maturity.

Even though your nominal return is pretty much guaranteed, there remains a big risk: inflation. That explains the appeal of inflation-indexed Treasury bonds.

Not so worried about inflation and happy to buy regular Treasury bonds? While there are mutual funds that invest in Treasurys, you may want to avoid fund expenses and instead purchase individual Treasury bonds directly from the government. That does, however, come with drawbacks. A fund allows you to reinvest your regular interest payments, no matter how small, in additional fund shares. But to reinvest in individual Treasury bonds, you'll have to wait until you have accumulated $100 in interest and until the next auction occurs. It's also more of a hassle to sell individual Treasury bonds.

223. INFLATION-INDEXED TREASURYS

Inflation-indexed Treasury bonds, formally known as Treasury Inflation Protected Securities, or TIPS, were first sold in January 1997, with the 10-year note initially yielding 3.45 percentage points more than inflation. Unfortunately, yields have been trending lower ever since. They did briefly spike above 3 percent in late 2008. But that rich yield didn't last long, and 10-year TIPS were yielding just 0.53 percent more than inflation at year-end 2014.

While the yield on regular 10-year Treasury notes is often depicted as the risk-free rate, arguably that distinction belongs to 10-year TIPS. Not only are you protected against defaults, but also you're protected against inflation. The principal value of an inflation-indexed Treasury bond is stepped up along with the inflation rate. The semiannual interest payment is then calculated by applying the bond's rate to this increased principal value. For instance, if inflation runs at 3 percent and you buy bonds yielding 1 percent, your annual total return would be 4 percent. One warning: If you own TIPS in a regular taxable account, you will owe federal income taxes each year on both the interest payments and the step-up in principal value.

Want to get a handle on expected inflation for the next 10 years? Take the yield on regular 10-year Treasurys, which was 2.17 percent at year-end 2014, and subtract the 0.53 percent offered by 10-year TIPS. The 1.6 percent difference is the annual inflation rate expected by investors over the next 10 years.

TIPS can be purchased directly from the government. But you might also check out low-cost mutual funds, such as Fidelity Spartan Inflation-Protected Bond Index Fund and Vanguard Inflation-Protected Securities Fund. There are also low-expense ETFs available, including iShares TIPS Bond ETF and SPDR Barclays TIPS ETF.

224. FLOATING RATE TREASURY NOTES

In January 2014, the U.S. Treasury began selling floating rate notes. The notes have a two-year maturity, with interest paid quarterly. Their yield changes based on the interest rate for 13-week Treasury bills. Through TreasuryDirect, the minimum purchase amount is $100. As with other Treasury bonds and many government agency bonds, the interest is taxable at the federal level, but exempt from state and local taxes.

With short-term interest rates currently so low, the yields on floating rate Treasurys are tiny. But the risk is also modest. Many bond investors fear rising interest rates, because it drives down the price of existing bonds. Yet owners of floating rate notes will benefit from a rise in short-term rates, because it will push up their yield. You can learn more at TreasuryDirect.gov.

225. SAVINGS BONDS

Savings bonds come in two flavors: EE and I. Series EE bonds pay a fixed interest rate for up to 30 years. For bonds purchased in the six months starting Nov. 1, 2014, that rate is a meager 0.1 percent. Meanwhile, I bonds increase in value along with inflation, plus holders can earn a small additional sum—but not always. Indeed, for bonds bought in the six months starting Nov. 1, 2014, there's no additional interest rate, over and above inflation. Still, with inflation higher than the 0.1 percent fixed rate on EE bonds, I bonds currently appear to be a far better deal.

With both EE and I bonds, you can defer paying taxes until you sell or the bond matures, at which point the accumulated interest is subject to federal income taxes, but not state and local taxes. You may, however, be able to avoid that tax bill if the proceeds are used for college costs. You can learn more in Part IV.

Savings bonds can be purchased in amounts as small as $25. An individual could potentially buy $25,000 of savings bonds in a year, with the maximum set at $10,000 for EE bonds, $10,000 for I bonds and $5,000 for I bonds bought with a federal tax refund.

You can sell a savings bond after holding it for one year. But if you sell within the first five years, you lose the last three months of interest. For more information, go to TreasuryDirect.gov.

226. MUNICIPAL BONDS

Municipal bonds can pay interest that's exempt from federal taxes and, if you own bonds from your own state, maybe state and local taxes as well. Sound appealing? Before buying, you should calculate whether munis make sense given your tax bracket. We tackle that topic in Part X.

If munis will give you a higher tax-equivalent yield, you might be tempted to purchase a muni fund that focuses on bonds from your state, so the interest is exempt from state as well as federal taxes. But these funds come with added risk. It isn't simply that you're focusing on bonds from a single state. Also, single-state muni funds often own relatively long-term bonds, so they could get hit hard by rising interest rates.

Many munis are issued with 20- or 30-year maturities. The issuer can often call the issue after 10 years. That means investors get their money back early, but could be giving up a bond with an attractive yield. Bond calls are less likely to happen if interest rates head higher from here, because municipalities will find it tough to replace the called bonds with lower-interest debt.

Don't want to take so much interest-rate risk? Some national municipal bonds funds—those that buy bonds from around the country—focus on short-term or intermediate-term bonds. This may be a safer option, though you'll pay a price in lower yields and less tax savings.

Vanguard Group has an impressive array of municipal bond mutual funds with low annual expenses, while both BlackRock's iShares and State Street's SPDR ETFs have a fistful of municipal bond ETFs. Prefer a state-specific muni fund? You may have to cast a wider net to find a fund that focuses on your state's bonds, including checking out closed-end funds, which are discussed later in this chapter.

What about individual bonds? Those can be a decent bet if you buy and hold new issues. To keep track of your portfolio, consider making use of BondView.com. What if you're buying or selling existing individual bonds in the so-called secondary market? Unscrupulous brokers may charge huge markups when you buy and hit you with large markdowns when you sell. To arm yourself with information before trading, check out recent activity using the Municipal Securities Rulemaking Board's EMMA (Electronic Municipal Market Access) system at MSRB.org.

227. MORTGAGE BONDS

New mortgages are often securitized, meaning they're packaged into bonds and sold to investors. An attractive investment? Mortgage bonds should yield more than comparable government bonds, in part to compensate investors for so-called prepayment risk.

That's the risk that homeowners will pay off their mortgages early, perhaps because they move or refinance or because they make extra principal payments. That early payment on a mortgage is more likely to happen if rates fall. Homeowners with older, higher-interest mortgages realize they could do better, so they refinance or pay ahead on their loan.

That creates an asymmetry in how mortgage bonds perform. When rates rise, mortgage bonds are likely to fall, just like other bonds. But if rates fall, mortgage bonds may not perform as well as other bonds, because of those prepayments. If you own mortgage bonds, what you really want is for interest rates to stay relatively constant.

Looking for a low-cost mortgage-bond fund? Check out mutual funds such as Fidelity GNMA Fund, Vanguard GNMA Fund and Vanguard Mortgage-Backed Securities Index Fund, and ETFs like iShares MBS ETF, SPDR Barclays Mortgage Backed Bond ETF and Vanguard Mortgage-Backed Securities ETF.

228. CORPORATE BONDS

As of late December 2014, top-quality corporate bonds were yielding 3.75 percent, while medium-grade bonds were yielding 4.71 percent, according to the Federal Reserve. That's more than you can earn on comparable Treasury bonds—with good reason.

When you buy both corporate and Treasury bonds, you take interest-rate risk, meaning your bonds could fall in price if interest rates rise. But corporate-bond investors take an additional risk that government bondholders don't have to worry about: There's a chance the companies involved could default on their interest payments.

In addition, corporate bonds are often callable before maturity, meaning an issuer can pay off its bonds early. This can be bad news for investors, who may have to surrender a bond with a relatively attractive yield. That's another risk Treasury investors don't have to worry about.

To compensate for these risks, holders of higher-quality corporate bonds might collect an extra one to two percentage points in annual yield compared to Treasurys. That extra yield should provide a partial buffer against rising interest rates. Given the risk of rising interest rates, you might reduce your interest-rate risk by favoring shorter-term bonds, but stick with corporate rather than government bonds, so you don't give up too much yield. There is, however, a price to be paid: When stocks next nosedive, corporate bonds will likely provide less protection than government bonds.

Vanguard Group has a variety of low-cost corporate-bond mutual funds, both actively managed and indexed, that target securities with different maturities. A host of exchange-traded corporate-bond funds are available from iShares, SPDR ETFs and Vanguard.

229. JUNK BONDS

High-yield junk bonds can offer impressive interest payments. The question is, how big a price will you pay in defaults? Junk bonds are rated below investment grade by credit-rating services such as Fitch Ratings, Moody's Investors Service and Standard & Poor's, meaning there is a serious risk you won't get your money back. Historically, some 5 percent of junk bonds have defaulted each year, though defaults in recent years have been running at more like 2 or 3 percent.

To compensate for the risk of defaults, junk bonds have, on average, yielded some 6 percentage points more than comparable Treasury bonds. But the spread over Treasurys has fluctuated widely. In June 2007, it was at an all-time low of 2.4 percentage points. Less than a year and a half later, in November 2008, the spread widened to almost 20 percentage points during the panic selling of the financial crisis.

At year-end 2014, the spread over Treasurys was at 4.9 percentage points, a little tighter than the historical average. The spread would have been even tighter if Treasury yields weren't so low. That means junk-bond investors have a relatively modest margin for error, should the default rate pick up. Junk bonds also tend to trade more like stocks than bonds, so a tumbling stock market could drag down junk bond prices.

While there are some ETFs that focus on junk bonds, most junk-bond funds are actively managed mutual funds. As you pick among them, pay attention not only to fund costs, but also to the credit quality of the portfolio. You can get the necessary information at Morningstar.com. A fund that focuses on lower-quality junk bonds will often sport a higher yield. But that higher yield may prove to be scant compensation if there's a flurry of defaults.

JONATHAN'S TAKE: While I have a small stake in junk bonds, I'm hardly a fan. The time to buy junk is during economic downturns, when concerns about defaults drive up yields. Problem is, that's also the time when you want to buy stocks—and stocks are likely to deliver better returns as markets rebound in anticipation of an economic recovery.

230. FLOATING RATE LOANS

As investors have sought both higher yields and protection against rising interest rates, some have turned to floating rate funds, also known as bank-loan or leveraged-loan funds. Examples include ETFs such as Highland/iBoxx Senior Loan ETF, PowerShares Senior Loan Portfolio ETF and SPDR Blackstone/GSO Senior Loan ETF, and mutual funds like Fidelity Floating Rate High Income Fund and Pimco Senior Floating Rate

Fund. There are also closed-end funds that focus on bank loans, many of which use leverage to goose their yield.

The loans held by these funds have their rates pegged to short-term interest rates. That means you aren't locked in at current yields, which is the danger faced by those owning regular fixed-rate bonds. But while bank-loan funds may be a good defense against rising interest rates, you could suffer if the economy turns down.

The reason: The loans involved are typically made to companies that are rated below investment grade. Because they're less financially strong, the risk of default is higher. In the event of a bankruptcy, bank loans typically have seniority over other debt, so holders are more likely to get their money back. Still, buyers of bank-loan funds should be prepared for a rough ride. How rough? In 2008, the funds lost almost 30 percent, according to Morningstar.

231. DEVELOPED MARKET BONDS

You should think of international bond funds not as a standalone investment, but as a further way to diversify a portfolio. Consider the T. Rowe Price International Bond Fund, which was launched in 1986. In the 28 full calendar years since then, the fund has lost money in 10 years, or more than a third of the time. That's hardly the sort of performance that would endear it to conservative investors.

On the other hand, the fund occasionally delivered strong returns at just the right time. During that 28-year stretch, the Standard & Poor's 500-stock index lost money in five years—1990, 2000, 2001, 2002 and 2008—and the T. Rowe Price Group fund posted gains in three of those five years, thus helping to bolster a diversified portfolio's performance at a time when its stock market investments were suffering.

An international bond fund can potentially post handsome gains either because foreign interest rates decline, pushing up the price of existing bonds, or because the dollar declines in value. The T. Rowe Price fund doesn't hedge its currency exposure. But some international bond funds do hedge, either occasionally or all the time. This will make the funds less volatile, which might appeal to conservative investors.

Among providers of ETFs, iShares and SPDR ETFs have an extensive array of international bond funds. In addition to the T. Rowe Price fund, you can purchase international or global bond mutual funds from companies such as American Century Investments, Fidelity Investments and Vanguard Group. International funds invest exclusively abroad, while global funds own a mix of U.S. and foreign securities.

232. EMERGING-MARKET DEBT

Emerging-market bonds have posted impressive returns over the past few decades, as emerging-market economies have grown more robust. That, in turn, has bolstered the credit quality of emerging-market debt, resulting in a narrowing of the spread between the yield on emerging-market debt and that available on U.S. Treasury bonds.

From here, however, returns are likely to be more muted. As of year-end 2014, emerging-market debt was offering relatively low yields. Moreover, the historical tightening of the spread between emerging-market debt and Treasury bonds was a onetime gain. The spread may tighten further, but the big gains have already been had. Also keep in mind that, in a crisis, emerging-market debt funds can suffer steep losses, such as 2008's 18 percent drubbing.

Two decades ago, emerging-market debt was often denominated in U.S. dollars, so investors didn't have to worry about currency risk. Today, emerging-market governments—which are easily the biggest issuers of emerging-market debt   are more likely to sell bonds denominated in their own currencies. These local currency bonds will be more volatile, but could prove to be a better diversifier for a portfolio that's mostly devoted to U.S. stocks and bonds.

Intrigued? Check out funds such as Fidelity New Markets Income Fund and Vanguard Emerging Markets Government Bond Index Fund. Before buying an emerging-market bond fund, find out whether the fund focuses on dollar-denominated bonds, local currency bonds or some combination of the two, so you know how much currency risk you're taking.

233. CLOSED-END FUNDS

Exchange-traded index funds have exploded in popularity since the first U.S. fund was launched in 1993. But ETFs weren't the first investment funds to be listed on the stock market. That distinction belongs to closed-end funds, which have traded in the U.S. since 1893. Today, there are some 600 closed-end funds, which collectively manage $300 billion in assets. For more information, check out the Closed-End Fund Center at CEFA.com.

Every closed-end fund has two prices. There's the price of the publicly traded shares—and then there's the value of the fund's assets expressed on a per-share basis, otherwise known as its net asset value. Closed-end fund shares are initially sold at a premium to net asset value, with the premium representing the money earned by the brokerage firms concerned. But often, funds quickly fall to a discount, at which point you might be able to buy a dollar of assets for just 90 cents.

A majority of closed-end funds focus on bonds, both taxable and tax-free. Indeed, the world of closed-end funds includes a vast array of single-state, tax-free municipal bond funds.

Be warned: Many closed-end bond funds use leverage to boost returns. The funds issue short-term paper at relatively low interest rates and then use the proceeds to buy longer-term bonds offering higher yields. The interest rate differential helps pad the yield paid to shareholders. But those higher yields come at a price: When bond prices fall, owners of leveraged closed-end funds will suffer steeper losses than those in unleveraged funds.

234. COVERED CALLS

In search of extra income, investors sometimes skip bonds—and instead sell call options against their stock portfolio. The buyers of these call options get the right to call away the underlying stock at a specified "strike" price either when the option expires or at any time up until the option's expiration date. In return for that right, the buyers pay a premium to the sellers.

Selling call options has two key drawbacks. First, trading options is a zero-sum game: For every winner, there's a loser. In fact, it's less than a zero-sum game once you factor in the trading costs involved. As a seller of call options, you're the winner if the underlying stock goes nowhere, because you make a little extra dough by pocketing the call premium. But you could end up as the loser if the stock climbs above the strike price. You might miss out on big investment gains—and the call premium you received may not come close to compensating.

That brings us to the second drawback. If you sell covered calls, you may see all of your good stocks called away and you might be left holding a bunch of duds. This could be more painful than you might imagine. How so? Most years, the market's performance is driven by a minority of stocks with strong performance, a phenomenon known as skewness. This shouldn't be surprising: The most a stock can lose is 100 percent of its value, but the potential gain is unlimited. In many years, there will be a small number of stocks that score gains of 200 percent, 300 percent or more. If you write covered calls, your stocks that get called away could be among the market's big winners.

Want more income from your portfolio? You'll likely achieve your goal at lower investment costs, and with fewer hassles, by simply keeping a little less in stocks and a little more in bonds.

235. CASH INVESTMENTS

Cash investments include things like Treasury bills, savings accounts, money-market deposit accounts, money-market mutual funds and certificates of deposit, where there's little chance you'll lose money and which can typically be sold at short notice (though, in the case of CDs, there will usually be an early-withdrawal penalty).

Historically, cash investments like Treasury bills and money-market mutual funds have paid a yield that roughly approximates the inflation rate. That means they can help preserve the spending power of your money before taxes, but you'll likely find you are losing money, once the taxman gets his share. In recent years, however, it's been far worse, with the Federal Reserve keeping short-term interest rates close to zero in an effort to stimulate the U.S. economy.

In addition to the long-run threat from inflation and taxes, holders of cash investments have also suffered the occasional short-term scare. During the 2008–2009 financial crisis, accountholders at failed banks had uneasy moments, even if they were eventually made whole, thanks to FDIC insurance. Over the past four decades, a few money-market mutual funds have "broken the buck," with their share price falling below the standard $1 net asset value. Perhaps the most notable failure was the Reserve Primary Fund, which slipped to 97 cents in September 2008.

Still, cash investments are far safer than stocks or bonds. Got money you expect to spend within the next year or two? Cash investments are typically the only prudent choice, given the chance of short-term losses with anything riskier. To find higher-yielding CDs and savings accounts, head to Bankrate.com.

What if you plan to hold cash investments as part of your longer-term portfolio? If you have a 401(k) plan at work that includes a stable-value fund, you might keep your cash allocation in the fund, which may offer a somewhat higher yield than, say, a money-market mutual fund. You could also keep longer-term cash holdings in short-term bonds, which will give you a higher yield, but there is a risk you'll have a year with modest losses. Alternatively, you might purchase longer-term CDs to get a higher yield, figuring that higher yield will compensate for any early-withdrawal penalty, should you need to cash out before maturity.

236. FDIC INSURANCE

The Federal Deposit Insurance Corporation provides protection for bank accounts, including checking accounts, saving accounts, money-market deposit accounts and certificates of deposit. In the event of a bank failure, you're insured for up to $250,000 per insured bank, with the insurance applying to each ownership category. Among the ownership categories are accounts solely in your name, accounts held jointly with someone else and bank products held in an IRA.

Suppose you have $250,000 in a savings account in your name and your spouse has a similar sum. You also both have IRAs that hold CDs worth $250,000. In addition, you have a joint account that holds $500,000. The FDIC would ascribe half the joint account to you and half to your spouse, and insure it for the full $500,000. Add it all up and you would together be covered for $1.5 million—and that's just at one bank. You could do the same all over again at a different bank. To increase FDIC coverage, some financial firms will help you set up a so-called sweep account, where your money is spread across a variety of banks to increase your FDIC coverage.

Keep two caveats in mind. First, FDIC deposit insurance only applies to bank products. FDIC insurance would cover a money-market deposit account, but not a money-market mutual fund. Second, before you purchase a certificate of deposit through a broker, ask whether it's covered by FDIC insurance. To learn more, go to FDIC.gov. In particular, check out the brochure entitled "Your Insured Deposits."

237. ALTERNATIVE INVESTMENTS

What counts as an alternative investment? Opinions differ. But the list might include gold, silver, stocks of mining companies that focus on these two metals, hedge funds, mutual funds that endeavor to act like hedge funds, timber, farmland, residential and commercial rental properties, real estate investment trusts, commodity funds that buy everything from agriculture to energy futures contracts, venture capital funds that invest in privately held companies, stocks of energy and natural-resource companies, and even bitcoins.

These various investments have one thing in common: They hold out the promise of performing well when stocks are getting crushed. Or, to use Wall Street lingo, these are potentially uncorrelated assets. That's a valuable quality. If you own something that rises in value when stocks fall, not only will you find investing less nerve-racking, but also you could turn this lack of correlation into additional investment gains through regular rebalancing.

Keep five caveats in mind. First, past correlations can be a lousy guide to future correlations. Take commodity futures. These are now widely owned by investors. As a result, not only are long-run returns from commodity-futures funds likely to be lower than history suggests, but also they are more likely to rise and fall with the same overall investor sentiment that's driving stock returns.

Second, in some cases, the diversification benefit may be an illusion. For instance, timber is seen by some institutional investors as a great way to diversify financial assets like stocks and bonds. But the apparent lack of correlation may simply reflect the absence of daily price information on your 100 acres of timber.

Third, many of these alternative investments come with steep investment costs. Hedge funds are the most notable culprit, though mutual funds that employ hedge-fund-like strategies are also far from cheap.

Fourth, some alternative investments can't be quickly sold, including rental properties, hedge funds and venture capital funds. That lack of liquidity makes rebalancing difficult.

Finally, never forget that low correlation is a double-edged sword. It may help when stocks are falling, but you could find yourself disappointed by your alternative investments as they tumble in value while stocks roar ahead.

238. GOLD

Many alternative investments can be slotted into one of two categories: They are either hard-asset plays, like commodities and real estate, or they are financially engineered to perform unlike conventional stocks and bonds, which is what you get with many hedge funds and hedge-fund-like mutual funds.

Among hard assets, the classic investment is gold, which is widely seen as a hedge against inflation and political turmoil, and viewed as a good diversifier for financial assets like stocks and bonds. Gold soared in the 1970s, collapsed in the 1980s and has come roaring back since 2001, eventually peaking close to $1,900 per ounce, before falling back to $1,184 at year-end 2014.

As gold soared, so too did the assets of SPDR Gold Shares, an exchange-traded fund backed by gold bullion. The fund, which was launched in 2004, became a popular alternative to owning gold itself, because it saved investors the hassles that come with storing, transporting and insuring their holdings of gold coins or bars.

While gold may provide offsetting gains when stocks and bonds are losing value, you may be disappointed with your long-run performance. Over time, price gains on gold should roughly match the inflation rate, which means all you're doing is preserving the spending power of your money—and maybe not even that if you buy at the wrong time and once you figure in taxes.

As an alternative, some investors focus instead on the stocks of gold-mining companies, which have the potential to outpace inflation over the long run. Gold stocks are more volatile than gold bullion, but this added volatility means they can be a better diversifier for financial assets. Many mutual fund companies offer funds that invest in mining stocks, including American Century Investments, Fidelity Investments and Vanguard Group. Also check out Market Vectors Gold Miners ETF.

JONATHAN'S TAKE: Gold stocks can be a great way to diversify a stock portfolio. But to turn this uncorrelated performance into greater wealth, you need to set a target portfolio percentage for your gold stocks and then regularly rebalance back to your target. All this takes a fair amount of investment courage: Many folks will find themselves unnerved by gold stocks' volatility—and frozen in place when they ought to be rebalancing.

239. BITCOINS

Bitcoins may be intended as a new currency, but they also have similarities to an alternative investment—and perhaps the closest parallel is gold. Neither bitcoins nor physical gold have any intrinsic value: They don't pay interest like a bond and they don't generate earnings and dividends like a stock. Instead, the value ascribed to both bitcoins and gold is born mostly of faith and trust.

True, gold has some limited use—mostly for jewelry—and historically it has been recognized as a store of value by some governments, while bitcoins can make neither claim. Still, like gold, bitcoins have a value largely because owners trust that the supply is limited and because they have faith that others will also view them as valuable.

In some ways, bitcoins are superior to gold. While both are recognized as a medium of exchange not controlled by any national government, bitcoins are a lot cheaper to buy, hold and sell. You don't have all the costs associated with trading and storing gold.

In recent years, bitcoins have been subject to large speculative swings in value. But assuming the market for the bitcoins isn't discredited or replaced by some other virtual currency, all you can expect from bitcoins over the long run is a return equal to the global inflation rate—which is exactly what you can expect from gold. As such, while you might be able to make a short-term speculative gain, it's unlikely to be a great long-run investment. What if you do make large gains? There's good news: The IRS has said that profits earned by bitcoin owners will be subject to capital gains taxes, not income taxes.

240. REAL ESTATE INVESTMENT TRUSTS

Real estate investment trusts come in two basic flavors. Mortgage REITs earn interest by providing financing to real estate owners and operators. Equity REITs purchase and operate properties such as apartment buildings, shopping centers, warehouses and office buildings. They collect rent and other income, which is then passed along to shareholders, and also occasionally make money by selling properties at a profit. Equity REITs account for 90 percent of REIT assets.

In the 1990s, equity REITs were laggards compared to the broad U.S. stock market. Since then, they have generated strong performance despite a few rough years, notably 2007 and 2008. The strong results continued in 2014, with a 26.4 percent total return through November. But that great performance means future returns are likely to be modest. Equity REITs, which were yielding almost 9 percent at year-end 1999, were paying out just 3.4 percent as of November 2014.

REITs must distribute at least 90 percent of their taxable income to shareholders each year. Those dividends can be deducted against a REIT's taxable income, so most REITs pay no corporate income taxes. Because of this favorable tax treatment at the corporate level, the dividends paid to REIT shareholders don't qualify to be taxed at the long-term capital gains rate. Instead, they're taxed as ordinary income. Because of that tax treatment and because REITs kick off so much income each year, you should probably hold your REITs in a retirement account.

Most major mutual fund companies, as well as the big ETF providers, now offer funds that invest in REITs. There are also many closed-end funds focused on real estate. For more on REITs, check out the website REIT.com/investing.

241. HEDGE FUNDS

For years, hedge funds were the status symbol of the investment world, promising superior returns to the lucky few who could afford the price of admission. But more often than not, the superior returns haven't materialized—and lately hedge funds have lost some of their luster.

These lightly regulated investment funds use a broader array of strategies than the typical mutual fund. For instance, a hedge fund might try to boost returns by borrowing money and then using that money to purchase additional investments. It might also buy some investments, hoping they'll rise in value, while also selling short other investments, in a bet they'll fall in value.

While hedge funds have a reputation for delivering outsized returns, that isn't always the objective. Yes, some funds gun for big gains, making large, leveraged bets. But others are focused on "absolute returns," meaning they aim to generate healthy returns year after year, no matter what's happening in the financial markets.

To invest in a hedge fund, you need at least a $1 million net worth, excluding your primary residence, or to have earned $200,000 in each of the past two years (or $300,000 together with your spouse). Many hedge funds, however, set the bar even higher, demanding huge initial investments that are only affordable by institutional investors and the extremely wealthy.

Hedge-fund ownership may be an exclusive club—but the membership fees are, alas, equally rich. Hedge funds typically charge 1 or 2 percent of assets each year, while also taking 20 percent of any gains. What if you buy a fund of funds, which is a hedge fund that invests in other hedge funds? You'll have to deal with a second layer of fees, which might take an additional 1.5 percent of assets and 10 percent of gains. Weighed down by fees with like that, it's hardly surprising that most hedge funds turn out to be poor investments.

242. HEDGE-FUND-LIKE MUTUAL FUNDS AND ETFs

A hedge fund might allow you to cash out just once every three months. By contrast, mutual funds need to provide daily liquidity, meaning you can get out at the end of any day that the market is open, while ETFs can be bought and sold throughout the trading day. For that reason, mutual funds and ETFs that pursue hedge-fund-like strategies are sometimes referred to as liquid alternatives or simply "liquid alts." What sorts of funds are available? Here is a sampler:

• Long-short funds, such as Schwab Hedged Equity Fund, which go long some stocks in the hope they'll rise, while shorting others in a bet they'll fall.

• Global macro funds, like William Blair Macro Allocation Fund and IQ Hedge Macro Tracker ETF. The latter seeks to mimic the performance of a hedge fund index. The index, in turn, tracks the results of hedge funds that have the freedom to invest anywhere.

• Managed futures funds such as WisdomTree Managed Futures Strategy Fund, an ETF that aims to generate positive returns that are uncorrelated to the financial markets. The ETF buys a mix of currency, commodity and Treasury bond derivatives.

• Merger arbitrage funds, like Arbitrage Fund and Merger Fund, which aim to make money by betting that mergers and acquisitions will be successfully completed.

Keep three caveats in mind. First, some liquid alt funds have steep annual expenses. Second, the strategies involved can generate big annual tax bills, so the funds are best held in a retirement account. Third, these funds all represent a bet on active management—a bet that historically hasn't panned out.

JONATHAN'S TAKE: You should never buy a fund unless you fully understand its strategy. If you don't, there's a risk you'll suffer an unpleasant surprise—and end up selling out, possibly at the worst possible time. That's why I think most investors should stick with easy-to-understand alternative investments, such as funds that focus on gold stocks and real estate investment trusts.

PART X

TAXES
PAYING UNCLE SAM,
BUT NOT UNTIL TOMORROW

There's what you make—and what you keep. Most folks don't spend nearly enough time focusing on the latter. That's a shame: If you can get a handle on our ridiculously complicated tax code and use that knowledge to manage your annual tax bill, you could add substantially to your wealth.

Imagine you invest $10,000 for 30 years and earn 8 percent a year. If you lost 25 percent of your gain to taxes every year, you would have $57,435 after 30 years, which is fairly impressive. Now, instead, suppose you could defer all taxes for 30 years, at which point you got dinged at 25 percent on your 30 years of tax-deferred growth. Result: You would walk away with $77,970, or 36 percent more.

There are two golden rules when managing taxes. First, it's usually better to pay taxes later. If you have a choice between paying taxes this year and paying in 10 years, you should take the second option. During the extra 10 years that you hang onto money earmarked for Uncle Sam, you can use that money to earn additional gains for yourself. This tax deferral is one of the compelling advantages offered by retirement accounts. It's also the reason people will realize investment losses and bulk up on tax deductions during the current tax year, while putting off income and capital gains until later.

Second, when you pay taxes, you want to pay at the lowest rate possible. That means favoring investments that are taxed less onerously. This should be a key factor when investing your taxable account. But it also means seizing the opportunity offered by years when you have little taxable income, which may include your early retirement years or a year when you're out of work. Indeed, while paying taxes later is rule No. 1, sometimes rule No. 2 means breaking rule No. 1.

Ready to get started? This chapter begins with an overview of the federal tax code and then offers a host of strategies for managing your investment tax bill.

243. FIVE STEPS FOR 2015

Want to boost your after-tax wealth? Here are five steps to get you started:

• Calculate your marginal tax rate. Knowing that rate will help you figure out whether it makes sense to buy municipal bonds, pay down mortgage debt, and fund Roth retirement accounts rather than the tax-deductible variety.

• Shovel as much money as you can into tax-sheltered accounts, including your employer's retirement plan and your individual retirement account.

• Not eligible for a tax-deductible or Roth IRA? Look into funding a nondeductible IRA and then converting it to a Roth.

• Use your retirement accounts to buy your portfolio's tax-inefficient investments, such as taxable bonds, real estate investment trusts and actively managed stock funds.

• Focus your taxable account investments on stock funds that are slow to realize capital gains, such as index mutual funds, exchange-traded index funds and tax-managed funds.

244. INCOME TAX BASICS

The federal tax code can be utterly baffling, which helps explain why 56 percent of individual tax returns are completed by a tax preparer and many of the rest use tax software. Still, while every nuance of the tax code won't be explained here, it's important to understand the basics so you can better manage your annual tax bill.

How is your federal tax bill calculated? You start by adding up your gross income. That means toting up the money you received over the past calendar year from your job, investments, rental properties and elsewhere.

Next, you figure out how much of this income is taxable by knocking off your personal exemptions, standard or itemized deductions, and any other deductions you have, including those for retirement account contributions. You will likely discover there's a large amount of income each year on which you pay no income taxes, though you may pay Social Security and Medicare payroll taxes on this money.

After that, you calculate how much you owe Uncle Sam on your taxable income. That isn't as straightforward as it seems, thanks to the multitude of different tax rates, including seven federal income tax brackets, capital gains taxes, the alternative minimum tax and the Medicare surtax.

Finally, once you have figured out your total tax bill, you may be able to trim it by claiming various tax credits, such as the child tax credit and the credit for daycare costs. There are also various education tax breaks, which are discussed in Part IV. All done? Unfortunately not. Many Americans then get to do it all over again, thanks to state income taxes.

If you want to learn more about the federal tax code, check out the interactive tax forms at TaxPolicyCenter.org. The Tax Policy Center is a joint venture of the Urban Institute and Brookings Institution. The interactive forms explain each line on the tax return, including how many people are affected.

245. FIVE FEDERAL TAXES

Your income could be subject to as many as five different federal tax systems. First, if you have a job, and hence you have what's called earned income, you pay Social Security and Medicare payroll taxes. For many folks, this is the biggest tax they pay.

Second, there's the federal income tax, which is why we spend the early months of each year sweating over Form 1040. Why is that form so complicated? One reason: In addition to payroll and income taxes, you may owe three other taxes, especially if you have a hefty income or you have so-called unearned income, which is income from investments.

That brings us to our third tax: If you have qualified dividends or you sell investments that you held for more than a year, you may pay taxes at the long-term capital gains rate, rather than at the higher income tax rate. The dividend and long-term capital gains rate is 0 or 15 percent for everyone except those in the top 39.6 percent tax bracket, who pay 20 percent. This potential tax advantage should heavily influence how you invest your taxable account.

Fourth, you may be subject to the Medicare surtax, which took effect in 2013 and was introduced to help pay for Obamacare. Unlike the standard Social Security and Medicare payroll tax, the Medicare surtax can ding not only your salary, but also your investment gains. In effect, it's two taxes—an additional payroll tax and an extra investment tax on high-income earners.

Fifth, there's the alternative minimum tax, or AMT. Initially introduced to help ensure those with high incomes paid at least a minimum amount of federal income taxes, the AMT now hits many middle-class families, especially those with a large number of dependents or sizable state and local tax deductions.

246. PAYROLL TAXES

Unless you're self-employed, it is easy to forget about the Social Security and Medicare payroll tax. Your employer takes the payroll tax from your paycheck before it does almost anything else, including deduct those 401(k) contributions. Those contributions may reduce your income for purposes of calculating income taxes, but they don't shrink the income that's subject to the payroll tax. Moreover, unless you have self-employment income, you won't even be reminded that you're paying the payroll tax when you fill out your federal tax return.

Yet, for many folks, the payroll tax takes a bigger bite out of their income than the federal income tax. Let's say you're the sole breadwinner in a family of four, you earn the U.S. median household income of $51,900, your only income comes from your job and you claim the standard deduction. In 2015, you would lose $2,572.50 to federal income taxes and $3,970.35 to the payroll tax—and this assumes your employer pays half the payroll tax.

Surprised? There may be seven federal income tax brackets ranging from 10 to 39.6 percent. But for many families, only the 10 and 15 percent brackets come into play, plus they can take advantage of exemptions, deductions and credits. That means their marginal tax rate is fairly low, and their average tax rate is even lower. By contrast, in 2015, the payroll tax for most folks is a flat 15.3 percent, with 7.65 percent paid by employees and 7.65 percent by employers. That tax is further divided, so that 6.2 percent of the 7.65 goes to Social Security and 1.45 percent to Medicare.

High-income employees get some relief from the payroll tax once their salary for 2015 crosses the $118,500 mark. At that juncture, they no longer have to pay any more Social Security tax, though they have to pay the 1.45 percent Medicare tax on every dollar of income they earn. If their total income—including investment income—is high enough, however, they may get hit with a nasty surprise: the Medicare surtax.

247. MARGINAL VS. AVERAGE TAX RATES

Imagine you're single, you claim the standard deduction and you have income of $50,000 in 2015. You would be in the 25 percent federal income tax bracket, but that isn't how much of your income you lose to taxes.

On the first $10,300 of income, you wouldn't owe any federal income taxes, thanks to your $6,300 standard deduction and your $4,000 personal exemption. The next $9,225 would be taxed at 10 percent and the subsequent $28,225 would be taxed at 15 percent. That gets you up to $47,750 in total income. It's only at that point that your income starts getting taxed at 25 percent. In other words, while you're in the 25 percent marginal federal income tax bracket, just $2,250 of your $50,000 income would be taxed at that rate. Your average rate is 11.4 percent for your $50,000 in gross income and 14.4 percent for your $39,700 in taxable income. For high-income earners, their marginal tax rate may differ from the rate for the top tax bracket that they're in, because each additional dollar of income also causes lost tax benefits, such as a reduction in the amount they can claim in itemized deductions and personal exemptions.

Your marginal tax rate is crucial for figuring out whether you should buy taxable or tax-free bonds, how much all that mortgage interest is costing you, and whether it makes sense to convert your traditional IRA to a Roth IRA. Most taxpayers pay federal taxes at a 15 percent marginal rate or lower. But your marginal rate isn't a good indicator of what your total bill will be for the year. For that, you'd want to know your average rate. For all taxpayers, the average federal tax rate in 2012 was 13.1 percent of total income.

248. STANDARD VS. ITEMIZED DEDUCTIONS

For 2014, the standard deduction is $12,400 if your tax-filing status is married filing jointly, $9,100 for heads of household and $6,200 for single individuals. For 2015, it's $12,600 for those married filing jointly, $9,250 for heads of household and $6,300 for single individuals. The standard deduction is slightly higher if you're elderly or blind. You take the standard deduction if it's greater than the sum of your various itemized deductions. The standard deduction is claimed on roughly two-thirds of individual tax returns.

Why is the standard deduction so important? Besides representing a sum you can earn each year without getting taxed, it also should guide your financial behavior. For instance, if you take the standard deduction, you aren't getting any tax benefit from the mortgage interest you pay, so it may make sense to pay off your mortgage more quickly. You only benefit from the mortgage-interest tax deduction if you itemize your deductions using Schedule A. Schedule A is also where you list other deductions, including those for property taxes, state income taxes, medical and dental expenses, and charitable contributions.

Even if you itemize, you may not get the full tax benefit from all the items listed on Schedule A. In 2014, your itemized deductions are reduced if your taxable income is above $305,050 and you're married filing jointly, above $279,650 and you're head of household, and above $254,200 and you're single. In 2015, the reduction will affect you if your income is above $309,900 and you are married filing jointly, above $284,050 if head of household and above $258,250 if single.

At these income levels, the value of your personal exemptions also phases out. The full value of each personal exemption is $3,950 in 2014 and $4,000 in 2015. You can typically claim a personal exemption for yourself, your spouse and all dependents.

249. MEDICARE SURTAX

The standard Medicare payroll tax is 2.9 percent, half of which may be paid by your employer, leaving your share at 1.45 percent. Add that to the 6.2 percent Social Security tax and you get the total 7.65 percent payroll tax. If you have a high income, you will notice that the Social Security tax stops getting collected once you hit that year's threshold, which for 2015 would be $118,500. But there's no cap on the Medicare tax, which is collected on every dollar you earn.

Sound rough? Starting in 2013, it got rougher. Once your taxable income gets above $200,000 if you're single or head of household and above $250,000 if you're married filing jointly, the Medicare tax jumps by 0.9 percentage point to 3.8 percent (though, again, 1.45 percent may be paid by your employer). Moreover, once you're at this income level, the 3.8 percent Medicare surtax doesn't just apply to earned income. Your net investment income is also taxed at these rates.

Net investment income includes your realized capital gains, dividends and interest, though not interest from municipal bonds. Let's say you realize a long-term capital gain that would otherwise be taxed at 15 percent. Now, you will also pay an additional 3.8 percent, bringing the total tax on the gain to 18.8 percent. Here's more salt for the wound: The income thresholds aren't indexed for inflation. That means that, in the years ahead, more folks will find themselves paying the 3.8 percent Medicare tax.

250. ALTERNATIVE MINIMUM TAX

The alternative minimum tax, or AMT, is a parallel tax system that forces you to calculate how much you owe in federal income taxes using a completely different set of rules. The Urban-Brookings Tax Policy Center estimates that 4.3 percent of taxpayers will pay the AMT in 2014, with the vast majority of those affected earning between $100,000 and $500,000. The AMT tends to hit folks who live in states with high state income taxes and include those taxes among their itemized deductions. It often also snags those who realize large capital gains or who have three or more children. If the amount owed under the AMT is greater than under the usual income tax calculation, you have to pay the difference.

For individuals, the AMT consists of just two tax rates, 26 and 28 percent. When calculating how much you owe under the AMT, you can't claim personal exemptions or the standard deduction. You can claim itemized deductions, though what counts is severely curtailed. For instance, no deduction is allowed for state, local or property taxes. You can still deduct charitable gifts and most mortgage interest. Deductible retirement plan contributions, which aren't reported as an itemized deduction, also reduce your income for AMT purposes.

While you can't claim personal exemptions when calculating how much you owe under the AMT, you do get the benefit of the much larger AMT exemption. That exemption is adjusted each year for inflation. For unmarried individuals, the exemption is worth $52,800 in 2014 and $53,600 in 2015. For married couples filing jointly, the exemption is $82,100 in 2014 and $83,400 in 2015. The AMT exemption phases out at higher income levels, so the effective marginal AMT tax rate is often higher than the notional 26 and 28 percent rates.

251. MANAGING YOUR EARNINGS

If you're like most employees, you don't have any control over when you receive your wages. Instead, as you seek to limit your annual tax bill, the key financial levers at your disposal include increasing your tax-deductible retirement account contributions, carefully managing your taxable investment accounts and making sure you take full advantage of the available tax deductions and credits.

What if you're a senior executive or a business owner who can influence the company's payroll policy? You might have added room for maneuver. For instance, if you know federal or state taxes are likely to rise next year, you might arrange for year-end bonuses to be paid this year.

If you're self-employed or own a small business, there's even more you might do. Got a lot of income in 2015 but suspect 2016 will be thinner? You might hold off billing clients so you get paid in 2016. Think 2016 will be a good year? You might wait until next year to buy new computer equipment or plan on maxing out your SEP IRA contributions.

252. MANAGING YOUR INVESTMENT TAXES

As a regular employee, you may find it tough to shift earnings from one year to the next. But there's plenty you can do to manage the tax bill generated by your investments. The rest of this chapter is devoted to the three strategies you ought to focus on.

First, make the most of the tax-sheltered retirement accounts available to you. That will mean not only stashing as much money as possible in these accounts, but also carefully weighing whether to fund traditional or Roth retirement accounts.

Second, ponder which investments to hold in your retirement accounts and which in your regular taxable account. In all likelihood, you'll want to use your retirement accounts to hold investments that would otherwise generate big annual tax bills, while keeping more tax-efficient investments in your taxable account.

Third, seize the opportunity offered by years when your income is relatively low. Those low-income years may allow you to generate additional taxable income, while still paying taxes at a relatively low rate. To that end, you might sell stocks with large unrealized capital gains that you no longer want to hold or perhaps convert part of your traditional IRA to a Roth IRA.

JONATHAN'S TAKE: Investors spend hours picking investments, while paying scant attention to taxes and investment costs. But the fact is, when you buy an investment, you never know whether you have yourself a winner. By contrast, managing your tax bill and holding down investment costs are two surefire ways to improve your portfolio's performance.

253. RETIREMENT ACCOUNTS

Retirement accounts come in a bewildering array of flavors. Employer-sponsored plans include 401(k), 403(b), 457 and profit-sharing plans, as well as the SIMPLE IRA and SEP IRA. On top of that, there are individual plans such as traditional and Roth IRAs, and also tax-deferred fixed and variable annuities.

How can you make sense of that mess? All these accounts offer tax-deferred growth, which means you don't have to pay taxes on any investment earnings until you draw them down, typically in retirement. At that point, withdrawals are usually taxed as ordinary income, which could mean a federal income tax rate as high as 39.6 percent. Sometimes, however, retirement accounts offer three additional benefits and one big drawback.

First, some accounts offer an initial tax deduction. That's the case with a tax-deductible IRA. Contributions to employer plans are often also effectively tax-deductible, because your contributions are taken out of pretax dollars.

Second, accounts such as the Roth 401(k) and Roth IRA won't give you an immediate tax deduction, but they offer the chance not just for tax-deferred growth, but tax-free growth. You may even have a choice between, say, a tax-deductible 401(k) and Roth 401(k) or between a tax-deductible IRA and Roth IRA. You can, alas, never get both a tax deduction and tax-free growth.

Third, your employer's retirement plan may include the chance to earn a matching contribution. Not contributing enough to your employer's plan to earn the full match? That ranks as one of the most foolish financial mistakes.

Finally, there's the big drawback: Some retirement accounts are inordinately expensive. That's an issue with some employer-sponsored plans. But the biggest culprits are many, but not all, tax-deferred annuities.

254. EMPLOYER PLANS

If you work for a larger employer, you might be offered a 401(k), 403(b) or 457 plan. The contribution limit for 2015 is typically $18,000. Those age 50 and up can make an additional catch-up contribution of $6,000, for a total of $24,000. Any matching employer contribution doesn't count toward these annual limits. Some companies also offer profit-sharing plans, which are funded solely by the employer, with no money expected from you.

If you work for a small employer, you might have access to a SIMPLE IRA. (SIMPLE is an acronym for Savings Incentive Match Plan for Employees.) The 2015 contribution limit is $12,500, with those 50 and up able to contribute an additional $3,000, for a total of $15,500. Employers are required to either contribute 2 percent of an employee's pay to a SIMPLE IRA or, alternatively, match 100 percent of each employee's contribution, up to 3 percent of pay.

If you're self-employed, you could fund a SEP IRA. (SEP stands for Simplified Employee Pension.) You can contribute as much as 20 percent of your net self-employment income, up to $53,000 in 2015. You can make this contribution even if you are covered by, say, a 401(k) at another job. Alternatively, if you're self-employed, you might consider a solo 401(k).

For most folks, funding their employer's retirement plan should be their top financial priority each year, not least because of the potential matching employer contribution. Failing to contribute isn't the only danger, however. You should also watch out for high investment costs and pay heed to vesting provisions if you're considering a new job. In addition, think twice before taking out loans from your retirement plan.

255. MATCHING CONTRIBUTIONS

It's hard to overemphasize the importance of putting at least enough in your employer's 401(k) or 403(b) plan to earn the full matching employer contribution. But to drive home the point, consider an extreme example.

Suppose your company is likely to have layoffs. Meanwhile, the local employment market is sufficiently depressed that you fear it will take many months to get a job. Your instinct is to hoard every dollar possible for what could be a lengthy period of unemployment. Nonetheless, if your employer offers a retirement plan with a matching contribution, you would likely be better off funding the plan, even if you fully intend to cash out your savings if you're laid off.

Let's say you are in the 15 percent federal income tax bracket and you put $2,000 in the plan. Your out-of-pocket cost would be $1,700, thanks to the initial tax savings. At the same time, your employer matches your contribution at 50 cents on the dollar, with the matching contribution vested immediately. Result: Your $2,000 investment gets you a $1,000 match, bringing your account balance to $3,000.

If you are then laid off and you cash out your retirement account balance, you might lose 15 percent to federal income taxes, plus another 10 percent to the tax penalty for making a retirement account withdrawal before age 59½. That combined 25 percent hit still leaves you with $2,250, well above your $1,700 out-of-pocket cost. Moreover, if you are unemployed for a long period, you may have little taxable income in the year you cash out your retirement account balance, so your income tax bracket could be below 15 percent.

256. LEAVING YOUR EMPLOYER

If you're changing jobs, take two steps to protect your retirement. First, if you have an outstanding loan from your 401(k) or 403(b) plan, get it paid off. If you don't and you leave your job, the loan will be considered a distribution, triggering income taxes and probably tax penalties. There's more on 401(k) loans in Part XI. Second, if there's a vesting schedule for your employer's contribution to the retirement plan, see when the next vesting occurs and, if it's soon, consider delaying your departure so you collect the extra money.

Once you leave your employer, you'll have a choice: You may be able to leave your retirement plan balance in your old employer's plan, move it to your new employer's plan or transfer it to an IRA. What's the right choice?

You'll probably want to move the money if your old employer's plan offers a limited selection of high-cost investment options. This, unfortunately, is often the case with small-business plans. You may also want to consolidate your retirement money in an IRA if simplifying your finances is a priority. Make sure you move the money using a trustee-to-trustee transfer or you could find yourself caught in a nasty tax trap. In addition, if you own your employer's stock in the plan, investigate the "net unrealized appreciation" strategy, which we discuss later in this chapter.

While consolidating in an IRA often makes sense, there are three reasons to keep your retirement money where it is or move it to your new employer's plan. First, it could mean a smaller tax bill if you have an IRA with nondeductible contributions that you plan to convert to a Roth IRA. Second, you might keep money in a 401(k) or similar employer plan—and out of an IRA—if you're worried about lawsuits, a topic we discuss in Part V. While both IRAs and 401(k) plans enjoy some creditor protection, the protection is greater for 401(k) and similar plans.

Third, some employer plans are particularly well-designed—and you could find it tough to do better with an IRA. A good plan may include a small but diverse list of institutional funds with rock-bottom annual expenses, making it relatively easy for employees to build sensible portfolios. For instance, Vanguard Emerging Markets Stock Index Fund charges 0.33 percent a year if you invest $3,000, but the biggest retirement plans can get access to a share class that costs just 0.1 percent. In addition, an employer's plan may include a stable-value fund that offers a combination of fixed share price and moderate yield that's hard to find outside a 401(k).

257. TRUSTEE-TO-TRUSTEE TRANSFERS

If you move money from one retirement account to another, try to arrange a trustee-to-trustee transfer, also known as a direct rollover. That involves asking your brokerage firm, mutual fund company, bank or former employer's 401(k) administrator to send a check that's made out to your new retirement plan custodian. For instance, the check might be payable to "First Fiduciary Trust Company FBO [for benefit of] Jane Smith." The check may be sent directly to your new retirement account provider or it could be mailed to you, and you then have to forward it.

Instead of a trustee-to-trustee transfer, some folks opt for a check made out to them personally, sometimes known as a 60-day rollover. Problem is, if you do a 60-day rollover from a former employer's retirement plan, you will typically receive a check for just 80 percent of the account balance, with the other 20 percent dispatched to the IRS. You can reclaim the other 20 percent on your next tax return—but only if you manage to roll over 100 percent of the account balance within 60 days. That won't be an issue if you have wads of cash sitting around.

But for most people, getting the money together will be a struggle. What if they fail? The 20 percent not rolled over will be considered a retirement account distribution, which means they will likely get hit with both income taxes and a 10 percent tax penalty. The bottom line: Don't let your old employer send you a check made out to you personally. Instead, go for the trustee-to-trustee transfer.

258. NET UNREALIZED APPRECIATION

Got company stock in your 401(k) plan? If you leave your employer, consider taking advantage of the net unrealized appreciation, or NUA, strategy. The idea is to transfer everything in your 401(k) to an IRA—except your employer's stock. These shares, instead, get deposited into a regular taxable brokerage account.

This triggers an immediate income tax bill on the stock's cost basis, which is the amount you paid for the stock or the amount it was worth when you received it as a matching employer contribution. If you are under age 59½, you will likely also have to pay a 10 percent tax penalty on the stock's cost basis. But in return for paying that tax bill, you get a tax break: All of the appreciation in the stock's value is potentially taxable at the long-term capital gains rate. This can be a significant advantage, because retirement account withdrawals are usually taxed at the higher income tax rate.

While the stock's appreciation within the 401(k) will be taxed at the long-term capital gains rate, the subsequent appreciation—after you pull the stock out of the 401(k)—will only be taxed at the capital gains rate if you wait a year before selling.

The NUA strategy makes most sense if the stock has greatly appreciated in value. What if the shares haven't climbed that much? You may want to avoid the immediate income tax bill and possible tax penalty by transferring everything, including the stock, into an IRA.

259. INDIVIDUAL RETIREMENT ACCOUNTS

IRAs come in two flavors: traditional and Roth. With a traditional IRA, you may get an initial tax deduction, but withdrawals are taxed as ordinary income. With a Roth, there's no upfront tax deduction, but all withdrawals in retirement can be tax-free.

For 2014 and 2015, you can contribute up to $5,500 to all IRAs combined, provided you have at least that much in earned income. (Investment income doesn't count.) If you're age 50 or older, you can make an additional catch-up contribution of $1,000, for a total of $6,500. You have until April 15, 2015, to make your 2014 contribution.

If you stash those dollars in a traditional IRA, you can always deduct your contribution if you aren't covered by an employer's retirement plan. What if you or your spouse has a retirement plan at work? You'll need to check the income limits for 2014 and 2015.

To fund a Roth, it doesn't matter whether you're covered by a workplace retirement plan. Instead, all that matters is whether you meet the income thresholds for that tax year.

If you're lucky enough to qualify for both a traditional and Roth IRA, you should weigh the choice carefully. What if you qualify for neither? You can always fund a nondeductible IRA. That may sound like a drab consolation prize—but it could open the door to a Roth conversion.

Finally, don't forget about your spouse. Even if your husband or wife has no earned income, he or she may still qualify for a so-called spousal IRA.

260. DEDUCTING IRA CONTRIBUTIONS

Suppose you aren't covered by an employer's retirement plan and—if married—your spouse isn't, either. In that scenario, you can take a tax deduction for your contribution to a traditional IRA, no matter how high your income.

But if you have a retirement plan at work, income thresholds come into play. If your tax-filing status is single or head of household, your ability to take a tax deduction for your IRA contribution phases out if your 2014 income is between $60,000 and $70,000. Above $70,000, you can't take a deduction, though you can still make nondeductible contributions. For 2015, the phase-out range is $61,000 to $71,000.

Meanwhile, if you are married filing jointly and you're covered by a retirement plan at work, your ability to deduct your IRA contributions phases out if your combined income is $96,000 to $116,000 in 2014. For 2015, the range is $98,000 to $118,000.

What if you aren't covered by an employer's plan, but your spouse is? In that situation, the deductibility of your IRA contribution phases out between $181,000 and $191,000 in 2014 and between $183,000 and $193,000 in 2015.

What if one spouse doesn't work? As long as the other spouse has enough earned income—remember, you can only make the full $5,500 or $6,500 IRA contribution if you have that much in earned income—the couple can fund an IRA on behalf of the nonworking spouse. If the spouse who works is covered by an employer's retirement plan, the deductibility of the nonworking spouse's IRA contribution phases out between $181,000 and $191,000 in 2014 and between $183,000 and $193,000 in 2015.

261. QUALIFYING FOR A ROTH IRA

To claim a tax deduction for your traditional IRA contribution, much hinges on whether you are covered by a retirement plan at work. That doesn't come into play with a Roth IRA. Instead, all that matters is your income.

If you are single or head of household and you have enough earned income, you can fully fund a Roth IRA in 2014 if your income is less than $114,000. The amount you can contribute is phased out if your income is between $114,000 and $129,000. Above $129,000, no contribution is allowed. For 2015, the phase-out range is $116,000 to $131,000.

If you are married filing jointly, your ability to fund a Roth phases out if your combined income is between $181,000 and $191,000 in 2014 and between $183,000 and $193,000 in 2015.

What if you're eligible to make only a partial Roth contribution of, say, $3,000 out of a possible $5,500? You can put the remaining $2,500 in a traditional IRA, though your contribution won't necessarily be tax-deductible.

262. TAX-DEDUCTIBLE VS. ROTH ACCOUNTS

You may qualify to fund both a tax-deductible and Roth IRA. Alternatively, perhaps your employer offers the chance to fund either a tax-deductible or Roth 401(k). Which should you go for?

A key factor is whether you think your tax bracket in retirement will be higher or lower. If you think you'll be in a lower bracket, you should opt for the traditional IRA, taking a tax deduction at your high tax rate today while knowing you'll pull those dollars out of your IRA at a lower tax rate once you're retired. Conversely, if you expect your tax rate in retirement to be the same or higher, you should favor the Roth, giving up today's tax deduction in return for tax-free growth. What if you're unsure what your retirement tax rate will be? You might hedge your bets, dividing your money between traditional and Roth accounts.

That said, there are some additional reasons to fund a Roth IRA. Unlike with a traditional IRA, you can withdraw your regular annual contributions from a Roth IRA at any time for any reason. Just put $5,500 in a Roth? You can pull that money out tomorrow with no taxes or penalties owed.

You also don't have to take required minimum distributions from a Roth IRA once you turn age 70½. That means you can leave the account to continue growing tax-free, and you might even bequeath the account to your children or other beneficiaries. A Roth IRA can make a wonderful inheritance, giving your beneficiaries years of tax-free income using a strategy known as the "stretch IRA," which we discuss in Part XII.

Like the idea of sidestepping required minimum distributions? If you fund a Roth 401(k), be sure to transfer it to a Roth IRA before you reach your 70s, because minimum distributions are required from a Roth 401(k). Avoiding required minimum distributions is also a reason to convert a traditional IRA to a Roth IRA.

263. HOW TO THINK ABOUT THAT TAX DEDUCTION

Assuming you follow the rules, a Roth IRA or Roth 401(k) will give you tax-free growth—and it doesn't get much better than that. But what about traditional 401(k) plans and IRAs, where you can get an initial tax deduction but everything withdrawn in retirement is taxable as ordinary income?

Occasionally, you'll hear so-called experts—who often have some other investment they're promoting—criticize tax-deductible retirement accounts, arguing that people are setting themselves up for huge tax bills in retirement. That may be the case. But if you run the numbers, you find the initial tax savings frequently end up paying for the final tax bill. Indeed, a tax-deductible account can give you tax-free growth, just like a Roth (though, as you'll discover in the next section, there's a subtle difference that nerdy types might want to consider).

Imagine you saved $8,000 in your employer's 401(k) plan and you're in the 25 percent federal income tax bracket. Thanks to the $2,000 in initial tax savings, your out-of-pocket cost is $6,000. Over the next 30 years, your $8,000 grows fivefold—or 400 percent—to $40,000. At that point, you cash it out, paying 25 percent in taxes, equal to $10,000.

That $10,000 represents 400 percent growth on your initial $2,000 in tax savings. In effect, the tax deduction paid the final tax bill, leaving you with tax-free growth on your $6,000 out-of-pocket cost. What if your tax bracket is lower in retirement, which is often the case? In that scenario, you'll have made out at Uncle Sam's expense.

Still, if you fund tax-deductible retirement accounts, it's worth keeping those embedded tax bills in mind as you approach retirement, so you have a better handle on the post-tax value of your retirement savings. The fact is, $10,000 in a tax-deductible retirement account will buy fewer groceries than $10,000 in a Roth.

264. FURTHER THOUGHTS ABOUT THAT TAX DEDUCTION

Okay, so you read the previous section and you see how a tax-deductible retirement account can give you tax-free growth, just like a Roth. In fact, if your tax bracket is lower in retirement, a tax-deductible retirement account can let you come out ahead at the taxman's expense. Meanwhile, if your tax bracket in retirement is higher, you'll be happy you funded a Roth.

But what if your tax bracket stays the same? All even? It depends. Go back and look at the previous section, where we assumed you were in the 25 percent tax bracket both when you funded the account and when you're retired. Suppose that, instead of putting $8,000 in your employer's traditional 401(k), you put $6,000 in the Roth 401(k). Your initial out-of-pocket cost would be the same in both instances and you would have the same after-tax sum in retirement. So, yes, it would be all even.

Now, imagine instead that you plan to max out your IRA. You have a choice: Put $5,500 in a tax-deductible IRA or $5,500 in a Roth. Either way, the account doubles in value between now and retirement, growing to $11,000. With the Roth, that will mean $11,000 in spending money.

With the tax-deductible IRA, you will owe taxes when you tap the account. If you're in the 25 percent tax bracket, you would be looking at a $2,750 tax bill. Fortunately, you also had the initial tax deduction, which would have been worth $1,375 if you had been in the 25 percent tax bracket when you funded the account. In an effort to cover the eventual tax bill on your IRA, you decide to invest the $1,375 tax savings in the same investments that you own in your IRA, so the $1,375 also doubles in value. That way, it would grow to $2,750 and cover the final tax bill, right?

Wrong. The problem: The $1,375 would be invested in a regular taxable account, where its growth would be taxed and hence it wouldn't grow to $2,750. That's why, if you suspect your tax bracket in retirement will be the same in retirement as it is now, you should favor Roth accounts over traditional retirement accounts.

265. ROTH CONVERSIONS

Why convert a traditional IRA to a Roth IRA? The rationale is similar to the reasons you might funnel your regular annual contributions into a Roth rather than a traditional IRA. There are, however, three additional considerations.

First, you might convert to a Roth if you have a year with low taxable income, so you pay tax on the conversion at a relatively modest rate. Remember, when you convert, you have to pay income taxes on the taxable sum converted.

That brings us to the second reason you might convert: Suppose that, in the past, you made nondeductible contributions to your traditional IRA. When you convert, you don't have to pay taxes on those nondeductible contributions. But be warned: For tax purposes, you can't pick which IRA to convert. Instead, you have to assume that the money comes proportionally from all your IRAs combined—which might mean a larger tax bill than you had hoped.

Third, you should only convert if you have money in a regular taxable account to pay the tax bill triggered by the conversion. Using this taxable account money to pay the conversion tax should, thereafter, lower your annual tax bill. How so? Not only will your IRA withdrawals no longer be taxable, but also you'll shrink the size of your taxable account, so that account is no longer generating as big a tax bill. Think of it this way: By converting to a Roth and paying the tax bill with taxable account money, you effectively move money from your taxable account—where it's getting taxed each year—to a Roth, where it can grow tax-free.

JONATHAN'S TAKE: I'm a huge fan of Roth accounts. If you have a year with relatively little taxable income, consider converting a portion of your traditional IRA to a Roth. In retirement, you might tap your Roth if you have a year with high expenses and you don't want to pull money from traditional retirement accounts, which could nudge you into a higher tax bracket. Better still, try not to spend your Roth—and instead bequeath it to your favorite relative. That's what I plan to do.

266. CONVERTING NONDEDUCTIBLE IRAs TO A ROTH

When you convert a traditional IRA to a Roth IRA, you don't have to pay taxes on your nondeductible contributions. Let's say that, over the years, you've made $20,000 in nondeductible contributions to an IRA that is now worth $30,000. When you convert, you don't have to pay taxes on the $20,000 in nondeductible contributions. Thus, the conversion would potentially add just $10,000 to your taxable income, while giving you a $30,000 Roth that will grow tax-free thereafter.

Sound appealing? Here's the hitch: Suppose that, in addition to your $30,000 nondeductible IRA, you also have a $170,000 rollover IRA from your old employer's 401(k). When you convert your $30,000, you have to assume that the money comes pro-rated from all your IRAs combined. That means it's coming out of the $200,000 total IRA. Result: Instead of just $10,000—or 33 percent of the sum converted—being taxable, you would find that $27,000, or 90 percent, would be taxed. The reason: The $20,000 in nondeductible contributions represents just 10 percent of your IRA's $200,000 total value.

What to do? If you have made nondeductible contributions and you're considering a Roth conversion, you might hold off rolling your former employer's 401(k) into an IRA. Alternatively, if you have that money already sitting in a rollover IRA, you may be able to move it into your new employer's retirement plan. That might leave you with just a single IRA, containing nondeductible contributions. You could then convert that account and pay a relatively modest tax bill.

267. ROTH'S FIVE-YEAR RULE

If you make regular annual contributions to a Roth IRA, you can withdraw those contributions at any time with no taxes or penalties owed. It's a different story, however, with the account's investment gains.

Those gains will be subject to both income taxes and tax penalties if you withdraw them within the first five years and if you are under age 59½ (or, to put it another way, you need to wait five years and until after age 59½ for the account's growth to be totally tax-free). The five-year clock starts on Jan. 1 of the tax year for which you made your first regular annual contribution—and it doesn't reset with each subsequent annual contribution or if you open a Roth at another financial firm.

What if you are over age 59½? From then on, if you made a withdrawal, you wouldn't owe a tax penalty if your first annual contribution had been made less than five years earlier. You could owe income taxes, but it's unlikely. How come? When you withdraw, the IRS lets you assume that any withdrawals initially consist of your original annual contributions. If you are drawing down the account relatively slowly, you probably wouldn't start pulling out the account's investment earnings until after you crossed the five-year mark.

Now, consider a different scenario: What if you convert a traditional IRA to a Roth? In that situation, a slightly different five-year rule comes into play. This time, the rule applies not only to the account's investment earnings, but also to the sum converted. In other words, if you withdrew the sum converted within the first five years, you would owe a tax penalty if you were under age 59½. You wouldn't, however, have to pay income taxes, because you would already have paid income taxes on the money involved when you did the original conversion. Unlike with regular annual contributions, a new five-year waiting period applies to each conversion.

What if you made a conversion more than five years ago and you're under age 59½? Because you've met the five-year rule, you can withdraw the sum converted with no penalty or income taxes owed. It's only if you touch the account's investment gains that taxes and penalties come into play—though you may be able to avoid the penalty if you meet one of the allowable IRS exceptions.

268. EARLY-WITHDRAWAL PENALTIES

If you withdraw money from a retirement account before age 59½, you typically have to pay both income taxes and a 10 percent tax penalty. But there are some situations where the penalty wouldn't apply:

• Distributions made after your death.

• Distributions made after you become permanently disabled.

• Withdrawals from an IRA to pay higher-education expenses. These withdrawals can hurt financial aid eligibility, a topic discussed in Part IV.

• Withdrawals of up to $10,000 from an IRA to buy a home. The $10,000 is a lifetime limit, and the provision can only be used by those who haven't owned a house within the past two years. Are you married? Together, you could withdraw $20,000.

• Distributions made as part of a series of substantially equal periodic payments over your life expectancy. If these distributions are from an employer's plan, you need to have left your job. Be warned: Calculating your annual withdrawal can be complicated.

• Distributions to pay deductible medical expenses that exceed 10 percent of your adjusted gross income. If you're age 65 or older, the threshold is 7½ percent.

• Withdrawals from an IRA to pay health insurance premiums while unemployed.

• Distributions from an employer's retirement plan made after you left your job at age 55 or older.

These exceptions to the penalty apply to both traditional and Roth accounts. But with the Roth, you may also avoid income taxes if you're under age 59½, though only in a few carefully defined scenarios, such as when withdrawing your regular annual contributions or when withdrawing the sum converted to a Roth after meeting the five-year rule.

269. MyRA

MyRA is a new retirement savings vehicle geared to those who don't currently have a retirement plan offered through their employer. Like a Roth IRA, there's no initial tax deduction, but all growth is tax-free. Indeed, to fund a myRA, you have to meet the same income thresholds as a Roth IRA.

Accounts are opened online. Subsequent investments are made by payroll deduction in any amount. The account is invested in a single investment whose earnings are driven by government bond yields. An account's balance is capped at $15,000.

The hope is that a myRA account may allow workers to get started with modest regular investments—something that's difficult to do at most financial firms, which often insist on steep initial minimums. Once the account has grown to a decent size, investors might roll over the account to a Roth IRA at, say, a mutual fund firm and then continue their regular savings program at the fund company. You can learn more about myRA at myRA.Treasury.gov.

270. TAX-DEFERRED FIXED ANNUITIES

Tax-deferred annuities come in two types: fixed and variable. Historically, fixed annuities have been pretty straightforward. You get a specified yield for the term of the annuity. Thus, it's a simple matter of deciding whether the yield seems attractive compared to the alternatives, whether the issuing insurance company appears to be financially strong and whether you're willing to lock up your money in the annuity structure until age 59½.

But picking among fixed annuities has grown more complicated, for two reasons. First, many annuities offer first-year teaser rates or other come-ons, which make it harder to compare one annuity with another.

Second, some insurers have been pushing a relatively new breed of fixed annuity known as an indexed annuity. These annuities offer returns that are pegged to a market index, such as the Standard & Poor's 500-stock index, while offering downside protection.

Problem is, investors never get the index's full annual total return. Instead, returns are based on the index with dividends excluded, plus the amount you can earn in any given year is often capped. On top of that, you typically face steep surrender charges if you try to cash out in the first 10 years or so. Those surrender charges are necessary because indexed annuities pay huge commissions to the salesmen involved, and the annuity needs to recoup that money from investors.

271. TAX-DEFERRED VARIABLE ANNUITIES

From a tax perspective, you can think of a tax-deferred variable annuity as similar to a nondeductible IRA. You won't get an initial tax deduction, but you do get tax-deferred growth.

Problem is, unlike a nondeductible IRA, you can't convert a variable annuity to a Roth IRA. On top of that, the variable annuity gives you much less investment choice and you'll face much higher expenses. Within the annuity, you get to choose from among a series of subaccounts that are similar to mutual funds. Each subaccount has its own investment expenses.

Layered on top of that is the expense of the variable annuity itself. This expense charge might be used to cover the annuity's administrative costs, compensate brokers who sell the annuity and pay for various guarantees, such as a guarantee that the annuity will have some minimum value when you die. It's debatable how valuable these guarantees are. But the net result is that variable annuities typically have total annual expenses that can approach 3 percent of assets per year, which makes it tough to earn healthy long-run returns.

JONATHAN'S TAKE: Not all annuities are a terrible investment. For instance, Fidelity Investments and Vanguard Group offer relatively low-cost variable annuities, and these might appeal to high-income earners who have maxed out their retirement accounts and are looking for additional ways to get tax-deferred growth. In particular, the tax deferral from a low-cost variable annuity may be attractive if you're inclined to buy taxable bonds, real estate investment trusts or actively managed stock funds, all of which tend to be relatively tax-inefficient.

272. TAXABLE ACCOUNTS

With a retirement account, your investments grow tax-deferred, so you don't have to worry about tax bills until retirement. But with a taxable account, trading too much or buying investments that pay a lot of immediately taxable interest can mean a heap of pain at tax time.

To avoid that pain, consider four strategies, which are discussed in the sections that follow. First, focus on generating long-term capital gains by hanging onto your individual stocks or stock funds for more than a year. The maximum long-term federal capital gains rate in 2014 and 2015 is 20 percent, well below the 39.6 percent maximum income tax rate. What if you hold your winning stocks or stock funds for a year or less? The higher income tax rate applies.

Second, periodically sell losing investments. The resulting tax losses can be used to offset realized capital gains and up to $3,000 in ordinary income each year. When taking tax losses, watch out for the wash-sale rule.

Third, when buying stocks and stock funds in a taxable account, favor those that pay qualified dividends. These dividends are taxed at the same rate as long-term capital gains.

Fourth, if you're in a high tax bracket and your taste runs to conservative investments, you might buy tax-free municipal bonds rather than taxable bonds. Munis pay interest that is typically exempt from federal taxes and, if you own bonds from your own state, potentially state and local taxes as well.

What does all this mean for your overall portfolio? That's where the crucial issue of asset location comes in—deciding which investments to hold in your retirement accounts and which in your taxable account.

273. INCOME VS. CAPITAL GAINS

The tax code is designed to encourage folks to save and invest. That's one reason for the wide array of retirement accounts. But it also explains the preferential tax treatment given to stocks and other longer-term investments held in regular taxable accounts. That preferential tax treatment shows up in two ways.

First, if you buy, say, a stock that appreciates in value and you hold that stock for more than a year, it's taxed as a long-term capital gain. In 2014, long-term capital gains are taxed at 20 percent if your taxable income is above \$457,600 and you're married filing jointly, above \$432,200 and you file as head of household, or above \$406,750 and you're single. In 2015, the 20 percent rate applies at \$464,850 if married filing jointly, \$439,000 if head of household and \$413,200 if single. For everybody else, the long-term capital gains rate will be 0 or 15 percent. That 0 percent rate on long-term capital gains is a handsome tax break enjoyed by those whose total taxable income falls within the 10 and 15 percent federal income tax brackets.

Whatever rate you pay, it should be well below the tax rate on your ordinary income. Moreover, that capital gains tax bill only comes due when you sell and realize your gain. Hanging onto winning investments in your taxable account effectively gives you tax-deferred growth, just like a retirement account.

Second, Uncle Sam rewards taxable-account investors for owning stocks that pay qualified dividends. Those dividends are taxed at the same rate as long-term capital gains. Most large U.S. companies pay dividends that are qualified, as do some foreign corporations. Real estate investment trusts typically don't pay qualified dividends, so you'll have to pay income taxes instead. Even if a corporation pays a dividend that's qualified, you also need to hold the shares for more than 60 days to get the favorable tax treatment.

In addition to these taxes, you may also be dinged for the 3.8 percent Medicare surtax. This surtax applies to income, including investment income, of couples filing jointly with modified adjusted gross incomes above $250,000. If you file as a single individual or head of household, the surtax kicks in once your income exceeds $200,000. Thanks to the 3.8 percent surtax, the top federal capital gains rate is effectively 23.8 percent, not 20 percent.

274. WASH-SALE RULE

If you own a stock that's fallen in value, you can take some of the sting out of that loss by selling your shares, realizing a capital loss and then using that loss to reduce your annual tax bill. A good idea? Problem is, selling means giving up any chance of making back the loss.

Many folks aren't keen to do that, so they often look to buy back the shares. But if you do that too quickly, you can invalidate the tax loss. At issue here is the wash-sale rule. If you buy the same or a substantially identical security within 30 days before or after you sold the losing stock, you aren't allowed to claim the tax loss. The rules for what's allowable and what's not are a matter of debate. Still, let's say you sell a stock and soon after buy options that give you exposure to the same shares. That would count as a wash sale and invalidate the loss.

That doesn't mean the loss can't ever be used. Instead, the earlier invalidated loss is added to the cost basis of the new security you bought. To make use of that loss, you'll have to wait until you sell the new security, assuming you do so without running afoul of the wash-sale rule.

275. MUTUAL FUND TAXATION

Got mutual funds in your regular taxable account? You can potentially get taxed either because of what the fund does or because of what you do.

Let's start with the former. Each year, a mutual fund is required by law to distribute virtually all of the interest and dividends that it earns, as well as any realized capital gains. Those are bundled together into periodic income and capital gains distributions. When these distributions are made, a fund's share price drops by a comparable amount, so investors are no better off in terms of their pretax wealth. Taxable shareholders, however, have to pay taxes on these distributions.

Bond and money-market funds typically pay income distributions every month, while stock funds might hold off until the end of year and then make a single set of distributions. If you own a fund when those distributions are made, you have to pay taxes on the sums involved, even if you only just bought the fund shares and even if you opt to reinvest the distributions back into the fund. For that reason, taxable account investors are often cautioned against making big stock mutual fund investments right before year-end.

Want to hold down the tax bill your funds generate? In your taxable account, you might favor stock funds that pursue a buy-and-hold strategy, such as index mutual funds, exchange-traded index funds and tax-managed funds. These funds are typically slow to realize their capital gains—and when they do, the gains are usually taxable at the long-term capital gains rate. By contrast, many actively managed stock funds have portfolio turnover of around 100 percent, which means they're typically holding shares for just 12 months.

While buying tax-efficient funds can help, you also need to temper your own behavior. In other words, even if your funds don't make big taxable distributions, you can end up with big tax bills if you're too quick to sell your funds. A silver lining: When you sell a fund, your cost basis for tax purposes includes not only the amount you invested, but also any distributions you reinvested in additional fund shares.

276. MUNICIPAL VS. TAXABLE BONDS

To figure out whether it makes sense to buy tax-free municipal bonds or taxable bonds, you first need to find out your marginal federal and state income tax bracket. Let's say you are in the 33 percent federal income tax bracket and a 7 percent state tax bracket. Meanwhile, suppose you are trying to choose between three bonds, which all have similar credit qualities and durations. There's a muni bond from your own state that's yielding 3.05 percent, a muni bond from another state that yields 3.42 percent and a corporate bond that pays 5.05 percent.

Which is the best bet, given your tax situation? To answer that question, you need to figure out the tax-equivalent yield on the muni bonds. To that end, take your tax brackets (33 and 7 percent), convert them to decimals (0.33 and 0.07) and then subtract them from 1. You would then divide the resulting number into the yield.

For the in-state bond, that would mean dividing the 3.05 percent yield by 0.6 (which you get by adding together 0.33 and 0.7 to get 0.4, and then subtracting that 0.4 from 1). The tax equivalent yield is 5.08 percent, which is more than the 5.05 percent yield on the corporate bond.

What about the out-of-state muni bond? Because the interest will only be tax-exempt at the federal level, you would need to divide the 3.42 percent yield by 0.67 (which is 1 minus your 0.33 federal tax bracket).

Result: The out-of-state bond has a tax-equivalent yield of 5.1 percen
hence might be the better deal. Or maybe not. You might also consider an
alternative strategy: buying taxable bonds in a retirement account, which we
discuss next.

If you need help calculating tax-equivalent yields, try an online
calculator, such as those offered by Bankrate.com and Fidelity.com. These
calculators can generate slightly different results, depending on each
calculator's embedded assumptions. Bear in mind that your tax bracket can
change from year to year. Even if munis make financial sense today, they
may not make sense when you retire. At that juncture, you might pocket
more income by buying taxable bonds, even after paying the resulting tax
bill.

277. MUNIS VS. TAXABLE BONDS IN A RETIREMENT ACCOUNT

If you're in a high income tax bracket, buying tax-free municipal bonds
in your taxable account might seem like a no-brainer. But there's a strategy
that could give you a better return: Use your taxable account to pursue a
tax-efficient stock strategy, while buying taxable bonds within your
retirement account.

The taxable bonds should have a higher yield than tax-free munis and,
because you're buying them in a retirement account, you don't have to
worry about paying tax each year on the interest generated. Meanwhile, in
your taxable account, you might favor stock investments that will be taxed
at the preferential long-term capital gains rate, including any qualified
dividends you receive.

This strategy doesn't sit well with some people, who prefer to have
bonds in their taxable account, where they can be easily sold if these folks
suddenly need cash. But you can effectively do the same thing, even if you
have stocks in your taxable account and bonds in your retirement account.
How? Suppose you suddenly need $20,000.

To generate the cash, you could sell $20,000 of the stocks you have in
your taxable account. If we're in the midst of a bear market, the timing
wouldn't be ideal. But in this case, it wouldn't matter because you would
simultaneously move $20,000 from bonds to stocks within your retirement
account. Result: Your stock exposure remains the same, you've sold
$20,000 in bonds—and you have the cash you need.

278. ASSET LOCATION

After reading Part VIII and Part IX, you know what sort of portfolio you want. But which investments should you hold in your retirement accounts and which in your taxable account? The goal is to minimize your investment tax bill by holding investments that generate a lot of immediately taxable income in your retirement accounts, while favoring relatively tax-efficient investments in your taxable account.

For your retirement accounts, that might mean holding taxable bonds, real estate investment trusts, actively managed stock funds and individual stocks you plan to trade actively. These investments will tend to generate a lot of ordinary income or short-term capital gains, so they would usually be taxed at income tax rates, rather than at the lower long-term capital gains rate. By keeping these investments in a retirement account, you defer that tax bill, plus you avoid the hassle of reporting all this activity on your tax return.

Meanwhile, in your taxable account, you might favor tax-efficient investments that you intend to hang onto for the long haul, such as stock index mutual funds, exchange-traded stock index funds, tax-managed stock funds and long-term individual stock holdings. These investments will tend to generate modest annual tax bills and, when there are taxes to be paid, they'll typically be paid at the long-term capital gains rate.

For your taxable account, you might also favor tax-free municipal bonds, especially if you are a conservative investor and you're in a high tax bracket. But also consider whether you would be better off sticking with long-term stock holdings in your taxable account, while buying taxable bonds in your retirement account.

JONATHAN'S TAKE: Don't let your mix of retirement and taxable money drive your asset allocation. Yes, it makes sense to hold tax-inefficient investments in your retirement accounts and tax-efficient investments in your taxable account. But if, say, you're young and inclined to put much of your money in stock index funds, you'll likely end up holding these tax-efficient funds in your retirement accounts.

279. LOW-INCOME YEARS

If you ever find yourself with a year when you pay no income tax, don't celebrate. Instead, rue the wasted opportunity.

Imagine it's December, you have been out of work all year and you have almost no taxable income. Or let's say you just retired, you haven't yet claimed Social Security and you are looking at a year with no money owed to Uncle Sam. To take advantage of these low-income years, you might convert part of your traditional IRA to a Roth IRA, knowing the tax bill will be relatively modest. Alternatively, if you have a stock in your taxable account that you've been reluctant to sell because you have a large unrealized capital gain, you might seize the opportunity to unload the position.

How much should you sell? Suppose you expect to be taxed at a 25 percent marginal rate once you find a job or once you turn age 70½ and start taking required minimum distributions from your retirement accounts. To head off big tax bills later, you might generate enough taxable income now to get to the top of the 15 percent tax bracket. In 2015, that would mean total income of $95,500 if you're married filing jointly, which would trigger a federal tax bill of $10,312.50. If you are single, it would take $47,750 in total income to get to the top of the 15 percent bracket, resulting in a $5,156.25 tax bill. These figures assume you take the standard deduction and personal exemptions, you have no children, and all tax is paid at ordinary income tax rates.

One caveat: If you're age 65 or older, a large Roth conversion or hefty realized capital gains may boost your income sufficiently that you end up not only paying a big tax bill, but also getting charged higher premiums for Medicare.

280. TAXES IN RETIREMENT

When drawing down a portfolio in retirement, the standard advice is to start with your taxable account, next turn to traditional retirement accounts and, finally, tap any Roth accounts. That way, you let traditional retirement accounts grow tax-deferred for longer and allow your Roth accounts to grow tax-free for longer still.

While that's generally good advice, you may want to tweak it. Retirement can prove surprisingly taxing, especially once you turn age 70½ and start taking required minimum distributions from your retirement accounts. All withdrawals from 401(k) plans, IRAs and their ilk are typically taxed as ordinary income. Moreover, those withdrawals could, in turn, drive up your taxable income so that up to 85 percent of your Social Security benefit is subject to taxes. This is sometimes referred to as the "tax torpedo."

How can you avoid the torpedo? Two strategies may help. First, endeavor to pay off your mortgage by retirement. That way, you'll avoid the need to draw down your retirement accounts to make mortgage payments. Those retirement account withdrawals could generate enough taxable income to trigger taxes on your Social Security benefit.

Second, you might use your early retirement years to trim the size of your retirement accounts by either drawing down those accounts or converting a portion to a Roth IRA. For instance, if you expect to be in the 25 percent federal tax bracket once you start required minimum distributions in your 70s, you might aim to generate enough income in your 60s to get to the top of the 15 percent bracket. To give yourself more room for maneuver, you could delay claiming Social Security until later in retirement—which, in any case, can be a smart thing to do. Strategies for claiming Social Security are discussed in Part II.

You might also look to take extra-large retirement account withdrawals if you have a year with large itemized deductions, perhaps because of medical expenses. These large itemized deductions could be offset against your taxable income, perhaps allowing you to tap your IRA at a relatively low tax cost.

✳ 281. SOCIAL SECURITY TAXATION

If your income is high enough, between 50 and 85 percent of your Social Security retirement benefit may be taxable. Don't be confused: There isn't an 85 percent tax rate on Social Security. Rather, we're talking about 85 percent of your benefit being subject to federal income taxes.

Will you get hit with this tax? Start by calculating your combined income, which is your adjusted gross income, plus any municipal bond interest and half your Social Security benefit. Your adjusted gross income would include distributions from a traditional IRA, but not from a Roth.

If you file as a single individual or head of household, and your combined income is between $25,000 and $34,000, up to 50 percent of your benefit may be taxable. If your combined income is above $34,000, up to 85 percent of your benefit may be subject to tax.

If you are married filing jointly, up to 50 percent of your benefit may be taxable if your combined income falls between $32,000 and $44,000, and up to 85 percent may be taxable if your combined income is above $44,000.

A majority of Social Security recipients don't pay tax on their benefit. But eventually, that's likely to change—because the various thresholds aren't indexed for inflation, so more and more folks will likely find themselves paying the tax.

282. REQUIRED MINIMUM DISTRIBUTIONS

Once you reach age 70½, you have to start taking required minimum distributions, or RMDs, from your retirement accounts. There are three exceptions. First, if you're still working at age 70½, you don't have to take distributions from your employer's 401(k) or similar plan until you retire, unless you own 5 percent or more of the company, in which case distributions must begin at age 70½. Second, you aren't required to take RMDs from so-called nonqualified variable annuities. These are annuities bought with after-tax dollars, as opposed to annuities bought through an employer's plan or in an IRA. Third, you never have to take distributions from a Roth IRA, though your beneficiaries—other than your spouse—will need to take RMDs. Be warned: RMDs must be taken from a Roth 401(k), which is a reason to roll over your Roth 401(k) to a Roth IRA.

If none of these three exceptions applies, you have to take distributions starting in the year you turn age 70½. You can put off taking your first distribution until April 1 of the following year. That, however, might not be a smart move: You'll have to take your second distribution before the end of the year, and the two distributions combined will likely be taxed more heavily than if you had taken them in separate years.

To calculate your RMD for the current year, you divide your retirement account balance as of the prior Dec. 31 by a life expectancy factor. You choose from among three different IRS life expectancy tables, depending on your financial situation. For instance, if your account balance was $500,000 as of year-end and you are age 75, the distribution period is 22.9 years if you're using the Uniform Lifetime Table. To figure out how much you need to withdraw, you would divide $500,000 by 22.9, giving you a minimum distribution of $21,834. You can withdraw more than this amount—but you should be careful not to withdraw less. The penalty for not taking a distribution is an amount equal to 50 percent of the sum that should have been withdrawn, but wasn't. Often, mutual fund companies and brokerage firms will calculate your RMD for you. There are also online calculators available, such as those offered at Fidelity.com and TRowePrice.com.

In December 2014, Congress voted to allow so-called qualified charitable distributions for the 2014 tax year. This provision lets those age 70½ and older contribute up to $100,000 directly from their IRA to a qualified charity and count the contribution toward their RMD. The charitable gift isn't tax-deductible—but the IRA distribution also isn't included in your taxable income. It isn't clear whether charitable contributions from an IRA will be allowed in 2015 and, based on recent history, we may not know until late in the year.

283. RECORDKEEPING

What tax information should you hang on to? Here are three pointers:
• Keep seven years of tax returns, including supporting materials. The IRS has three years to audit your tax return or six years if it suspects

substantial underreporting of income. What if you have been playing fast and loose with your taxes? You probably shouldn't throw anything away.

• Keep cost-basis information for assets held in your taxable account. This should include how much you paid for your house, plus the cost of any subsequent home improvements. You may be able to add those improvements to your home's cost basis when you sell and thereby reduce any taxable gain. You should probably also keep records of how much you paid for individual investments, unless your financial firms provide it. Mutual funds are now required to provide cost-basis information for funds bought in 2012 or later, and many firms provide information for funds purchased prior to that year.

• Keep a record of all nondeductible IRA contributions—and make sure your heirs know where to find the details. If you bequeath your IRA, your beneficiaries won't have to pay taxes when they withdraw those nondeductible contributions.

PART XI

BORROWING
BUY NOW,
PAY BY THE TIME YOU RETIRE

Starting in college and continuing through your 20s and 30s, the debts might pile up thick and fast: first college loans, then a car loan, next a mortgage and perhaps a second mortgage. Frightening? You should consider borrowing early in your adult years as a rational strategy—and, once again, your human capital plays a central role. By borrowing, you are able to purchase items you can't currently afford, thus smoothing out consumption over your lifetime. With decades of paychecks ahead, you should have plenty of time to pay off these loans before you quit the workforce, so you can retire debt-free.

That, at least, is the theory. In practice, many folks end up borrowing too much. The vast majority of American households have some form of debt. While overall household debt has been trending down since 2008, many observers have recently sounded the alarm about student loans. It's crucial to avoid borrowing more than you can comfortably handle.

It's also crucial to hold down your borrowing costs. You can do that by regularly checking your credit reports for errors, maintaining good credit scores, favoring secured loans, considering taxes, refinancing when the opportunity arises and paying down debt when it makes sense. You might view your debts as "negative bonds" and pay them off ahead of schedule if that offers a higher post-tax return than the investment alternatives. Indeed, ridding yourself of all debt by retirement can make a ton of sense, both because it eliminates a major expense and because it can help you avoid the "tax torpedo," a nasty retirement tax trap described in Part X. Got too much debt? We offer some strategies at the end of this chapter.

An organizational note: This chapter discusses all kinds of borrowing—except education loans. Because education loans are an integral part of college financial aid packages, it made more sense to include them in Part IV, the chapter on paying for college. There, you'll also find some tips on how to trim your monthly loan payments if you've already graduated.

284. AMERICA'S DEBTS 2014

Almost 75 percent of American families are in debt, according to the Federal Reserve's 2013 Survey of Consumer Finances. The most common types of borrowing are mortgage debt, installment loans like car and student loans, and credit card balances.

Every three months, the Federal Reserve Bank of New York puts out a report on household debt. As of September 2014, the overall picture was heartening. Over the five years through September 2008, the amount of debt carried by American families soared 68 percent. That was a key cause of the financial crisis that hit with full fury in late 2008.

In the five years that followed, Americans shed debt, as they both paid back the money they borrowed and also defaulted on loans. As of September 2014, Americans were carrying 8 percent less debt than in September 2008, despite a modest uptick in borrowing since mid-2013. According to the New York Fed, the typical American family had $45,600 of loans outstanding, including mortgage debt, home equity loans, car loans, credit card debt and student loans. That might seem modest given the large mortgages often needed to buy homes in major East and West Coast cities. But remember, homes are substantially cheaper in many parts of the country, plus the median is influenced by retirees with little or no debt and by the third of American households that don't own a home and hence have no mortgage.

Indeed, not all the news is good. While most types of debt have been shrinking over the past six years, student loans have soared 84 percent. The money borrowed should help make the U.S. economy more productive and help the students involved earn higher lifetime incomes. Still, this burgeoning debt speaks to the financial sloppiness of the baby boomers, who are providing notably little financial help to their college-bound teenagers, thus compelling their children to borrow more. Today's big fear: The current crop of college graduates won't be able to handle the debts they've taken on, triggering a new financial crisis.

285. FIVE STEPS FOR 2015

Not sure you're handling your debts properly? Here are five steps to get you back on track:

• Get free copies of your credit reports from the three major credit bureaus by heading to AnnualCreditReport.com.

• Make sure you're using a rewards credit card for all your daily spending. You should be getting at least 1 percent cash back, or the equivalent in other rewards, such as frequent-flier points or rewards points. Also look to pay off your credit card balance in full every month. This should be a top financial priority. Probably the only higher priority is putting at least enough in your employer's retirement plan to get the full matching contribution.

• With 30-year fixed-rate mortgages still available at around 4 percent, see if it's worth refinancing. Explore whether you could afford the payments on a 15-year or 20-year loan, so you get your mortgage paid off more quickly.

• Set up a home equity line of credit in case you're hit with a financial emergency. You might also use this credit line to pay off any credit card balances and possibly as an alternative to other borrowing, such as car loans.

• See if you're on track to get your mortgage paid off by retirement and, if not, consider making extra principal payments.

286. CREDIT REPORTS

Every year, you are entitled to a free copy of your credit report from each of the three major credit bureaus: Equifax, Experian and TransUnion. Your all-important credit score is based on the information in these reports. To view your three reports, go to AnnualCreditReport.com. Consider checking your credit reports every year, especially if you plan to borrow a large sum to buy, say, a house or car.

What should you look for? See if there are any accounts you don't recognize. That could be an indication that you're a victim of identity theft.

Also check your credit reports for inaccuracies, such as incorrect information about debt payments, past employers or places where you have lived. Look for any debts that are listed more than once. Filed for bankruptcy more than 10 years ago? That should no longer appear in your credit reports.

If you spot erroneous information in any of your three reports, contact either the credit bureau itself or the company that supplied the incorrect information. Through their websites, Equifax.com, Experian.com and TransUnion.com, all three credit bureaus allow you to submit an online request to have inaccuracies fixed.

287. CREDIT SCORES

Credit scores are a source of shame for some, pride for others and confusion for pretty much everybody. Whatever the case, it's worth understanding how they're calculated, because your credit scores don't just affect whether you get accepted for a loan or a credit card and what interest rate you'll pay. They're also looked at by insurers, employers before making job offers and landlords when vetting tenants.

There are multiple credit-scoring systems, though the FICO score is easily the most widely used. Even FICO scores come in different flavors: The score looked at by a credit card issuer may differ from that looked at by an auto lender. Even when using the same scoring system, the three credit bureaus can come up with different results if they have different information in the credit report they maintain for you.

FICO scores range from 300 to 850. The typical score is around 690 and a score above 720 indicates you're considered a very good risk. How can you improve your credit score? Whether you pay your bills on time is the biggest factor affecting your FICO score. Lenders, in particular, are quick to report late payments to the credit bureaus.

How much you owe is also important. For instance, it's best to use 10 percent or less of the available borrowing limit on your credit cards, and that's true even if you pay off the balance in full every month. In fact, canceling a credit card can hurt your credit score because you will likely end up using a higher percentage of your remaining available credit, and that will make you appear financially stressed. It's also helpful to have a long credit history and to use different types of credit, including both credit cards and installment loans like mortgages and auto loans. In addition, you should avoid applying for credit too often.

Typically, you have to pay to learn your credit score. Even websites that promise to reveal your credit score for free often come with some catch. That, however, isn't the case with educational sites such as Credit.com, CreditKarma.com, CreditSesame.com and Quizzle.com. You can also learn your credit score for free if you use certain financial institutions, such as carrying a credit card from Citigroup or Discover Financial Services.

288. WHAT WON'T HURT YOUR CREDIT SCORES

Your credit reports and credit scores are, more than anything, a reflection of how responsible you are in handling your debts. Lenders are quick to report late payments and other issues to the credit bureaus.

What about other aspects of your financial life? When it comes to your credit scores, the items that don't matter are quite surprising:

• Your income and net worth don't directly influence your credit scores or appear in your credit reports. Your credit reports, however, may list current and former employers.

• Overdrawing your bank account won't affect your credit scores unless your bank brings in a collection agency to collect the debt.

• Late payments on bills from your insurance company, cell phone provider or local utility won't ding your credit scores. Ditto for paying the rent late. If, however, you're really late on a bill and it ends up with a collection agency, your credit scores could take a hit.

289. IDENTITY THEFT

Identity theft occurs when someone uses your name, address, Social Security number and other personal information to borrow money, open a credit card account or commit fraud in some other way.

To guard against identity theft, review financial statements carefully for any charges you don't recognize. Regularly check your credit reports for accounts you didn't open. Become concerned if you receive a bill from a company you don't recognize. That may mean someone has opened an account in your name. Also be concerned if you receive a letter saying a loan application has been rejected. That could indicate someone is trying to use your identity to borrow money.

What if you believe you are the victim of identity theft? Contact the companies where accounts have been opened and ask that they be closed. File a report with the Federal Trade Commission at FTCcomplaintAssistant.gov and call the local police to report the crime. Place a fraud alert on your file at the three major credit bureaus. To find out how, go to Equifax.com, Experian.com and TransUnion.com. You might even consider freezing your credit.

To learn more about identity theft, check out the Federal Trade Commission's site at Consumer.gov/idtheft.

290. FREEZING YOUR CREDIT

If you fear your identity has been stolen or you're very concerned about the risk, one option is to freeze your credit. Once your credit is frozen, the credit bureaus can't release information from your credit reports without your permission, effectively stopping someone from borrowing money using your identify.

To freeze your credit—also known as a security freeze—you have to contact the three major credit bureaus. You can get details at each of their websites, Equifax.com, Experian.com and TransUnion.com.

The cost to freeze your credit varies by state. Often, it's free for victims of identity theft and sometimes also for seniors. Even if there's a fee, the three bureaus typically charge just $5 to $10 to freeze your credit and a similar fee to unfreeze it. The latter will become necessary if, say, you apply for a mortgage or a new credit card. Keep in mind that it isn't just lenders who look at your credit reports. A credit freeze could also interfere with a job application or renting an apartment.

291. DEBT RATIOS

How much can you prudently borrow? You might check on yourself the way a banker would. If you apply for a mortgage, lenders will often assess your borrowing ability using two key measures: your housing and debt ratios. The housing ratio looks at your expected or current monthly mortgage payment, including principal, interest, property taxes and homeowner's insurance. As a rule, this shouldn't be more than 28 percent of your pretax monthly income. For instance, if you earn $60,000 a year or $5,000 a month, your total mortgage payment shouldn't be above $1,400.

The debt ratio looks at all your debt payments, including mortgage, auto loans, student loans and minimum credit card payments. If you are divorced, the debt ratio will also include any child support and alimony you pay. Typically, these various obligations shouldn't be above 36 percent of your gross monthly income, which would equal $1,800 if you earn $5,000 pretax every month. What if you apply for a mortgage and you don't have any other debts? A lender may be willing to lend you more, so your monthly mortgage payments are above 28 percent of your gross income.

Even if you aren't applying for a mortgage, keep these ratios in mind. For instance, the difference between the housing ratio's 28 percent and the debt ratio's 36 percent is 8 percentage points. The implication: Lenders don't want borrowers devoting more than 8 percent of their gross income to nonmortgage debt. Let's say you are taking out an auto loan. You might calculate whether the auto loan will push your nonmortgage debt payments above 8 percent of income. Alternatively, imagine you're advising your children on college borrowing. You might calculate whether your children's eventual student-loan payments will be more than 8 percent of their likely income.

292. SECURED VS. UNSECURED DEBT

It's helpful to think about your debts in two buckets: secured and unsecured. What's the difference? Secured debt is backed up by an asset you own. For instance, your mortgage is secured by your home, your brokerage-account margin loan by your portfolio and, in most cases, your auto loan by your car. Because lenders have an asset they can seize if you fail to make your debt payments, the interest rate tends to be relatively low.

Personal bank loans and credit card debt are unsecured, hence the relatively high interest rates charged. Those high rates are needed to compensate lenders for the money lost to defaults. What about education loans? Those might also appear to be unsecured. But with federal education loans, the government has ways of reclaiming its money—including asking your employer to garnish your wages, taking your federal and state tax refunds, and even garnishing your Social Security retirement benefit.

If possible, avoid unsecured debt and instead favor debts that are secured by an asset, so you pay a lower interest rate. That, however, isn't the only consideration: You'll also want to consider taxes.

293. TAX-DEDUCTIBLE INTEREST

You can potentially deduct the interest on the three types of loans: education loans, mortgages and margin debt. Education loans are discussed in Part IV.

Suppose you take out a loan costing 6 percent and you're in the 25 percent federal income tax bracket. If the interest is tax-deductible, your after-tax cost is just 4.5 percent. Keep that tax-deductibility in mind as you consider how best to borrow. Tax deductibility also comes into play as you weigh which debts to pay down first or whether, instead, you should invest your spare cash.

You can deduct the interest on up to $1 million borrowed to buy, build or improve a first or second home. You can also deduct the interest on an additional $100,000 of home equity borrowing used for any other purpose, unless you're subject to the alternative minimum tax. For AMT purposes, you can only deduct mortgage interest if the loan was used to buy, build or improve a home.

You can also deduct the interest on loans used to buy taxable investments. In other words, you can take out a margin loan against your portfolio's value and deduct the interest if you buy stocks—but you can't deduct the interest if you use the money to buy municipal bonds or a new car. An important detail: You need to offset deductible investment interest against net investment income. The latter includes taxable interest that you earned, and perhaps also dividends and realized capital gains.

294. MORTGAGES

The Federal Reserve's 2013 Survey of Consumer Finances found that 65.9 percent of homeowners had a mortgage or other debt that was secured by their home. That isn't surprising, given how much homes cost. It also isn't especially alarming: A mortgage is typically the cheapest way for most folks to borrow. Because your home is collateral for the loan, the interest rate will usually be low—and it's even lower once you figure in the tax deduction.

Could you trim your cost further? The larger your house down payment, the lower your rate will potentially be. A larger down payment may also either reduce the cost of private mortgage insurance or, if you put down 20 percent or more, allow you to avoid it all together. In addition, in the months leading up to your mortgage application, you might check your credit report for errors and work to raise your credit score, so you qualify for a preferential rate.

It's possible to lower the rate on a new mortgage by paying points. Each point is equal to one percent of the loan's value, so paying one point on a $200,000 loan would cost you $2,000. A smart move? Paying points might look like a big money saver if you keep the loan for 15 or 30 years. But there's a good chance you will refinance or move long before then, so paying points may not make financial sense. According to a 2014 survey by the National Association of Realtors, recent home sellers had typically owned their property for 10 years—and presumably many had refinanced once or more during the time they owned their homes.

You could also cut your initial mortgage rate by skipping a fixed-rate mortgage and instead opting for an adjustable-rate loan. But that comes with extra risk.

295. FIXED VS. ADJUSTABLE

Most folks instinctively opt for a fixed-rate mortgage, where your principal-and-interest payment stays the same every month. But in all likelihood, an adjustable-rate mortgage, or ARM, will be cheaper. ARMs are priced off short-term interest rates, while fixed-rate mortgages are priced off intermediate-term rates—and short-term rates are generally lower than intermediate-term rates.

With an ARM, there's a risk that the interest rate you're charged will increase at the next adjustment date. ARMs often have both periodic and lifetime caps that limit how much the rate can increase. Let's say an ARM has a two-percentage-point periodic cap, a six-point lifetime cap and a one-year adjustment period. Every year, the rate you're charged could climb two percentage points, though it can never climb more than six points above your initial rate.

Not sure you want to take that much risk? Instead of a pure ARM, many homebuyers take out a 3/1, 5/1, 7/1 or 10/1 hybrid ARM. With these loans, your rate is fixed for the first three, five, seven or 10 years, and then the rate adjusts every year thereafter. At that point, the rate could climb sharply. But there's also a good chance you might move or refinance within the first five or six years, so you may never feel the bite from the mortgage's adjustable rate.

As you ponder what mortgage to get, give some thought to your job situation. If you have a secure job with a steady paycheck, you might take the risk of an ARM and, fingers crossed, get rewarded with a lower average rate over the course of the mortgage. But if your income fluctuates, you should probably look for predictability in the rest of your financial life, including favoring fixed-rate mortgages.

296. CONFORMING VS. NONCONFORMING

A conforming loan is one that meets the standards used by Freddie Mac and Fannie Mae, making them eligible to be purchased by either institution. Result: A conforming loan often charges a somewhat lower interest rate, perhaps 0.25 percentage point less than a comparable nonconforming loan.

To qualify as a conforming loan, a mortgage has to meet a number of conditions, the most notable of which is size. According to the Federal Housing Finance Agency, for 2015, a conforming loan for a single-family home typically has to be $417,000 or less. In more expensive parts of the country, however, a single-family home loan can be as large as $625,500 and still qualify as conforming. In Hawaii, the conforming loan limit goes as high as $721,050.

What if a loan is larger than these limits? It's considered a jumbo loan. Such loans are more difficult for lenders to securitize, by packaging them into mortgage bonds and then selling these bonds to investors. Instead, lenders will often keep a jumbo mortgage on their own books, hence the higher cost and stricter scrutiny of borrowers.

297. CLOSING COSTS

As you struggle to save enough for a house down payment, it's easy to forget that the down payment is just the beginning. To close the deal, you will face a slew of other costs, including legal fees, mortgage-application costs, title insurance and a home inspection. Together, these costs might add up to $3,000 to $6,000, though they can be substantially more. One rule of thumb puts closing costs at 2 to 5 percent of a home's purchase price.

How can you trim that cost? Try shopping around for title insurance, which many experts view as overpriced. Additional competition has emerged from a new breed of online title insurers, notably EntitleDirect.com, which operates in 40 states and Washington, DC. There are also regional firms such as TitleForward.com, which handles transactions in Florida, Georgia, Maryland, Pennsylvania, Virginia and Washington, DC, and OneTitle.com, which does business in New York.

Your real estate broker may happily offer the names of a local home inspector and mortgage banker. But you will likely fare better if you do your own search. In fact, it's probably a bad idea to use a home inspector who lives in the town where you're buying. The inspector is no doubt anxious to win referrals from local real estate agents and may be reluctant to issue a tough assessment. Meanwhile, there's a good chance you can get a cheaper mortgage by skipping both local banks and well-known national banks. Instead, look for lenders offering competitive rates by checking websites such as Bankrate.com and HSH.com.

As you budget for a home purchase, keep in mind that you may face additional costs, including moving costs and the expense of some initial redecorating. In addition, there will often be at least a few immediate home repairs, because of problems the seller neglected to mention and the home inspector failed to spot.

298. REFINANCING

If interest rates have fallen since you took out your mortgage, you may find it's worth refinancing, which involves swapping your current mortgage for one with a lower interest rate. But check that it really is worthwhile.

To that end, you need to make an apples-to-apples comparison. Let's say you have had your current 30-year fixed-rate mortgage for six years, so what you now effectively have is a 24-year loan. If you refinance and replace that 24-year loan with a new 30-year loan, you will lower your monthly payment, even if the mortgage rate is exactly the same. The reason: You're taking your current principal balance and spreading its repayment over six additional years.

Instead, to see how much you are truly saving every month, compare your current payment to the payment on a hypothetical 24-year loan at the new, lower interest rate. You can calculate the latter by playing around with the mortgage calculator at Bankrate.com.

Next, take the expected closing costs for the refinancing and divide it by the reduction in your monthly payment. That will tell you how many months it'll take to break even. For instance, if the closing costs are $4,000 and you'll save $150 a month, it will take you some 27 months to break even. As long as you don't expect to move before the 27 months are up, refinancing probably makes sense.

When refinancing, consider taking out a mortgage that will be paid off by the time you retire, and preferably earlier. In the above example, where you have 24 years left on your current mortgage, you might opt for a 20-year or 15-year loan.

What if you find it isn't worth refinancing because your remaining mortgage balance is fairly small? Consider taking out a home equity line of credit—often called a HELOC—and using that to pay off your current mortgage. HELOCs are cheap to set up and the rates are typically low, in part because they are priced off short-term interest rates. There is a risk that the rate on your HELOC could rise. Still, if your mortgage is small and you expect to have it paid off within the next three or four years, that might be a risk worth taking.

299. HOME EQUITY LOANS

If you need to borrow, tapping into your home's value can be one of the cheaper options. The interest rate will tend to be low, because the loan is secured by your house, and the interest could be tax-deductible.

What sort of loan should you take out? You can choose between a home equity loan and a home equity line of credit. In terms of the interest rate, it's similar to choosing between a fixed-rate and an adjustable-rate mortgage.

The interest rate on a home equity line of credit, or HELOC, is pegged off short-term rates, just like an adjustable-rate mortgage. Usually, the rate charged by a HELOC is set at some discount or premium to the prime rate. The rate can change every month and could climb quickly if short-term interest rates rise. You won't be charged interest until you use the credit line. When you first apply for a HELOC, the bank will put a cap on how much you can borrow, such as $50,000 or $100,000. Occasionally, a bank may cancel a credit line or reduce its size.

The interest rate is typically fixed on a home equity loan, just like it is on a fixed-rate mortgage, and that rate will usually be higher than the rate on a HELOC. That extra cost buys you protection against rising rates. Unlike a HELOC, you have to decide how much you want to borrow. You would then need to repay the loan on a predetermined schedule, just as you would with a fixed-rate mortgage.

A HELOC can be useful both as a source of emergency money and for major expenditures, such as buying a car or remodeling the kitchen. You might also use a home equity loan for major expenditures, especially if you have a firm idea of how much you need to borrow.

300. PRINCIPAL AND INTEREST

Most mortgages are designed so that, with each payment, you not only pay the interest owed on the outstanding loan balance, but also you pay down part of the loan's principal balance. That means that, in the following month, the principal is slightly smaller, so you owe less interest and even more of your monthly payment can go toward reducing the loan balance.

As time goes on, the amount earmarked for principal starts growing by leaps and bounds. Suppose you borrowed $300,000 through a 30-year fixed-rate mortgage costing 5 percent. Assuming you didn't make any extra principal payments, it would take 15½ years to pay back the first $100,000 and another 8½ years to pay off the next $100,000. What about the final $100,000? That's paid off in the mortgage's last six years because, by then, most of your monthly payment is going toward principal and not interest.

This shifting mix of principal and interest often creates confusion among mortgage borrowers. One misconception: It isn't worth making extra principal payments when a mortgage is close to being paid off because, at that point, you aren't getting charged much in total interest.

That's true—except you are still getting charged the same interest rate. Suppose you have a fixed-rate mortgage costing 5 percent. Whether you make an extra principal payment in year one or year 30, the annual pretax return is still the same 5 percent. The only difference is that the extra principal payment early in the life of a mortgage saves you 5 percent in annual interest for more years.

301. PREPAYING A MORTGAGE

Is paying ahead on a mortgage a good investment? We have more on the "invest vs. pay down debt" question later in this chapter. But even if prepaying a mortgage isn't your best investment, retiring debt-free should be a priority. That way, you'll eliminate a major expense and avoid the retirement tax trap described in Part X. What if your last scheduled mortgage payment is after your likely retirement date? Consider making extra principal payments.

When you make additional principal payments on a fixed-rate mortgage, you pay off the mortgage more quickly. When you pay extra on an adjustable-rate mortgage, you trim the loan balance faster than scheduled, and that should result in lower monthly payments when your rate next adjusts—unless the interest rate adjusts higher and that swamps the impact of your extra principal payments.

Your mortgage lender might pitch you a "biweekly mortgage," where you pay half the mortgage payment every two weeks, rather than the full payment every month. That pays off your mortgage faster, because you end up making an extra month's mortgage payment every year. Alternatively, some dubious financial firms might offer "mortgage acceleration" services. Either way, don't bite. You can achieve exactly the same result, and avoid the fees charged for these services, by simply adding extra money to your monthly mortgage payment.

What if there's no way you will get your mortgage paid off by retirement or soon after? You might take the opposite tack. As you approach retirement, consider refinancing your mortgage with a new 30-year loan. That should sharply reduce your monthly payment, thereby trimming your retirement living expenses. Handling home loans in retirement is also discussed at the end of Part II.

302. CREDIT CARDS

Credit cards have become so integral to American life that some folks almost never pay cash for anything and instead charge even the smallest expense. That's convenient, it can be safer than carrying cash and it could come with a monthly bonus, in the form of credit card rewards. Set against that is the well-known downside: If you aren't careful, you will charge too much, won't be able to pay off the balance in full and get walloped with finance charges.

There is no legal maximum interest rate that a credit card can charge, though many card issuers appear to charge no more than 29.99 percent. Minimum payments are typically set so that your balance should shrink over time, assuming you aren't adding more debt. That might mean the minimum payment is 1 percent of the balance plus that month's interest and fees, which all told might come to around 2 percent of the balance.

How many people carry a balance? Reliable statistics are surprisingly hard to come by, but it seems a little over half of all Americans carry a credit card balance and the average debt per cardholder is around $5,000.

Carrying a card balance, while sometimes unavoidable, isn't smart. Today, a credit card might charge an interest rate of 12 to 20 percent—an exorbitant sum, especially when you consider that today's savings accounts and short-term certificates of deposit pay less than 1 percent. Credit card debt is the classic example of bad debt: The interest rate charged is steep, the interest isn't tax-deductible and the money was typically used to buy nothing of lasting value.

Want to avoid charging so much that you end up with a bill you can't pay in full? Try deducting your credit card charges from the balance in your check book. That way, when the bill arrives, you won't be unpleasantly surprised—and you should have the money to pay off the entire sum owed.

303. CREDIT CARD REWARDS

If you use a credit card, you should use one that gives you rewards, whether it's cash back, rewards points, frequent-flier miles or some other bonus. Typically, these rewards are worth around 1 percent of the amount you spend, though some cards give as much as 2 percent and others have rotating categories where you can earn extra rewards, such as 5 percent cash back on restaurant purchases or at the grocery store.

Many rewards credit cards don't charge an annual fee. That isn't, however, true of cards that pay airline miles, so you need to weigh carefully the annual fee against the value of the frequent-flier miles you're likely to earn during the year.

While it's appealing to earn rewards, the value of those rewards pales next to the interest you'll pay if you carry a balance. Suppose you have a card that charges 18 percent in annual interest and pays you back 1 percent in cash. If you spend $1,000 and carry that balance, the 1 percent cash back on your $1,000 of spending will be less than one month's interest expense. And if you carry that balance month after month, the math only gets worse.

JONATHAN'S TAKE: Credit cards are a financial nightmare for many Americans because they make it so easy to overspend and end up in a financial hole. It doesn't have to be that way: If you funnel as much spending as possible through a rewards credit card and you're careful to pay off the balance in full every month, you will avoid the downside of credit cards, while collecting the equivalent of 1 percent back on every dollar you spend and perhaps more.

304. CREDIT CARD PERKS

Credit cards don't just offer rewards. They also offer a slew of perks, many of which aren't heavily promoted, so you may not be aware of them. Check to see whether your credit cards offer these benefits:

• Extended warranties on items you purchase with the card.

• Price protection if you buy an item and then see it advertised at a lower price soon after.

• Protection if an item you buy quickly breaks or is lost or stolen.

• Assistance if you have a dispute with a retailer over, say, the quality of something you purchased. A credit card representative may be able to help get your money back.

• Discounts if you buy items through the credit card's website.

• Accidental death and dismemberment insurance. The insurance may pay out if you are injured or killed in an accident that occurs while on a trip that was paid for with the credit card.

• Travel emergency assistance, including help with lost luggage and possibly even compensation for the items lost.

• Rental car insurance may be provided by your credit card. You may also be covered for rental cars by your auto insurer.

• Roadside assistance, including towing, tire changing and jumpstarting a battery, though you will likely pay a fee for these services.

• Concierge services, such as help getting tickets to shows or making restaurant reservations.

305. MARGIN LOANS

If you hold your investments in a margin account at a brokerage firm, you can typically take out a margin loan equal to 50 percent of the account's total value. This is the so-called initial margin requirement, and it effectively allows you to control investments worth twice as much as you could otherwise afford.

A margin loan doesn't have to be used to purchase additional investments. Some folks use margin loans to buy cars or pay the kids' college bills, in part because the alternative may be to sell winning stocks and thus trigger capital gains taxes. Your interest costs, however, are only tax deductible if the margin loan is used to buy taxable investments.

Whatever your reason for borrowing, a margin loan has the potential to boost your returns if the market rises—and magnify your losses if it goes against you. Once you take out a margin loan, make sure your account continues to meet the margin maintenance requirements. Under FINRA rules, a margin loan must equal no more than 75 percent of your account's total value. But brokerage firms can impose their own stricter rules, often insisting the loan be no more than 70 percent of the account's value and sometimes less.

Suppose you deposited $10,000 in a brokerage account and then borrowed another $10,000 to buy additional stocks, so you controlled $20,000 of shares. If your stocks fall 29 percent, to $14,200, your $10,000 loan would equal more than 70 percent of the account's total value—and, depending on the brokerage firm's rules, you could receive a margin call.

At that juncture, you would need to reduce the loan as a percentage of the account's total value by either adding securities or cash to the account or by selling holdings to repay part of the margin loan. Be warned: Your brokerage firm may not call you before selling securities to meet margin requirements, so it's best to monitor the account carefully and take action before a margin call is a possibility.

Margin borrowing is often viewed as an indicator of investors' appetite for risk. As of November 2014, there was $457.1 billion in margin debt outstanding, compared with $444.9 billion at year-end 2013, $330.4 billion at year-end 2012 and $267 billion at year-end 2011.

306. LOANS FROM 401(K) PLANS

Many folks find 401(k) and 403(b) loans appealing, in part because the loans are easy to obtain and the interest that's charged goes back into their account, so they're effectively paying interest to themselves. But the loans can quickly lose their luster. A 2014 study by TIAA-CREF found that 29 percent of Americans who were participating in a retirement plan said they had taken out a loan from their plan. But 44 percent of those who had borrowed regretted doing so.

Why the regret? Borrowing has two costs. First, a 401(k) loan isn't really a loan. Instead, the money you're supposedly borrowing is actually removed from your account, which means you lose out on any investment returns the money might have earned. Second, while the money you originally contributed to your 401(k) plan came out of pretax dollars, you have to repay a 401(k) loan from post-tax income. In retirement, when you withdraw the money, you'll have to pay taxes on these dollars again, so they're effectively taxed twice.

Still like the idea of 401(k) loans? The good news is, they're typically easy to apply for, with no credit check required and often no loan application fee. You can usually borrow up to $50,000 or half your account balance, whichever is less, though plans can impose stricter rules and some don't allow loans. The money borrowed has to be repaid within five years, unless it's used to buy a home, in which case the repayment period can be longer.

If you leave your employer and don't promptly repay a 401(k) loan, it'll be considered a distribution and subject to both income taxes and probably tax penalties. Thinking of changing jobs? You should make a concerted effort to pay back the loan.

307. HARDSHIP WITHDRAWALS

If you have maxed out on 401(k) loans and you have an urgent financial need, you may be able to take a hardship withdrawal from your employer's plan. Hardship withdrawals are typically allowed for unreimbursed medical expenses, college bills and funeral expenses, to prevent foreclosure or eviction, or to buy or repair your principal residence. Similar rules apply to 403(b) plans.

While hardship withdrawals are legally permissible, your employer isn't obligated to allow them. Moreover, you may have to jump through various hoops, such as documenting your financial need.

With hardship withdrawals, the real hardship may be the cost involved. You will have to pay income taxes on the sum withdrawn, plus a 10 percent tax penalty if you are under age 59½. If you're in the 25 percent tax bracket, a $10,000 withdrawal could leave you with just $6,500 to spend after federal taxes and penalties, and even less if you have to pay state income taxes. In addition, you may be barred from making contributions to your 401(k) for the next six months.

308. LIFE INSURANCE LOANS

If you have a permanent life insurance policy and you've built up some cash value, you could potentially borrow against the cash value. The loans are easy to obtain, with no credit check required, because you're effectively borrowing from yourself.

Still, tread carefully. In theory, you don't have to repay life insurance loans. But any loan outstanding at the time of your death will reduce the policy's death benefit. Even if you don't repay the loan itself, think twice before skipping the interest payments. If you don't make the interest payments, those will get added to the loan balance—and you'll incur interest charges not only on the original sum borrowed, but also on any unpaid interest.

If the outstanding loan grows too large, so that the amount owed is greater than the policy's cash value, your policy could lapse, triggering a hefty tax bill. You would typically owe income taxes on the policy's cash surrender value, less the total premiums paid into the policy. That income tax bill would be avoided if you kept the policy until you died.

309. CAR LOANS

Need a car loan? Banks provide more auto loans than anybody else. Other major players include credit unions, auto-finance companies, car manufacturers and car dealers.

It might be convenient to get financing through the dealership. But you will likely get a better rate if you shop for a low-cost loan before you head to the car dealer. With a preapproved loan in your back pocket, you will be in a stronger bargaining position with the dealership, and you could parlay that preapproved loan into an even better deal.

The dealership might offer you the choice of a rebate or a 0 percent loan. To figure out which is best, simply compare the monthly payments on the 0 percent loan with the payments on the alternative loan, which would be a smaller amount borrowed—thanks to the rebate—but at a higher interest rate. That higher rate might not be so high if you bypass the dealership's financing department and get a low-cost loan elsewhere.

An auto loan won't necessarily be your best bet. Also consider whether it would be cheaper to buy the car with a home equity loan or line of credit. The rate may be lower than on an auto loan, plus the interest could be tax-deductible. The downside: You put your home at risk if you fail to make the required payments on your home equity borrowing.

310. BUYING VS. LEASING

According to Edmunds.com, 26 percent of all new cars were leased in 2013, versus 16 percent a decade earlier. A good idea? Leasing may allow you to drive a car that you couldn't afford to buy. Historically, most leases have been for luxury cars, though consumers have lately been leasing less expensive vehicles. With a lease, there's usually a mileage limit, such as 36,000 miles on a three-year lease, and insurance is typically more costly than it is for owners.

Still, leasing can be cheaper if you plan to get a new car every three years. Upfront costs on a lease, if any, should be far smaller than the down payment on a car loan, and the monthly lease payments ought to be less than a car loan payment. Because you might get a new car every three years, maintenance costs are likely to be modest and any major repairs could be covered by the warranty. And if you really like the car, you can usually buy it at the end of the lease at a preset price.

Problem is, getting a new car every three years is an expensive habit—and you'll likely fare better financially if you buy a car and hang on to it for longer. Remember, at the end of a lease, you don't own anything. But as a buyer, you could sell the car and use the proceeds to make a down payment on a new vehicle. Better still, you might keep the car until the loan is paid off, at which point you can enjoy driving the car with no monthly payments to worry about.

311. INVEST OR PAY DOWN DEBT?

Suppose you have $200,000 in bonds—and you also have $200,000 in mortgage and other debt. Arguably, your net bond position is zero. After all, your bonds are paying you interest, but your debts are costing you interest. In fact, the interest rate charged on your debts is likely greater than the interest you are earning on your bonds.

The implication: Instead of buying more bonds, you might use your extra savings to pay down debt. You may even find that, because your debts are costing you more than your bonds are earning, it makes sense to sell your bonds and use the proceeds to reduce debt.

But what if we're talking about mortgage debt, with its tax-deductible interest? Let's say you have a 5 percent mortgage and you're in the 25 percent federal income tax bracket, so the effective cost of your mortgage is just 3.75 percent. Fingers crossed, you should be able to earn more than that over the long term by purchasing a diversified collection of stocks.

What if the alternative is to buy bonds? Suppose you can buy bonds that yield 4 percent, which is higher than the 3.75 percent after-tax cost of your mortgage. That might seem more attractive. But if the 4 percent bonds pay taxable interest and you hold them in a regular taxable account, you might be left with just 3 percent after paying taxes—which means paying down the mortgage will give you a better return.

JONATHAN'S TAKE: Even if the potential gain from investing is higher, I still think there's great virtue in paying down debt, even low-cost, tax-deductible mortgage debt. The return is guaranteed, it makes your overall finances less risky and ridding yourself of all debt is a crucial step on the path to a comfortable retirement. Not sure whether it's a good time to buy stocks or bonds? When in doubt, you can do a lot worse than pay down debt.

312. STRUGGLING WITH DEBT

If you are well above the debt ratio used by lenders, which means you're devoting more than 36 percent of your pretax monthly income to servicing your debts, there's a good chance you have borrowed too much. But you probably don't need the debt ratio to tell you that because it's already painfully obvious.

What to do? The first step is to put yourself on a cash diet, which means not spending more than you earn and avoiding all new borrowing. Next, start to tackle your debts. Focus on paying down your highest-cost debt first, which will likely be your credit card balances. You might, however, take a slightly different approach if you have, say, student loans or car loans that are almost paid off. If you can get those paid off quickly, it might substantially improve your monthly cash flow, and then you can focus in earnest on paying off those credit cards.

Another possibility: If you have built up some home equity, set up a home equity line of credit or refinance your current mortgage. Either way, you could borrow against your home's value and use that money to pay off higher-cost debt. If you'll struggle to cope with the resulting monthly mortgage payments, refinance with a 30-year mortgage rather than anything shorter. That should help hold down the monthly payments.

As an added bonus, the interest on any home equity borrowing could be tax-deductible. Also consider other ways to consolidate debt, such as borrowing from your 401(k) plan or cash-value life insurance, and using that to pay off higher-interest debt. You might even apply for a bank loan, though that may be difficult to get if your finances are in rough shape.

Steer clear of debt-consolidation companies or other firms promising to help you pay off your debts. All too often, their loans come with exorbitant fees, high interest rates and other drawbacks. What if your debts are so great that you can't see any way to get yourself back on track? It may be time for more drastic action.

313. OVERWHELMED BY DEBT

Got so much debt that you can't see any way out? To find a reputable nonprofit credit-counseling agency, try the National Foundation for Credit Counseling (NFCC.org) or the Association of Independent Consumer Credit Counseling Agencies (AICCCA.org). Identify a local credit-counseling agency and ask for a list of fees. If the fees aren't modest, you may have mistakenly contacted a for-profit credit counseling agency, debt-settlement firm or some other company hoping to profit from your misfortune.

If your debts are overwhelming, a nonprofit credit-counseling agency can help you settle on a debt management plan, which typically involves making loan repayments over a three- to five-year period. A debt management plan can lower your finance charges, reduce collection calls and help to repair your credit.

If part of your debt is forgiven, there could be tax consequences. You may receive a form 1099-C for the amount of the cancelled debt, on which you might then have to pay income taxes. Talk to your credit counselor about whether there's an exclusion or exception that may allow you to avoid the tax on this phantom income.

Even before you contact a credit-counseling agency, you might be tempted to raid your retirement accounts to cover the mortgage or pay the credit cards. Don't do it. Not only would your retirement account withdrawals likely trigger income taxes and tax penalties, but you would also be spending money that would otherwise be protected from your creditors. If you end up in bankruptcy, you will probably be able to hang onto money you have in 401(k) plans and IRAs.

314. BANKRUPTCY

If your debts are too large to pay down and creditors are unwilling to forgive enough debt to make it manageable, you may need to file for bankruptcy. This isn't a step to be taken lightly. The bankruptcy will stay on your credit report for up to 10 years, and you will likely have little or no access to credit for a number of years.

If an individual files for bankruptcy, it's typically under either Chapter 7 or Chapter 13 of the bankruptcy code. With a Chapter 7 bankruptcy, your assets can be liquidated to pay off unsecured debt. In practice, any assets owned are often protected and thus nothing gets sold. Meanwhile, with your secured debts, such as your auto loan that's backed by your car or your mortgage that's backed by your home, you can either turn over those assets to the lenders involved or try to strike a deal where you keep the assets in return for making some sort of payment.

While a Chapter 7 bankruptcy deals with your debts through liquidation, a Chapter 13 bankruptcy tackles your debts through some form of payment plan. Chapter 13 bankruptcy is designed for those with regular incomes, who are then expected to complete a monthly payment program that lasts three to five years. How much you will be expected to pay will depend, in part, on how much you earn and how much you owe.

If you file for bankruptcy, you'll need an attorney's help. Whom should you hire? You can search for lawyers through NACBA.org, the website of the National Association of Consumer Bankruptcy Attorneys. Also check out BankruptcyResources.org.

PART XII

GIVING

NOW YOU'VE FINALLY GOT IT, MAYBE IT'S TIME TO GIVE IT BACK

Amassing wealth may be comforting. But there's also pleasure in giving it away, whether to family members or your favorite charity.

You'll want to consider how much you can afford to give away during your lifetime or whether you ought to wait until after your death. You should also think about whether you want to nudge the recipients to use the money in a particular way and what's the best gifting strategy, given your goals, and also the possible tax and other benefits.

For gifts to family members, that'll mean developing an estate plan, which might include making regular gifts during your lifetime. As you craft your plan, also give some thought to end-of-life decisions, such as who will make medical and financial decisions on your behalf if you become incapacitated. These various estate planning issues are tackled in the pages ahead.

For charitable gifts, which we discuss toward the end of this chapter, you'll want to consider the potential tax savings. Your gifts might also be part of your retirement-income strategy: You might purchase a charitable gift annuity or create a charitable remainder trust, both of which can give you a combination of tax benefits and regular retirement income.

But whether the gifts are to charity or to family members, your primary motivation should be generosity, not the tax savings or other benefits. Yes, it's nice if you get a tax deduction in return for your charitable contribution. But you'll still end up with less money than you started.

315. FIVE STEPS FOR 2015

If you haven't given much thought to estate planning and charitable giving, here are five steps that can help jumpstart your thinking:

• Ponder how much money you might have at the end of your life and whether you can afford to give some away now—and then discuss your intentions with your family.

• Check you have the right beneficiaries on your retirement accounts. Your individual retirement account and employer's retirement plan might hold the bulk of your savings, so it's crucial these accounts pass to the right folks.

• If you want to create a legacy for your children or other family members, consider funding a Roth 401(k) or Roth IRA, or converting a traditional IRA to a Roth, and then leave the account untouched for your heirs.

• Think about who, at the end of your life, you want to make medical decisions on your behalf and how far you would like doctors to go in attempting to prolong your life. You should codify these wishes in a health care power of attorney and living will.

• Investigate the charities you currently support by heading to CharityNavigator.org and GuideStar.org. A crucial question: What percentage of the dollars you donate ends up in the hands of the people you're hoping to help?

316. NOW OR LATER?

As discussed in Part II, most of us are ill prepared for retirement. During our lifetime, we probably should be modest with our gifts to family and to charity. Instead, we might focus on how we'll disburse our wealth after our death. Our kids and other family members won't appreciate it if we give them a big hunk of our wealth today—and then ask for it back a decade later, when we're impoverished retirees.

What if you have done a fine job of saving for retirement and other goals, and you can afford to give away money now, rather than waiting until after your death? There are good arguments for giving away part of your wealth during your lifetime.

If you give money to family members while you're alive, you'll get to share in their delight, and you might help them enjoy the sense of financial security you've achieved. In addition, you'll get money out of your estate, including the future investment growth. That might reduce the potential bite from both federal estate taxes (though that won't be an issue for the vast majority of Americans) and your state's estate tax (which can be a big issue in some states).

Similarly, if you give to charity now, you'll have the pleasure of knowing you are doing some immediate good. Whether you give money to charity now or at death, you will shrink your taxable estate. But by giving during your lifetime, you could also cut your federal income tax bill, assuming you itemize your deductions. By contrast, if you make a bequest upon death, there are no income tax savings.

317. ESTATE PLANNING

The primary goal of estate planning is simple: You want to make sure your assets end up with the right folks.

In all likelihood, you have already made a slew of estate planning decisions, perhaps without fully appreciating it. For instance, when you and your spouse bought the house and the car jointly with right of survivorship, you ensured your spouse would inherit both items should you die first.

Remember the IRA you opened years ago, with your sister named as beneficiary because you hadn't yet met your spouse? Unless you change the beneficiary, your sister will likely get that money after your death. Beneficiary designations also determine who will inherit trust assets, payable-on death accounts and the proceeds from any life insurance.

What about your will? That determines who receives assets that go through probate. But as you might have gathered, assets like retirement accounts and property owned jointly with right of survivorship go directly to your heirs, and aren't subject to probate.

While estate planning is mostly about who gets what, you'll also want to give some thought to end-of-life decisions and to taxes. Federal estate taxes aren't an issue for 99 percent of Americans, thanks to 2015's $5.43 million estate tax exclusion. But your heirs could face state estate taxes, which can be owed on even midsize estates. In addition, you may want to think about taxes as you consider which assets to spend down your lifetime and which ones to bequeath to your heirs. Want to make sure your estate plan is fully fleshed out? You might start with our checklist.

318. ESTATE PLANNING CHECKLIST

Listed here are some key components of an estate plan. If you're under age 50, you might focus on the first three items. Those already retired or approaching retirement should probably consider every item listed here·

• A will that specifies who should inherit those assets subject to probate. Drawing up a will becomes especially crucial once you have children, not least because you'll want to name guardians for your kids.

• The right beneficiaries listed on your life insurance and retirement accounts.

• Correct titling on major assets, such as your home and cars.

• Regular gifting to take advantage of the annual gift-tax exclusion.

• A revocable living trust if probate is a cumbersome process in your state or you own property outside the state where you have your primary residence.

• Trusts to control how your assets are disbursed, which could be crucial if, say, you are remarried but you want your assets eventually to go to your children from an earlier marriage.

• Steps to reduce federal and state estate taxes, if either could be an issue.

• Financial and medical powers of attorney in case you become incapacitated.

• A personal letter, or letter of last instruction, that provides additional details and spells out how your personal possessions should be disbursed.

319. GIFT-TAX EXCLUSION

In 2015, you can give $14,000 to as many individuals as you wish, without worrying about the gift tax. This is the annual gift-tax exclusion. Do you and your spouse have three kids? You could together give each of them $42,000 this year, thus shrinking your estate by $84,000. As described in Part IV, there's even a special provision just for 529 college plans that allows you to contribute five times the gift-tax exclusion in a single year and count it as your gift for the next five years.

Even if you give more than the gift-tax exclusion, you likely won't pay gift taxes. Instead, the amount above the exclusion will reduce the sum you can leave to your heirs tax-free upon your death. Only if you manage to eat through your entire federal estate tax exclusion—$5.43 million in 2015— would you have to start paying gift taxes.

In other words, let's say you're a single parent and you gave your only child a gift of $1,014,000 in 2015. That gift would be $1 million above the $14,000 gift-tax exclusion, so it would reduce the amount you can leave tax-free at death to $4.43 million. The super-wealthy sometimes make such large gifts because it gets the money, including subsequent investment growth, out of their estate, thus trimming the eventual estate tax bill.

An interesting wrinkle: While you can only give $14,000 to another person each year without worrying about the gift tax, there's no limit on the sum you can pay toward another person's medical or education expenses, provided the money is paid directly to the medical provider or educational institution involved.

JONATHAN'S TAKE: Giving away money is perhaps the cheapest and easiest way to shrink an estate. There are no fancy estate planning techniques involved and no legal fees, which may explain why this strategy isn't given more publicity. If you can afford to make regular gifts to family members, seriously consider doing so.

320. SMART GIVING

If you give money to your children, either now or when you die, there's a risk they will quickly spend the money you so painstakingly amassed. Faced with this risk, some folks set up spendthrift trusts that parcel out the trusts' assets to the beneficiaries slowly over time. You could avoid that complicated and costly step if you raise financially responsible children, a topic we touched on in Part VII.

In fact, you might use your gifts both to help your children financially and also teach them about money. For instance, if your teenage children have earned income—perhaps from a summer job—you could fund a Roth IRA on their behalf, contributing up to the amount they earned. A Roth, with its tax-free growth, will likely make more sense than a traditional tax-deductible IRA, because the tax deduction won't be worth much if your children have only modest income.

When you fund the Roth, you might talk to your kids about how compounding works and perhaps use an online calculator to illustrate how much the money could be worth when they retire. An added bonus: The 10 percent tax penalty on early withdrawals may deter your children from raiding the account, though that penalty would only apply if they withdrew the Roth's investment earnings, not the original contributions.

Alternatively, once your children are in the workforce, you might encourage them to contribute to their employer's 401(k) plan by offering to reimburse 25 or 50 cents for every $1 they put in their 401(k). Similarly, to encourage your kids to save for a house down payment, you might offer to contribute $1 to their savings account for every $1 they contribute. With both strategies, you're encouraging good savings habits while also promoting worthy goals like saving for retirement and buying a home.

321. GIVING APPRECIATED STOCK

Instead of giving cash, you could give away investments that have appreciated in value. This can work well with charities, as we'll explain later in this chapter. But with your children or other family members, it can be a mixed blessing.

Let's say you give your children some shares you own. If you had paid $10 a share for the stock and it's now worth $50, your children will assume your $10 cost basis. If they sell, they'll owe taxes on the $40 per share in capital gains, assuming the stock is still worth $50. This isn't great—but if their tax bracket is lower than yours, there will be some tax savings. Your children will also assume your date of purchase, which will affect whether the gain is taxed at the short-term or long-term capital gains rate.

What if the stock has fallen in value? If, when sold, the stock is still worth less than your cost basis but more than the value when gifted, there's neither a gain nor a loss. In that situation, you would have been better off selling the stock first, taking advantage of the capital loss and then giving the proceeds to your children. If, however, the stock continues to fall in value, your children will be able to realize a capital loss, but only based on the difference between the value when gifted and the sale price.

If you hang onto the stock until you die, none of this matters. Your heirs inherit the stock at its current market value, thanks to the step-up in cost basis. At that point, any potential capital-gains tax bill disappears—but so, too, does the chance to use any unrealized capital loss.

322. WILL

There's a decent chance that your will won't determine what happens to the bulk of your wealth, because the fate of many assets depends on how they're titled and the beneficiaries named. Still, it's crucial to have a will that spells out who should receive those assets that are subject to probate.

Without it, you will die intestate. That means the disposition of your probate assets will be determined by state law—and your assets may not be divvied up the way you would have wanted.

In your will, you should also name a personal guardian for your minor children, which will be crucial if you and your spouse die prematurely. You will likely also want to specify that your wealth should be held in trust for your children until they reach age 18, 21 and possibly later, and also name someone to manage this money. That someone doesn't have to be your children's personal guardian.

As your life changes, you'll likely want to change your will. In particular, you will probably need to revise it if you marry, have children or divorce.

You should also revise your will if the executor dies and possibly if one of your beneficiaries dies. Moving to a different state is another reason to revisit your will. While it may be acceptable in the new state, settling your estate could take longer. Revising your will is especially important if you're married and move from a community property state to a common law state, or vice versa.

323. DISCLAIMING

You can disclaim assets that are left to you in a will. At that point, the money disclaimed passes to the other heirs as though you had predeceased the person who had just died. A will might even have a disclaimer clause that specifies what will happen if money is disclaimed. When disclaiming, you can't specify who should receive your portion of the inheritance, so the wording of the will is critical.

What's the advantage of disclaiming? Let's say your mother leaves you $100,000. You don't need the money and, indeed, you fear the money will be subject to federal or state estate taxes when you die and leave it to your kids. Depending on how your mother's will is written, you may be able to disclaim the inheritance, with the money going directly to your children.

Similarly, you might disclaim part of the inheritance from your spouse, perhaps so the money ends up with your children now, while also reducing the risk that estate taxes will be due upon your death. You might do this if your spouse hadn't taken steps to use his or her estate tax exclusion—though you could also take advantage of the portable estate tax exclusion, discussed later in this chapter.

324. ESTATE PLANNING WHEN MARRIED

If you're married, you enjoy certain tax privileges, such as the unlimited marital deduction, which we'll tackle later in this chapter. But there is also a key obligation: You have to bequeath a minimum amount to your spouse. Exactly how much varies from state to state.

There are nine community property states: Arizona, California, Idaho, Louisiana, Nevada, New Mexico, Texas, Washington and Wisconsin. Puerto Rico is also a community property jurisdiction. In Alaska, spouses may create community property by entering into a community property agreement, but such agreements are optional. In a community property state, the wealth acquired during the course of the marriage—except gifts and inheritances—is considered equally owned by you and your spouse. That means you need to leave at least that much to your spouse.

The remaining states are common law states. In these other states, your spouse isn't entitled to an automatic 50 percent of the marital property. Instead, the minimum—typically a third of the deceased spouse's property—is specified by state law.

You are also required, under federal law, to name your spouse as beneficiary of your 401(k) plan and other "qualified" employer-sponsored plans, unless your spouse signs a waiver. This isn't true of an IRA. That said, if you live in a community property state, your spouse may be entitled to a portion of your IRA if you made contributions to the account while you were married.

325. TITLING

Think about the assets you own that aren't in a trust or inside a retirement account. We are typically talking about items such as your home, car and taxable financial accounts. Will these assets pass directly to your heirs, or will they go through probate and be governed by your will? It will depend on how they're titled.

Assets held solely in your name will go to whomever you named in your will. One exception: If you title your bank and investment accounts as *payable on death*, those assets will bypass probate and go directly to the named beneficiaries.

What about jointly owned assets? If you own, say, a home with your spouse and you're listed as *joint tenants with right of survivorship*, your house will pass directly to your spouse, assuming you die first.

There's a variation on joint tenancy with right of survivorship that is known as *tenancy by the entirety*. Only spouses can use this ownership arrangement. It isn't recognized in most community property states and also some common law states. What's the advantage of tenancy by the entirety? Unlike with joint tenants with right of survivorship, you can't transfer your ownership stake without the consent of your spouse. This can provide protection from creditors if one of you is sued.

Finally, if you own property as *tenants in common*, there is no right of survivorship. While joint tenants are equal owners of a property, tenants in common can have ownership stakes that are different in size. If you own assets as a tenant in common, they would pass to whomever you named in your will.

326. BENEFICIARY DESIGNATIONS

When you open a retirement account or purchase life insurance, you usually name beneficiaries to inherit these assets. This is also true when you set up a trust.

Because much of your wealth may be in IRAs, 401(k) plans and similar accounts, it's crucial you have the right beneficiaries listed. Divorced? If you don't change the beneficiaries on your retirement accounts, your ex-spouse may get the last laugh.

Whoever inherits your retirement accounts has to follow special rules when making withdrawals. They will also have to pay income taxes on those withdrawals, unless the money is coming out of a Roth account. Still, even with an embedded income tax bill, a retirement account can make a fine inheritance if your beneficiaries take advantage of the so-called stretch IRA.

By contrast, your beneficiaries typically won't have to pay income taxes on life insurance proceeds. There could, however, be estate taxes owed—unless you arrange for the life insurance to be owned by somebody other than yourself. That somebody is usually not a person, but rather an irrevocable life insurance trust.

327. STRETCH IRA

You might have heard financial experts claim that IRAs, 401(k) plans and other retirement accounts are terrible assets to bequeath, because the government will end up with more than 80 percent of the money. This is just a scare tactic: Unless you're subject to federal estate taxes and the account's beneficiaries are in the top income tax bracket, the tax bill will be considerably smaller—and, with proper handling, the account's subsequent growth could more than compensate.

Spouses who inherit a retirement account can transfer the money into their own IRA, which would allow them to postpone taking distributions until age 70½. Meanwhile, everybody else should consider taking advantage of the so-called stretch IRA.

That means moving the money into an inherited IRA and beginning distributions in the year after the original IRA owner's death. Spouses who are under age 59½ and need income right away might also choose this route, because it will allow them to avoid the 10 percent tax penalty on early withdrawals.

Each year's required minimum withdrawal is based on the beneficiary's life expectancy. That could mean a modest distribution. Meanwhile, the money remaining in the account can continue to grow tax-deferred. If handled properly, an inherited IRA can provide beneficiaries with decades of tax-deferred growth. Because the stretch IRA can be such a financial bonanza for beneficiaries, there's been talk in Washington of clamping down on the strategy's use.

Three tips: First, it's crucial that beneficiaries follow the rules carefully—or they might disqualify themselves from using the stretch IRA strategy. Second, check whether the original owner of the IRA made nondeductible contributions. If so, you won't have to pay taxes on a portion of each year's withdrawals. Third, if the IRA was part of an estate that was subject to federal estate taxes, you may be eligible for a tax deduction known as "income in respect of a decedent."

Beneficiaries who inherit Roth IRAs will also need to take minimum distributions (unless you're the spouse and choose to treat the Roth as your own). But in the case of the Roth, the annual distributions and the growth of the remaining money will be tax-free.

328. FEDERAL ESTATE TAXES

You can leave any amount to a spouse who is a U.S. citizen without worrying about federal estate taxes, thanks to the unlimited marital deduction. But if you bequeath a total of more than $5.43 million to other folks in 2015, federal estate taxes kick in at a 40 percent rate. This $5.43 million is sometimes referred to as the unified credit.

Don't have anything close to $5.43 million? Taxes could still take a bite out of your estate—for two reasons. First, your estate could be taxed at the state level. About a third of states levy either an estate tax or an inheritance tax, and sometimes both. Second, if you bequeath retirement accounts, other than Roth accounts, your heirs will owe income taxes as they draw down those accounts.

What if you leave your heirs your home, which is worth far more than you paid? What if you bequeath regular taxable accounts where you hold, say, stocks with large unrealized capital gains?

For those investments and for your home, there's good news: These assets enjoy a step-up in basis, which means their purchase price for tax purposes becomes the price as of your death. Result: Unlike with a retirement account, the embedded tax bill disappears. You may want to factor this into your planning as you consider which accounts to spend down during your lifetime and which to bequeath.

329. UNLIMITED MARITAL DEDUCTION

Spouses are free to give as much money as they wish to each other, both while they're alive and also upon death. In other words, as long as your spouse is a U.S. citizen, you aren't constrained by 2015's $14,000 gift-tax exclusion or $5.43 million federal estate tax exclusion.

Moreover, your federal estate tax exclusion is "portable." Let's say you die first and leave everything to your spouse, who is a U.S. citizen. Upon your spouse's death, the amount that can be bequeathed free of federal estate taxes would be twice as much, or $10.86 million, and probably more because of intervening inflation adjustments to your spouse's estate tax exclusion. (Your unused exclusion amount, however, wouldn't increase with inflation after your death.) Portability isn't automatic, so it's important that your spouse and executor consult a qualified attorney. To claim the unused exemption, your spouse will typically have to file Form 706 with the IRS within nine months of your death.

What if your spouse is a U.S. resident, but not a citizen? You can't take advantage of the unlimited marital deduction, but you could still benefit from the usual $5.43 million federal estate tax exclusion, so estate taxes shouldn't be an issue for most couples. While you're alive, you are also limited in how much you can give each year, without worrying about the gift tax, to a spouse who isn't a U.S. citizen. But again, the limit is high— $147,000 in 2015.

330. STATE ESTATE TAXES

Roughly a third of states have either an estate tax or an inheritance tax, and two of them have both. These taxes are separate from the federal estate tax—and they typically kick in at much lower asset levels.

Iowa, Kentucky, Nebraska and Pennsylvania all have inheritance taxes. An inheritance tax is levied not on the estate, but on those who inherit the money. Depending on the state, certain heirs may be exempt from the tax, such as your spouse and children. If you're a married same-sex couple and your state doesn't recognize same-sex marriages, the exemption likely won't apply. Because of the complexity of estate planning for same-sex couples, it's important to talk to a knowledgeable attorney.

State estate taxes are levied in Connecticut, Delaware, Hawaii, Illinois, Maine, Massachusetts, Minnesota, New York, Oregon, Rhode Island, Tennessee, Vermont and Washington, as well as in Washington, DC. Exclusions from state estate taxes are almost always much lower than the $5.43 million federal estate tax exclusion, which means your estate could avoid federal taxes, but still get hit at the state level.

Finally, for the lucky residents of Maryland and New Jersey, there is both a state estate tax and an inheritance tax to contend with.

Some good news: A number of states are reviewing their estate tax, possibly with a view to raising their exclusion so it's more in line with the federal level.

331. WHAT TO BEQUEATH

Your heirs will, most likely, appreciate anything you leave them. But some bequests may be more appreciated than others.

At the top of the list would probably be a Roth IRA. Yes, estate taxes could be owed if your overall estate is large enough and, yes, your heirs will have to draw down the account gradually over their lifetime. But there will be no income taxes owed on those withdrawals, and the money that remains in the account can continue to grow tax-free.

Life insurance can also make an attractive inheritance, especially if you are subject to estate taxes. Why? The proceeds will be income-tax-free to your beneficiaries and, if properly structured, the policy won't be part of your taxable estate. Still, given how expensive life insurance becomes as you age, you probably shouldn't buy it solely to ensure an inheritance, unless estate taxes are an issue.

You might keep highly appreciated investments and bequeath those. That way, you'll avoid the embedded capital gains tax bill, thanks to the step-up in basis upon death, and that will leave more money for your heirs. Keep in mind that you should sell underwater investments, not bequeath them. You can use the tax losses to reduce your income tax bill while you're alive, but those losses have no tax value after your death.

What if you are faced with a choice between bequeathing a traditional retirement account and bequeathing money in a taxable account? Despite the embedded tax bill, the traditional retirement account might make the better inheritance, especially for younger beneficiaries and those in low tax brackets—but only if you think your heirs will take advantage of the stretch IRA.

Finally, your heirs will probably be less happy to inherit assets that are difficult to sell. At issue here are not only illiquid investments, but also time shares, antique cars and second homes. Clearly, if you're making full use of these assets while you're alive, you should keep them. But your heirs would probably prefer to receive cash.

332. TRUSTS

When folks hear that someone has set up a trust or is the beneficiary of a trust, one thought often comes to mind: We're talking about serious money. In the lexicon of wealth, the term "trust" is as evocative as "hedge fund," "private equity" and "overseas bank account."

In truth, a trust is just an estate planning tool, one that someti
sense even for families with relatively limited wealth. Why would
this tool? There are four reasons:

• Assets held in a trust can avoid probate. This is the reason some
people set up revocable living trusts.

• A trust can allow you to control how the assets you bequeath are used
after your death. For instance, folks will often use trusts when leaving
money to children, including those with special needs, or to family
members who are financially irresponsible. They might also use trusts if
they're remarried and trying to provide for both a new spouse and children
from an earlier marriage.

• Trusts can help if you fear you might be subject to estate taxes. Two
popular tax-cutting strategies including using bypass trusts and setting up
irrevocable life insurance trusts.

• For those worried about lawsuits, trusts can help with asset protection.

Depending on the type of trust, hefty costs can be involved. This
shouldn't be an issue with, say, a revocable living trust used simply to avoid
probate. But let's say you bequeath money to your children in a trust. The
trust could pay substantial annual fees for administration and money
management, and also need to file its own tax return.

333. REVOCABLE LIVING TRUSTS

Like a will, a revocable living trust is a way of detailing who should
inherit your wealth after your death. But unlike a will, assets bequeathed via
a living trust don't go through probate. It's also harder for disgruntled
family members to challenge the terms of a living trust, and there isn't the
potential publicity that accompanies the probate process.

Why are these trusts referred to as revocable? Assets placed in the trust
can be removed at any time. Is it really that advantageous to avoid probate?
Much will depend on where you live. In some states, probate is a quick and
easy process. In others, it's costly and cumbersome.

Even if probate isn't a great hassle where you live, you may want to
establish a revocable living trust if you own a vacation home or other
property in a different state from where you have your principal residence.
If the trust holds this out-of-state property, your estate won't have to go
through probate in two separate states. A living trust can also help if you
become incapacitated. Depending on the terms of the trust, your spouse or
successor trustee should be able to manage the trust's property without
going to court to get the necessary authority.

Even if you have a living trust, you still need a will. Inevitably, there will be some probate assets that are outside the trust at the time of your death. Your will can specify who should receive those assets. Also keep in mind that a living trust, on its own, doesn't do anything to reduce estate taxes.

334. CHILDREN'S TRUSTS

While children can own property, they can't legally enter into contracts. That makes it difficult for them to manage an investment portfolio, because they can't buy or sell. This is the reason a child's investment account needs an adult custodian—and the reason substantial sums bequeathed to children who are under age 18 or 21 are often placed in a trust, with a trustee overseeing the assets involved. Trusts for children are typically testamentary trusts, meaning they're set up according to the instructions in your will, rather than being established before your death.

While your children could receive their trust assets once they reach the age of majority, which is typically 18 or 21 depending on the state, all the money doesn't necessarily need to be disbursed at that point. Instead, you might specify that the trustee should use the trust's assets to pay living expenses and education costs, with the remaining balance distributed when your children reach age 25 or even age 35. That will give them a chance to mature and, you hope, become a little more sensible about managing money.

While you may not want the trust to hand over great chunks of money to your children in their early 20s, you probably want the trust to disburse a little money every year for tax reasons. If a trust disburses its investment income, that income is taxable to the beneficiaries. But if the trust retains dividends, interest and realized capital gains, it can quickly find itself paying taxes at a steep rate. In 2015, a single individual needs taxable income of $413,200 before he or she is in the top 39.6 percent federal tax bracket, but a trust will be in that tax bracket if it retains more than $12,300 in taxable income.

You might be able to sidestep this problem by focusing the trust's investments on tax-efficient stock funds and tax-free municipal bonds. If you establish the trust while you are alive, you could also set it up as a grantor trust, which means that during your lifetime the trust's retained income would be taxable on your return.

335. SPECIAL NEEDS TRUSTS

If you have a child with a physical or mental disability who is unlikely to be self-supporting, you might set up a special needs trust, either during your lifetime or upon your death. By placing money in the trust, not only can you specify how the money should be spent, but also you won't disqualify the child from receiving means-tested government benefits.

Typically, if a child has more than a modest amount of cash in his or her name, the child will be disqualified from receiving Medicaid and Supplemental Security Income. The SSI program pays benefits to disabled adults and children with modest incomes and few assets. To avoid disqualification, you might encourage family and friends to make gifts to the trust, rather than directly to your son or daughter.

The trust shouldn't disburse money to the beneficiary, because that could also disqualify the child from receiving government benefits. Instead, the money should be used to pay directly for goods and services for the child, such as education costs, entertainment, vacations, a personal attendant and out-of-pocket medical expenses.

Make sure you use a qualified attorney to set up the trust. Carefully consider whom to appoint as trustees. You might pair a corporate trustee, such as a bank or trust company, with a family member. Look closely at the costs charged by the corporate trustee. Also ask the attorney whether the trust will be required to reimburse Medicaid after the beneficiary's death—and whether it's possible to sidestep this requirement.

336. SPENDTHRIFT TRUSTS

Suppose you plan to leave a healthy sum to your adult children, but you're worried they'll quickly fritter away the money. Perhaps they have a problem with drinking, drugs or gambling. Perhaps they spend compulsively. Or perhaps you fear the inheritance will make them the target of scams or lawsuits.

One possibility is to leave money for their benefit in spendthrift trusts, from which the beneficiaries have no right to make withdrawals. Instead, money is only disbursed according to the terms you have drawn up. You can even specify that the trust shouldn't disburse money and instead should use its assets to pay certain living expenses for the beneficiary.

Because the beneficiary isn't allowed to make withdrawals, the assets should be protected from creditors if, say, the beneficiary is subject to a lawsuit or ends up in debt. Still, you will likely want the trust to disburse some money each year or purchase some goods and services for the beneficiary. As explained in the section above on children's trusts, a trust can find itself paying taxes at a steep rate if it retains even a modest amount of income.

337. IRREVOCABLE LIFE INSURANCE TRUSTS

Life insurance proceeds are almost always income-tax-free to the beneficiaries. But will estate taxes be owed? This is an issue for a small fraction of estates. If it is, you might consider an irrevocable life insurance trust. The insurance proceeds might then be used to cover estate taxes. That could, for instance, avoid the need to sell the family business to pay the taxman.

Why use a trust to hold life insurance? If you own a policy when you die, the proceeds could be subject to estate taxes. But if insurance on your life is owned by somebody else—or some other entity, such as a trust—no estate taxes are owed.

If you buy life insurance within a trust, you might pay the premiums by making use of the annual gift-tax exclusion, which is $14,000 in 2015. To make use of the exclusion, your attorney will need to create a trust with so-called Crummey powers. That means the beneficiaries have the right to withdraw the money gifted—a right you hope they don't exercise.

If you transfer an existing policy into the trust, you need to live another three years beyond the date of the transfer for the change of ownership to be effective for estate tax purposes. Alternatively, you might cancel your current insurance and have the trust buy a new policy, assuming it makes financial sense and you can pass the necessary medical exam.

The tax advantages of life insurance are impressive, but so too are the premiums, especially as you get older. Still, for wealthy families facing estate taxes, it might be worth paying those premiums. If you're married, you may be able to trim the premiums by using your irrevocable life insurance trust to purchase second-to-die life insurance, which doesn't pay out until the second spouse in a couple dies.

338. BYPASS TRUSTS

Suppose you and your partner have substantial wealth, but you aren't legally married. To ensure you both take advantage of the federal estate tax exclusion, you might use a bypass trust, which is funded upon your death under the terms of your will or living trust.

Let's say you die first. Upon your death, your will might direct that a sum equal to the federal estate tax exclusion—$5.43 million in 2015— should go into a bypass trust, with the money perhaps earmarked for your favorite niece but with your partner still able to receive income from that money. Upon your partner's death, another $5.43 million (though likely more, thanks to inflation adjustments) would pass free of federal estate taxes, for a total of $10.86 million.

Thanks to the portability of the federal estate tax exclusion, wealthy married couples have less need to use bypass trusts. Still, by stashing assets in a bypass trust upon the death of the first spouse, you sidestep the risk that those assets might appreciate substantially in the years between the first spouse's death and the second. If that happens and the bypass trust is not used, federal estate taxes may be an issue upon the death of the second spouse, even though the second spouse's estate gets to make use of both spouses' estate tax exclusions, thanks to portability.

On the other hand, if the assets are held in a trust and they increase substantially in value, your beneficiaries may have a different problem: capital gains taxes. That problem would be avoided if you simply leave the money to your spouse, because the assets would have their cost basis stepped up to the current market value upon your spouse's death. Your estate planning attorney can help you figure out whether capital gains taxes or estate taxes are the bigger issue.

The answer will hinge partly on the size of your estate and how assets are invested. A bypass trust could also help with state estate taxes, where portability may not be allowed. In addition, a bypass trust might make sense if you're remarried and have children from an earlier marriage. The trust could provide income to your new spouse after your death, while ensuring that your children ultimately inherit the assets involved. This is often also the motivation behind setting up a QTIP trust.

339. QTIP TRUSTS

A Qualified Terminable Interest Property, or QTIP, trust can provide income for your spouse, while also naming the ultimate beneficiaries of the trust's assets. Sound like a bypass trust? It is—except a bypass trust makes use of your federal estate tax exclusion, while a QTIP trust takes advantage of the unlimited marital deduction.

This might seem unnecessary. After all, you could simply leave the money to your spouse, and that also would take advantage of the unlimited marital deduction. But let's say you have been married before and you want to ensure that your wealth eventually ends up in the hands of your children from your earlier marriage or marriages. By using a QTIP trust, you can ensure that whatever assets remain in the trust after your spouse's death will go to them.

Unlike the money in a bypass trust, there may be federal estate taxes owed on the money in a QTIP trust.

340. ASSET PROTECTION TRUSTS

If you're worried about lawsuits, an asset protection trust could put your wealth beyond the reach of your creditors. For a trust to provide this sort of protection, it has to be irrevocable and needs to have spendthrift provisions. In other words, you can't reclaim the money put into the trust and you can't control how much the trust distributes each year. Instead, distributions will be at the discretion of an independent trustee, who might cease all distributions if you're the subject of a lawsuit.

An asset protection trust isn't necessarily a bulletproof defense against a legal judgment. But it's enough of a deterrent that plaintiffs may decide it isn't worth pursuing their case or they may settle for a modest sum. An overseas asset protection trust will likely be less vulnerable to legal challenges, but these are more expensive to set up and administer than domestic asset protection trusts.

Indeed, before you rush to set up an asset protection trust, carefully consider the costs involved. The initial and ongoing fees are likely to be substantial, including costs for legal work, administration and money management. Moreover, you are giving up control over your assets—not a step you want to take lightly.

341. DURABLE POWERS OF ATTORNEY

If you become incapacitated toward the end of your life, it may be difficult for your family to make financial and medical decisions on your behalf unless you have durable powers of attorney drawn up.

You will likely want two powers of attorney, one for health care matters and the other for financial decisions. These powers of attorney are often "springing," meaning they don't become effective until a doctor certifies that you are incapacitated.

With a durable power of attorney for financial matters, you specify what your "agent"—who might be your spouse or an adult child—can do on your behalf. This might include paying bills, making portfolio decisions, handling bank transactions and filing taxes. If you don't make such an arrangement and you become incapacitated or incompetent, your family may have to go through the cost and hassle of asking the court to appoint a guardian.

Meanwhile, a health care power of attorney (sometimes called a health care proxy) allows your agent to make medical decisions. As part of the health care power of attorney, or in a separate living will, you can detail your wishes concerning life-prolonging medical procedures.

342. LETTER OF LAST INSTRUCTION

A letter of last instruction isn't a substitute for a will. Still, it's worth drawing up, because it will help your family settle your affairs in the weeks and months after your death. In our paperless world, a letter of last instruction—sometimes called a doomsday letter—has become especially important, because you may not have paper statements lying around to help your family identify your assets and liabilities.

What should your letter include? It's up to you, but the more detailed it is, the better. You might include:

• Funeral instructions, who should be notified upon your death and which publications you would like your obituary sent to.

• A list of financial accounts, including credit cards, insurance, and bank and investment accounts, as well as the location of any safe-deposit box. Also include the names and contact information for your insurance agent, financial advisor, lawyer, doctors and any other professionals you regularly deal with.

• Details of where key papers can be found, such as your birth certificate, car registrations, will, trust documents, tax returns and financial account statements.

• The usernames and passwords for various email programs and websites you use.

• An inventory of household items and who you would like to receive them. You might specify who should inherit certain jewelry, furniture and paintings. If some items are particularly valuable, you may want to include them in your will, so your wishes are less likely to be contested.

Don't forget to tell your executor and other key family members where the letter is located—or all your hard work could go to waste.

343. GETTING ORGANIZED

As you look to get your financial affairs organized, start with that letter of last instruction. Do you find yourself writing a lengthy description of where all key papers are located and how you want matters handled after your death? That's probably a sign that you need to organize and simplify.

While folks are often advised to keep key documents in a safe-deposit box, this has a downside. After your death, the box may be sealed, and your family may not have access until they get a court order. A representative of the local tax authority may need to be present when the box is unsealed.

At a minimum, don't keep your will and burial instructions in the safe-deposit box. Your family will want immediate access to those—but it could take weeks to view these documents if they're in a safe-deposit box. Instead, keep them at home in a fireproof filing cabinet or metal box.

344. HAVING THE TALK

Many folks are uncomfortable discussing their finances. Still, you should seriously consider talking to your children and other affected family members about your financial situation and especially your estate plan.

Why? For starters, it'll give your family an idea of what they can expect to inherit, and they can then factor that into their own financial decisions. It can also give you a chance to explain your bequests, especially if you plan to give more to some family members than others.

In addition, you can talk about end-of-life medical decisions, what sort of funeral you want and where key papers are located. You might even discuss what you would like your children to do with their inheritance. Perhaps you are anxious for them to buy their own home or for your grandchildren to go to good colleges.

There could also be other nitty-gritty financial details you want to tackle. For instance, you might explain the benefits of doing the stretch IRA, especially with a Roth. Alternatively, perhaps you plan to bequeath appreciated stock, but you want to emphasize that this is simply to get the step-up in cost basis, and your children should sell the shares immediately and buy a more diversified portfolio.

JONATHAN'S TAKE: Most of us won't leave millions of dollars to our heirs. But we can all make sure that our affairs are well organized, that there's a detailed letter of last instruction, and that our families know our wishes regarding life-prolonging medical procedures. These steps—and more—can save our families from extra anguish during an already difficult time.

345. INVESTIGATING CHARITIES

Before giving to a charity, you want to be confident the money will end up helping your favorite cause, rather than being lavished on handsome salaries for the charity's staff and other administrative costs.

Doing an online search may turn up any complaints about the charity. Your state government or the Better Business Bureau might also have complaints on file. Check out the BBB website for charities and donors at Give.org. In addition, you might review the charity's Form 990, which it is required to file with the IRS and which might be available on the charity's website. This will give you details on its finances.

Make sure the organization is not just tax-exempt, but that it carries the Internal Revenue Service 501(c)3 designation, which means your contributions will be tax-deductible. The charity's website should tell you. If you're uncertain, go to IRS.gov/charities and click on "EO Select Check."

As you investigate a charity, look for concrete results from the past year, rather than just a nebulous statement of purpose. You might try using CharityNavigator.org, CharityWatch.org and GuideStar.org. CharityWatch.org includes a list of top-rated charities by category. GuideStar.org allows you to download a charity's Form 990. Charity Navigator.org details how much of a charity's budget goes to administrative expenses, how much to fundraising costs—and how much to the charity's programs. The most efficient charities spend 10 percent or less of their revenue on administration and fundraising.

One tip: If a telemarketer calls seeking a donation for a charity, say "no," even if you're inclined to give. Telemarketers often take a large cut of any money they raise. If you want to contribute, give directly to the charity.

346. DEDUCTING CHARITABLE CONTRIBUTIONS

Charitable contributions should principally be motivated by generosity. Still, don't overlook the tax advantages.

If you give cash, you can deduct the entire contribution. For instance, if you're in the 25 percent federal income tax bracket, a $1 contribution will save you 25 cents in taxes. You only get this tax benefit if you itemize your deductions, rather than taking the standard deduction. If you usually take the standard deduction, you might bunch two or three years of charitable contributions into one tax year and see if that allows you to itemize. In any one year, the deduction for cash donations is capped at 50 percent of your adjusted gross income. Any excess can be rolled over and used during the subsequent five years.

Looking to save even more in taxes? Often the smartest strategy is to give appreciated assets that you have held for more than a year and which would otherwise be taxed at the long-term capital gains rate. Donating appreciated assets can have three tax benefits.

First, you can deduct the value of your contribution. That deduction, in any given year, is capped at 30 percent of your adjusted gross income. Second, you avoid paying capital gains taxes on the assets involved. To avoid the tax, don't sell the assets yourself, but instead let the charity do so. Third, you reduce the size of your taxable estate, which could ultimately mean paying less in federal and state estate taxes.

Want the tax savings today, but not sure which charities to support? You might contribute to a donor advised fund, such as those operated by FidelityCharitable.org, T. Rowe Price Group's ProgramForGiving.org, SchwabCharitable.org and VanguardCharitable.org. Your money can collect investment gains while you decide which charities to give to. What if you have a loss on, say, a stock? Don't donate the shares. Instead, sell the stock yourself so you get the tax benefit from the loss, and then donate the cash proceeds.

If you're retired or approaching that stage, here's another option: In return for your charitable contribution, you could get a tax deduction and generate retirement income—by making use of charitable gift annuities and charitable remainder trusts.

347. CHARITABLE GIFT ANNUITIES

A charitable gift annuity is similar to a plain-vanilla, immediate fixed annuity purchased from an insurance company. You hand over a chunk of money to a charity, which then pays you income for the rest of your life. But there are five key differences from an insurance company's annuity:

• A charitable gift annuity can give you an immediate tax deduction, which is based on how much the charity estimates it will have left upon your death.

• The annuity can be funded with appreciated property, such as stocks or mutual funds with large unrealized capital gains. This saves you selling the property and paying the capital gains tax bill. But if you fund the annuity with appreciated property, you will have to pay tax on a larger portion of each annuity payment.

• These annuities typically treat men and women equally, which is beneficial to women. With a commercial annuity, women usually receive less income than men of the same age, because the insurance company factors in their greater life expectancy.

• Whether you are a man or a woman, a charitable gift annuity will typically give you less monthly income than a commercial annuity. Yes, this is a charitable gift, so a charitable gift annuity shouldn't be your first choice if you're looking for maximum retirement income.

• If you die young, your untimely demise will benefit the charity, not an insurance company. This may make it a little more palatable to plunk down a large sum, knowing you would collect scant income from the annuity if you go under the next bus.

For further information, check out the website of the American Council on Gift Annuities at ACGA-web.org.

348. CHARITABLE REMAINDER TRUSTS

A charitable remainder trust is similar to a charitable gift annuity, but you retain greater control over how the money is invested, who the trustee is and which charity ultimately benefits. The downside: A charitable remainder trust is more involved, and you'll likely need legal help to set it up.

How does a charitable remainder trust work? You transfer assets to an irrevocable trust, which then pays you income for a fixed time period or until you die. All the income you receive will likely be taxable. The money that's left in the trust then goes to the charity named.

A charitable remainder trust makes most sense if you can fund it with assets that have increased in value, such as stocks or real estate. By donating the assets, you avoid capital gains taxes and receive an immediate tax deduction, which is based on an estimate of the sum that the charity will eventually receive.

You have a variety of income choices. For instance, you might opt for a fixed annual amount, like you would receive from an annuity. Alternatively, your annual income might be set at, say, 5 percent of the beginning-of-year value of the assets you donated. That means your income will fluctuate from year to year—but, if the trust's investments perform well, it might rise over time.

Sound too involved? You could opt for a charitable gift annuity instead. Some charities also have pooled income funds, which operate like charitable remainder trusts, but the charity assumes the administrative duties in return for a fee.

349. CHARITABLE BEQUESTS UPON DEATH

If you decide to make a charitable donation upon your death, you won't get an income tax deduction, which you could receive if you made the gift during your lifetime. You will, however, shrink the size of your taxable estate.

You could simply name a charity in your will to receive some portion of your estate. But here's an intriguing possibility: Donate your traditional IRA. As mentioned earlier in this chapter, beneficiaries (other than a spouse) of a traditional or Roth IRA have to draw down the account, but they can do so over many years. Those who inherit traditional IRAs will have to pay income taxes on the taxable portion of the withdrawal. Still, if your beneficiaries are smart, they can draw down the account slowly and get the benefit of decades of tax-deferred growth.

What if you doubt your beneficiaries will take advantage of the stretch IRA or you would rather save them the hassle? You might name a charity as beneficiary of your traditional IRA, while bequeathing your Roth IRA and other assets to your children or other family members. By giving your traditional IRA to charity, you'll shrink your taxable estate and get rid of the IRA's embedded income tax bill.

PART XIII

LIFE EVENTS
GOOD STUFF, BAD STUFF AND ALL THOSE PESKY FINANCIAL DECISIONS

The earlier parts of this book have tried to educate you about various personal-finance topics and then help you settle on the right strategy for tackling the financial task at hand. This chapter is a little different. Here the focus is on specific steps you might take at key points in your life:

- Graduating college
- Getting started as an investor
- Coping with market declines
- Moving in together
- Getting married
- Having a baby
- Sending children to college
- Getting divorced
- Changing jobs
- Losing your job
- Nearing retirement
- Helping elderly relatives
- After a loved one's death

As you busy yourself dealing with these changes, keep an eye on the big picture. Moments of transition and turmoil are often a great time to reconsider your overall finances, and for that you'll want to turn to other parts of this book.

350. GRADUATING COLLEGE

As you leave college and enter the work world, money will likely loom large—or, to be more precise, the lack thereof. Still, don't let a modest paycheck deter you. With the right steps, you can put yourself on the fast track to achieve two of life's most important financial goals: buying a home and retirement.

Live beneath your means. As you consider what sort of place to rent and what other expenses to take on, aim to keep your cost of living low. That'll give you more financial breathing room, make your life less stressful and, as the pay increases come through, you can start socking away serious money for a house down payment and other goals.

Pay all bills on time. We're talking about things like rent, utilities, student loans and credit card bills. Where possible, set up automatic payments, so you're less likely to be late. Paying your bills on time is typically the biggest factor affecting your credit score. If you nurture your credit history and credit score now, you should be in good shape when you apply for a mortgage.

Take on debt cautiously. You likely already have student loans, and you might need to borrow to buy a car. If you can, avoid taking on other debts, so mortgage lenders won't have any concerns when you ask for that hefty home loan.

Use credit cards sparingly. To build a good credit score, it's helpful to charge a small sum every month and then pay off the credit card balance in full. Try not to let that small monthly charge become a large one. If you use too high a percentage of your available credit limit, it'll make you appear financially stressed and it could hurt your credit score. More important, if you charge too much, you may not be able to pay off the balance in full—and you'll likely incur steep finance charges.

Contribute to your employer's retirement plan. With retirement so far away, this might seem like a low priority. But be sure to contribute at least enough to get any matching employer contribution. You will soon get used to living without the money. The earlier you start saving, the more you'll potentially accumulate, and you could set yourself up for early retirement.

351. GETTING STARTED AS AN INVESTOR

If you don't have much money, it can be tough to get started as an investor. Many brokerage firms and mutual funds require an initial investment of $2,500, $3,000 and sometimes more. What to do? Consider these steps:

Fund that 401(k). If you're in your 20s, there's a decent chance your first foray into investing will be through your employer's retirement plan. That's a great place to start, and not just because of the tax benefits and any matching employer contribution. You'll likely find the plan includes a limited list of mutual funds, which makes the choice more manageable, and you don't have to worry about meeting some required minimum initial investment.

Look for low-minimum funds. For $100, you can buy one of the Charles Schwab mutual funds. Schwab's fund lineup includes index funds, fundamentally weighted index funds and target-date retirement funds. For $500, you can get into the Homestead Funds and some of the Nicholas Company funds. Artisan Funds, Buffalo Funds and Scout Investments will waive their regular minimums if you agree to a $50- or $100-a-month automatic investment plan.

For $1,000, you can purchase one of T. Rowe Price Group's target-date retirement funds in an individual retirement account, while $1,000 will allow you to buy a Vanguard Group target-date fund in either an IRA or a regular taxable account. If you have relatively limited savings, you won't be able to buy many investments, so you should probably stick with mutual funds that give you broad market exposure—which is what you get with a target-date fund.

Buy exchange-traded funds. Instead of mutual funds, you could open a brokerage account and purchase ETFs. Merrill Edge, ShareBuilder, TD Ameritrade and TradeKing have no required minimum to open a brokerage account. ETrade will let you open an account for $500, while Charles Schwab requires $1,000, though Schwab will waive that minimum if you commit to adding $100 a month to your account. Some brokerage firms have a select list of ETFs that you can purchase without a commission.

Save for the house. To amass money for a future house down payment while also accumulating a pool of emergency money, try shoveling cash into a savings account or certificates of deposit. You won't earn much interest these days. But given that you can't afford to take much risk when pursuing short-term goals, a high return was never in the cards. Instead, your regular savings will be the key driver of the account's growth.

352. COPING WITH MARKET DECLINES

Most investors grow exuberant as share prices climb and fearful when they tumble. But to be a successful investor, you need to reverse those feelings, so you stand pat during market declines and, better still, seize the opportunity and invest more. That's tough to do—but these strategies may help:

Before selling stocks, talk to someone. That someone might be your spouse, a friend or colleague. Don't just talk about why you're fearful now. Also discuss why you're inclined to ditch the strategy in which you had so much confidence just a few months earlier. As you try to articulate what has changed, you may realize that not much has.

Think about value. Stocks aren't just pieces of paper. Rather, they represent partial ownership of corporations that often have growing profits and pay regular dividends. When share prices fall, stocks become better value relative to those profits and dividends—and the rational response is to buy more, not sell.

Look at the big picture. Your stock portfolio is likely a small part of your total wealth. While your shares may be falling in value, your other assets—including your bonds, your home and your human capital—may be more valuable than ever.

Force yourself to rebalance. You should have a target percentage for your portfolio's allocation to stocks. A market decline will likely leave you underweighted. That means you ought to buy stocks as part of your regular rebalancing program. In fact, if the market drops severely, you may want to rebalance immediately, even if your next scheduled rebalancing is months away. If the market continues to fall, you can always rebalance again.

To read more about investors' mental mistakes, rebalancing and portfolio building, check out Part VIII.

353. MOVING IN TOGETHER

If you're in a relationship and decide to move in together, you may want to take things slowly—at least when it comes to your finances.

Rent a place you could afford on your own. That way, if the relationship doesn't work out, you won't be saddled with a lease neither of you can afford.

Divide up financial responsibilities. Before moving in together, decide how you'll split the bills and who will be responsible for paying them. The more you discuss ahead of time, the less room there will be for misunderstanding.

Don't combine your finances unnecessarily. Initially, there's no need to entwine your finances by, say, opening a joint checking account or buying a car together. There just isn't much to be gained, except extra hassles if the relationship doesn't work out.

Gauge your partner's financial habits. Money is one of the biggest sources of tension in relationships, so it's important to get a handle on your partner's money habits. Is he or she careful about spending? Is your partner an aggressive investor? What's his or her attitude toward carrying credit card debt?

If your partner isn't careful about money, you'll avoid financial headaches—and heated arguments—by keeping your finances separate. On the other hand, if it's clear you are both financially prudent and you believe the relationship will last, you might start marrying your finances, even if you don't envisage ever getting married. For instance, after a year or two, you might consider buying a home together and naming each other as beneficiaries of your retirement accounts and life insurance.

354. GETTING MARRIED

If you decide to marry, you'll have a lifetime of financial decisions ahead of you. But there are some items you should probably tackle right away:

Budget the wedding. Weddings are said to cost an average $25,000. Half of workers approaching retirement have less than $50,000 in savings. An obvious question: Would it make more sense to opt for the cheaper wedding and save the rest for longer-term goals?

Get to know each other financially. Find out how much you each save regularly and have set aside for retirement, and how much you each have in debt. Also learn about each other's attitudes toward spending, credit cards and investment risk. It's worth checking out your future in-laws and how they handle money, because there's a good chance your future spouse has adopted many of his or her parents' financial attitudes.

Change beneficiary designations. You will likely want to name your new spouse as the beneficiary of your life insurance and retirement accounts. You both should also get new wills drawn up.

Rethink your life insurance. You may need to take out more life insurance, especially if you're planning to buy a home together, one of you plans to stop working or you intend to start a family.

Look for cost savings. You might save money by sharing phone plans and digital subscriptions, and by getting both of you onto whichever health plan offered by your respective employers is least expensive. Be warned: One cost could rise, which is the amount you pay in federal and state income taxes. In 2015, if you marry and your combined income is greater than $172,000 or so, your total federal income tax bill could be higher than if you remained single.

355. SAME-SEX MARRIAGE

Much has changed for married same-sex couples since the Supreme Court ruled in 2013 that the Defense of Marriage Act was unconstitutional. But the changes aren't over yet—and, in the meantime, same-sex couples need to tread carefully.

Prepare for tax headaches. Thanks to the Supreme Court ruling, married same-sex couples can now file joint federal tax returns. But if you live in a state that doesn't allow or recognize same-sex marriage, you will likely have to file separate state tax returns, which will mean additional tax hassles.

Keep an eye on Social Security. The Social Security Administration is now paying spousal benefits to same-sex couples who are in a legal relationship and live in states that recognize their relationship. What about married same-sex couples who live in other states? Can they claim spousal and survivor benefits based on the earnings record of the other spouse? The Social Security Administration has encouraged these couples to file for benefits so they establish their claim, but for now it's deferring to state law.

Plan ahead for medical emergencies. If your spouse was hospitalized in a state where same-sex couples don't enjoy marriage equality, would you be able to visit him or her? You might both sign hospital visitation authorizations, specifying that your spouse can visit you in hospital. In addition, consider drawing up health care powers of attorney, where you name the other spouse to make medical decisions on your behalf, should you become incapacitated.

Bulletproof your estate plan. If you live in a state with laws that are unfriendly to gay couples, your spouse may not receive anything if you die without a will, so it's crucial you both get wills drawn up. Even if you have wills, hostile family members might challenge them.

What to do? Consider talking to a knowledgeable attorney about drawing up revocable living trusts, which are tougher to challenge. You might also consider owning assets jointly with right of survivorship, and you should make sure you have the right beneficiaries listed on retirement accounts and life insurance.

356. HAVING A BABY

Once a baby arrives, you quickly discover two things are in short supply: time and money. According to the Department of Agriculture's Expenditures on Children by Families study released in August 2014, it costs $245,340 for a middle-income family to raise a child through age 17, figured in today's dollars. Costs in the first few years are pegged at $12,940 per year. How can you prepare your finances?

Stockpile cash. The more you have in a savings account, the easier it'll be to handle medical costs, buy all the baby paraphernalia, pay for babysitters and daycare, and more.

Assess living expenses. A pile of savings will help if one parent won't be working for a few months. What if one of you plans to stay home for the foreseeable future? You could quickly run through your savings, unless you take steps to cut back your living expenses. That isn't easy to do when you have an extra person to clothe and feed, and you might also need a larger home. Still, you will likely enjoy your new child more if you aren't financially stressed.

Check your employers' policies. See what the rules are regarding maternity and paternity leave. Find out what childbirth expenses will be covered, how much it will cost to get your new baby added to the health plan and what out-of-pocket medical costs you might face.

Revise your wills. Both of you will need to update your wills to name a guardian for your newborn, just in case you both die prematurely.

Boost life insurance coverage. You may have some coverage through your employer. But with the arrival of the baby, you will likely need a larger policy. Don't necessarily purchase this additional coverage through your employer. The premiums could be relatively high because they reflect the health of all employees, who on average may be older and some of whom will smoke. You will probably want coverage not only on the life of the employed parent, but also for the stay-at-home parent. A death in either case would mean significant additional ongoing costs.

357. HAVING A BABY WHEN YOU'RE A SAME-SEX COUPLE

What happens if you're part of a same-sex couple and you have a child—but you aren't the adopting or biological parent? The legal issues can be tricky, so be sure to seek advice from a qualified attorney.

Apply for a second-parent adoption. If you aren't the adopting or biological parent, you may not have any rights if you get divorced, the other spouse dies or you simply want to visit your child in hospital. As a precaution, you might establish your rights by applying for a second-parent adoption.

Draw up a custody agreement. If a second-parent adoption isn't an option in your state, consult a lawyer who specializes in same-sex couples. The lawyer might suggest steps to secure your child-custody rights in case you get divorced or in case your child is hospitalized and the staff prevent you from visiting.

For instance, you might draw up a co-parenting or similar agreement. A co-parenting agreement is a declaration that you both consider yourselves parents of the child. While courts don't necessarily have to respect such agreements, they should help, as should any evidence that the nonadopting or nonbiological parent has behaved as though he or she is a parent to the child.

Name the other parent as guardian. Your lawyer might also suggest that the biological or adopting parent name the other parent as legal guardian in his or her will. This should secure the rights of the parent in the event the other dies prematurely.

358. OFF TO COLLEGE

When you send your teenagers off to college, you might include four tools in their financial backpack: a checking account, credit card, renter's insurance—and some sound advice.

Checking accounts. Favor checking accounts where your kids won't get charged a monthly maintenance fee and where they have access to a large number of fee-free ATMs at both college and home. Also make sure the account is set up so your children can't overdraw, and hence incur hefty fees, with ATM withdrawals or debit card purchases.

Credit cards. Many financial companies offer credit cards specially geared to students. This can be a good way for your kids to start building a credit history.

Alternatively, if your credit card company allows it, you might add your teenager as a joint accountholder to a credit card you already have. This can have a magical effect: You may discover that the card's entire history is added to your kid's credit report—and suddenly it will look like your teenager has been responsibly using a credit card for many years.

Instead of adding your student as a joint accountholder, you could add him or her as an authorized user. This, however, probably won't be as helpful in establishing your child as a good credit—and it may not help at all.

Renter's insurance. This is often recommended for college kids, so they're covered if their bicycle is stolen or their computer is destroyed in a fire. Would replacing your student's possessions cause real financial hardship? If the answer is "no," maybe you should skip the coverage.

Have the talk. Spend some time talking to your kids about the dangers of overspending. Discuss what they can charge to the credit card. Emphasize that they should tell you early on if anything goes awry—financially or otherwise—at which point the problem may be more easily fixed.

Not sure your teenagers will be financially responsible? You might keep them on a shorter leash by giving them spending money every two weeks or every month, rather than giving them a big chunk at the start of each semester.

For general information about paying for college, spend some time with Part IV.

359. GETTING DIVORCED

If you're getting divorced, be careful—but also try to be civil. Here are some steps to take in the initial weeks after the breakup:

Draw up a financial inventory. Make copies of financial account statements, tax returns, pay stubs and anything else that documents your collective income, assets and debts. Create a list of valuable household items. You might even photograph or videotape them. Don't discount the possibility that your spouse is hiding assets.

Disentangle your ongoing finances. Get your own checking account and credit cards, while cancelling joint cards. Your goal is to ensure you aren't responsible for any financial missteps that your spouse makes in the weeks and months ahead. At the same time, make sure the household bills get paid, or you may both see your credit scores plummet.

Find the right lawyer. While a courtroom battle is sometimes necessary, you probably don't want a lawyer for whom that seems to be the first option, not the last resort. The less time you spend in court and the more details you and your spouse can hash out on your own, the less costly your divorce is likely to be.

Avoid unnecessary arguments. Unfortunately, many divorces degenerate into needless bickering that leaves both parties worse off and the lawyers considerably richer. If you can manage to be civil, you will both benefit financially.

A modicum of civility is especially important if you have children. In the years ahead, you will need to make countless joint decisions regarding your children, plus you may need your ex-spouse's cooperation if, say, you suddenly need to work late and can't pick up the kids. Those conversations will be far easier if you haven't torn each other to shreds during the divorce proceedings.

Civility, however, doesn't mean you shouldn't be firm in seeking a fair settlement. The division of property, as well as the amount paid in child support and alimony, are crucially important. State law goes a long way toward deciding these issues. Still, think carefully about what's equitable and which assets to request.

360. SPLITTING FINANCIALLY

In a divorce, you should be able to keep any assets you owned at the time of the marriage, plus any gifts and inheritances you received while married. What about other assets acquired during the marriage? How those are divided will depend on state law, especially whether you live in a community property or common law state. Even then, it's important to pay close attention to the financial details:

Get all joint debts paid off. If you rely on your ex-spouse to continue making payments on loans that are in both your names, you're putting your credit history and credit score at risk.

Decide which assets you want. Many folks want to keep the family home, so they have a sense of stability and continuity. But if you do that, are you locking up too much of your wealth in your home—and could you afford the property taxes, maintenance and homeowner's insurance? If the property is worth more than you paid, you may want to sell it while still married. You can avoid taxes on $500,000 of home price appreciation if you're married, but that drops to $250,000 once you're single.

Consider embedded tax bills. Suppose you have two stock holdings valued at $20,000 each. One is worth less than the price paid and the other is worth more. The latter is less desirable, because you'll owe taxes when you sell, while the stock with a capital loss will give you a tax break.

Similarly, a traditional IRA or 401(k), with its big embedded income tax bill, is worth less than a comparable sum in a Roth account. Need to move retirement account money from one spouse to the other, so you equalize your assets? If done properly, you can avoid triggering an immediate income tax bill or tax penalty.

Think about the transition. If a divorce will compel you to return to work, you may want to seek taxable account money in the divorce, rather than retirement account money. This will give you savings you can easily draw on, should it take you longer than expected to find a job.

What if you're receiving money from your spouse's 401(k) or similar plan under a QDRO (qualified domestic relations order) and you think you'll need to spend it? You can take the money as a lump sum and avoid the usual 10 percent tax penalty on withdrawals before age 59½, though you will owe income taxes. Be warned: If, instead of taking the lump sum, you transfer the 401(k) assets to an IRA and then try to spend it, you'll likely get hit with tax penalties.

361. DIVORCE AND STATE LAW

While divorces often trigger endless wrangling, there's less room for maneuver than you might imagine—because much depends on state law:

Community vs. common law states. There are nine community property states: Arizona, California, Idaho, Louisiana, Nevada, New Mexico, Texas, Washington and Wisconsin. Couples in Alaska can also create community property if they opt to enter into a community property agreement. In a community property state, the wealth acquired during the course of the marriage is considered equally owned by you and your spouse, and would usually be divided equally.

Other states are so-called common law or equitable distribution states. If you end up in court because you can't reach an agreement, a judge will order what he or she believes is an equitable division of the wealth acquired during the marriage. Equitable won't necessarily mean equal. You may not like the result, which creates a strong incentive to settle matters yourself. To learn more about divorce law in your state, head to DivorceNet.com.

In community property and most common law states, you should be able to keep the wealth you brought to the marriage, as well as gifts and inheritances received during the marriage. But if this separate property was mixed with marital property—let's say you put it in a joint account with your spouse—then you may lose a portion in the divorce proceedings.

Alimony. Today, stay-at-home and lower-earning spouses are less likely to receive alimony and instead are expected to return fulltime to the workforce unless, say, they're in their 50s. But it's hard to generalize. If the marriage lasted more than 10 years and one spouse will find it tough to support himself or herself, alimony might be awarded, but perhaps only for a limited time.

Child support. Unlike alimony, which is hard to predict, child support payments are typically driven by state formula, so there's little room for contention. State formulas are based on the notion that one parent is the custodial parent, which can seem unfair when the parents have joint custody and want an equal say in how to spend money earmarked for the children's benefit. While alimony is tax-deductible for the payer and taxable to the recipient, child support is neither tax-deductible nor taxable.

If you have a child, negotiate who gets to claim the kid as a dependent for tax purposes. If you have two children, you might each claim one as a dependent. That will allow both of you to file as head of household, which will trigger a smaller tax bill than filing as a single individual.

362. CHANGING JOBS

If you change jobs, it's likely for a more enjoyable or more senior position—and it may mean more money. But don't focus just on the size of your new paycheck. Also give some thought to your new job's health, life and disability insurance, as well as the retirement benefits.

Health insurance. If it will take a few months before you are eligible for health care coverage at your new job, you might be able to continue your old employer's health benefits by taking advantage of so-called COBRA coverage.

Life and disability insurance. You'll want to consider what sort of disability and life insurance coverage your new employer provides, and whether you should supplement this with individual policies. You can read more about life, disability and health insurance in Part V.

Your old employer's retirement plan. If your current employer has a vesting schedule for its retirement plan contributions, see if delaying your job change by a few weeks will garner you additional retirement money. Also, be sure to pay back any 401(k) loans—or you could find yourself facing income taxes and tax penalties.

Consolidate retirement accounts. Got retirement savings in your old employer's plan? You could transfer the money to an IRA, which will simplify your finances, give you more investment choice and may lower your investment costs. If you move your 401(k) to an IRA, be sure to do a trustee-to-trustee transfer or you could end up with a nasty tax conundrum.

Before moving the money, give some thought to how this will affect future Roth conversions, what it means for creditor protection, what's the best strategy if you have your old employer's stock in the plan—and whether your old 401(k) is so good that you shouldn't move the money. All of this is covered in detail in Part X.

Your new employer's retirement plan. Your new employer may automatically enroll you in its retirement plan. But if you sign up yourself, you may get into the plan more quickly and at a higher contribution rate. If your new employer's plan is top-notch, you might even transfer your 401(k) balance from your old employer to the new plan.

363. LOSING YOUR JOB

If you lose your job, you may want to consolidate your 401(k) money in an IRA and you might continue your current health benefits by taking advantage of COBRA coverage, discussed in Part V, just like those who are changing jobs. But also consider taking these other steps:

Prep your finances for hard times. If you have an inkling that layoffs are in the works, save whatever you can, pay back 401(k) loans, and trim the balance on your credit cards and home equity line of credit. Don't, however, rush to pay off car loans and student debt. While you can always run up the balance again on your home equity line of credit and on your credit cards (though it isn't advisable), you can't "re-borrow" your auto and student loans.

Slash your living expenses. Instead of opting for COBRA coverage, see whether you can trim your health insurance premiums by purchasing a policy through your state's insurance exchange. Also, cut out discretionary spending, so you only have fixed costs to worry about. That way, you should be able to make your savings and any severance payment last longer.

Apply for unemployment benefits. Depending on state law, if you receive a severance payment from your employer, you may not be immediately eligible to receive unemployment benefits. Still, apply as soon as you lose your job, so payments start once you're eligible.

Manage your tax bill. Because you have lost your regular income, you may find you're in a surprisingly low tax bracket. To take advantage of your low tax bracket, think carefully about the timing of stock sales and any retirement account withdrawals. For instance, if you are laid off late in the year and you are compelled to dip into retirement accounts to pay living expenses, the income tax cost may be lower if you delay any retirement account withdrawals until after Dec. 31, at which point the withdrawals could be taxed at a lower rate.

364. NEARING RETIREMENT

You can learn more about preparing for retirement and generating retirement income in Part II. But here are some additional steps you might take in the year or two before you quit your job:

Check the employee handbook. By delaying retirement by just a few weeks or months, you may qualify to get cashed out on vacation days for the current year or to receive money held in the company's deferred compensation plan. You might also become vested for part of your employer's matching contribution to the 401(k).

Exercise employee stock options. You may have been awarded options years ago and never given them much thought, perhaps because the amount involved was small and the stock hasn't been much of a performer. Still, the options may be worth a modest sum, so be sure to exercise them before you quit.

See the doctor and dentist. If you have good medical and dental coverage through your current employer, get health issues tackled now, before you retire.

Refinance your mortgage. Ideally, you should get your mortgage paid off before you retire. But if that won't happen any time soon, it may be worth refinancing. It'll be easier to get approved for the loan if you still have a job and a regular income.

Set up a home equity line of credit. With any luck, you'll never have to use it. But it could come in handy if you suddenly need cash—and, as with a refinancing, it's a lot easier to get approved for a home equity line of credit while you still have a regular paycheck coming in.

365. HELPING ELDERLY RELATIVES

Looking after your parents or other elderly family members? In all
likelihood, it's a team effort, with perhaps your siblings involved and others
whom you have hired. To help matters run more smoothly, consider these
steps:

Create a list of experts. Pull together the names and contact information
for doctors, dentists, lawyers, tax preparers, financial advisors and anybody
else who assists your parents. Make sure your siblings and other caregivers
have the list.

Find a backup. If you and your siblings don't live near your parents, find
somebody local who can check on your parents if you become concerned.
Make sure that person has a set of keys to your parents' home.

Agree on how to share costs. If your parents don't have enough money for
their own care, you and your siblings may have to pick up part of the cost.
Early on, discuss how much you can afford to spend and create a system of
monthly accounting, so nobody ends up shortchanged.

Watch for abuse. There might be physical or emotional intimidation or,
alternatively, perhaps someone is stealing from your parents. If you think
something is awry, be quick to alert others.

Have a contingency plan. What if things deteriorate with your parents—and
it's suddenly clear they can no longer live independently? Ideally, you
should discuss this with your parents ahead of time. For instance, if the
next step is an assisted living facility, it will be easier if you check out a few
places ahead of time and get your parents' opinion.

Throughout, keep the focus on what your parents want. Emphasize that
you're trying to help them maintain their independence. As we age, we have
a sense that we're losing control. If you start making decisions without
consulting your parents or you push them too hard to make changes, they
will likely feel as if they're being forced to surrender yet more control—and
the conversations could quickly turn contentious.

366. AFTER A LOVED ONE'S DEATH

Death, unfortunately, is often accompanied by a slew of practical details.
Where to begin?

Look for funeral instructions. You may discover they're in the deceased's
will or letter of last instruction.

Consider the cost. This is hardly the moment when most folks are up for
price shopping, yet it pays to keep your wits about you. Funeral homes
often nudge the family to spend more than is necessary. To read more
about funeral expenses and how you can lower the bill, check out the

Funeral Consumers Alliance at Funerals.org.

Order death certificates. The funeral home may ask how many copies of the death certificate you want. Don't skimp. Depending on the complexity of the deceased's finances, you might order 10 or more. You'll need these certificates whenever you claim benefits or property on behalf of the deceased's beneficiaries. It's often cheaper and easier to order death certificates from the funeral home than to obtain them later.

Watch out for theft. Burglars occasionally target the homes of the recently deceased, so you might ask the police to keep an eye on the house. Perhaps more alarming, family members sometimes feel they're free to grab whatever they want without asking. If the deceased had valuables of any kind, consider getting them out of the house.

Locate key papers. In particular, find the will and see who is named as executor. What about other financial or legal papers? For now, set them aside. You don't want to throw anything away until you're confident you have identified all assets and have the account statements you need.

367. SETTLING AN ESTATE

Are you named as executor of an estate? Here are some steps you'll likely need to take:

Hire an attorney. Don't feel compelled to use the deceased's lawyer, especially if he or she doesn't specialize in settling estates. A lawyer might charge a flat fee, a percent of the estate's gross value or by the hour. Try to avoid an hourly fee, because it's hard to know what you'll end up getting charged.

If the deceased has investments in a regular taxable account, ask the attorney whether you should sell the assets. That may be an especially smart move if the deceased's portfolio consists of large investments in just a few stocks. Thanks to the step-up in cost basis upon death, the capital gains tax bill should be little or nothing. You may also want to diversify the deceased's retirement account if the investments don't appear prudent.

Gather financial papers. Find the latest statements from the deceased's bank, credit cards, mortgage companies, mutual fund companies, brokerage firms, insurance companies and any other financial firms the deceased had dealings with. See if there's a safe-deposit box. Also study the deceased's most recent tax return and see what arrives in the mail. That way, you can make sure you've located all assets.

Check with financial advisors. If the deceased used a broker, financial planner, insurance agent or accountant, these folks may be helpful in locating assets and settling the estate. Ask the insurance agent about any life insurance. Talk to the accountant about filing final federal and state income tax returns for the deceased and, if necessary, federal and state estate tax returns.

Call current or former employers. If the deceased was still working, he or she may be due a final paycheck and a payout on employer-provided life insurance. Even if retired, the deceased may have 401(k) assets at an old employer, or heirs might be eligible for survivor benefits from the pension plan.

Contact Social Security. You'll need to stop benefits and see about any survivor benefits. If the deceased served in the armed forces, also call the Department of Veterans Affairs.

Think before you spend. If you're the executor, you are likely also one of the estate's beneficiaries. It can take a few months before you receive a distribution from the estate. That's good news—because it will give you time to contemplate what to do with the money. This could be the windfall that puts you on track for retirement, so think twice before going on a spending spree.

As executor, you might want a quick education on estate planning. For that, check out Part XII.

PART XIV

RULES OF THE ROAD
KEEPING YOURSELF
ON TRACK IN 2015

L ooking to improve your money management in 2015? Here are 31 rules for the financial road ahead:

1.   Check your retirement progress by taking your nest egg and applying a 4 percent annual portfolio withdrawal rate, equal to $4,000 a year for every $100,000 saved. Will you have enough retirement income—or should you be saving more?

2.   Don't automatically claim Social Security at age 62. It often makes sense to delay benefits so you get a larger monthly check, especially if you're married and have been the main breadwinner.

3.   Never buy a home unless you expect to stay put for at least five years and preferably seven years or longer. Between mid-2006 and early 2012, the S&P/Case-Shiller U.S. National Home Price Index plunged 27.4 percent. Enough said.

4.   Planning to remodel your home in 2015? If you'll get a lot of pleasure from the improvements and you can afford the cost, go ahead. But don't kid yourself that you're making an investment.

5.   Never use a custodial account to save for college costs. Instead, open a 529 college savings plan or a Coverdell education savings account. Both will give you tax-free growth and shouldn't badly hurt financial aid eligibility.

6.   Don't let your children take on more student loans than they can reasonably handle, given their expected career and likely earnings.

JONATHAN CLEMENTS

7. Insure against the big financial risks in your life, while skipping the small stuff. Extended warranties, trip-cancellation insurance and low auto-insurance deductibles? Just say no.

8. If you aren't rich, buy term life insurance to protect your family. If you're super-rich, consider cash-value life insurance to save on estate taxes. Either way, never buy life insurance purely as an investment.

9. Worried about layoffs? Limit your fixed living costs to 50 percent or less of your pretax income. Fixed costs include expenses such as mortgage or rent, property taxes, debt payments, groceries, utilities and insurance premiums. At the 50 percent level, you know you could get by on half your old income if you lose your job.

10. Think about which expenditures gave you a lot of pleasure in 2014 and which were quickly forgotten. Use that to guide your spending in 2015.

11. Always contribute at least enough to your employer's 401(k) plan to get the full matching contribution. Even if you leave your employer, immediately cash out your 401(k), and pay taxes and penalties, you'll likely still come out ahead after figuring in the employer match.

12. Expect modest returns from stocks and bonds. The worst that will happen is you'll save too much for retirement and other goals.

13. Think about your paycheck—and how secure it is—as you decide how much to invest in stocks, how big an emergency fund to hold and how much debt to take on.

14. Avoid investments you don't completely understand. Among other financial products, that likely means skipping equity-indexed annuities, leveraged exchange-traded index funds, hedge funds and the mutual funds that mimic them, and variable annuities with living benefits.

15. Shun investments with high expenses or whose costs you don't fully grasp. Examples? See previous point.

16. Never keep 100 percent in stocks—or 100 percent in bonds. A well-designed portfolio will always include both investments.

17. Don't buy individual company stocks, and think hard before purchasing actively managed mutual funds. After investment costs, you're highly unlikely to beat the market, which is why market-tracking index funds make so much sense.

18. Check that you have tax-efficient investments in your taxable account, while using your retirement accounts to hold investments that generate big annual tax bills.

19. When did you last rebalance your portfolio back to your target weights for stocks, bonds and other investments? If it's been a year or more, you probably have too much in stocks. Look to get your investment mix back on track—preferably sooner rather than later.

20. If rich stock valuations and skimpy bond yields make you nervous, you can always pay down debt instead.

21. Never have a year when you pay nothing in income taxes. If you expect to have little or no taxable income in 2015, take advantage of your low tax bracket by converting part of your traditional IRA to a Roth.

22. Check your credit reports for inaccuracies. You can get free copies through AnnualCreditReport.com.

23. Always pay your bills on time. This is likely the biggest factor affecting your credit score. In particular, late payments on credit card bills and loan payments are quickly reported to the credit bureaus.

24. Are you on track to pay off your mortgage by retirement? If not, consider making extra principal payments.

25. Never carry a credit card balance, which might cost you 20 percent or more in annual interest. You won't earn that sort of return in the financial markets over the long haul.

26. If you have more than enough saved for your own retirement, consider taking advantage of the 2015's $14,000 gift-tax exclusion to make gifts to your children and other family members. It's a great way to brighten their lives—and the cheapest and easiest way to reduce the potential hit from state and federal estate taxes.

27. Get a will. You've been promising to do so for years. Make it happen in 2015.

28. Check you have the right beneficiaries listed on retirement accounts, life insurance and any trust documents. Let's face it: You probably don't want your ex-husband inheriting your individual retirement account.

29. Try not to spend money in Roth IRAs. Instead, leave these accounts untouched for your beneficiaries, who could enjoy decades of tax-free withdrawals. They'll remember you fondly.

30. When giving to charity, consider gifting appreciated investments. You'll potentially enjoy three tax benefits: an immediate tax deduction, avoiding capital gains taxes on the investments donated, and a smaller taxable estate.

31. In 2015, keep an eye on the big picture: You want to design a financial life for yourself where money worries are minimized, you have special times with friends and family, and you devote your days to activities that you think are important and that you're passionate about.

ABOUT THE AUTHOR

Jonathan Clements is the personal-finance columnist for *The Wall Street Journal Sunday*, a special section carried in 70 U.S. newspapers with a combined circulation of almost seven million. His weekly column also appears on WSJ.com and MarketWatch.com.

Born in London, England, Jonathan graduated from Cambridge University. He spent 18 years at *The Wall Street Journal* in New York, where he was the newspaper's personal-finance columnist, before joining Citigroup in 2008. He worked at the bank as Director of Financial Education for the U.S. wealth-management business until early 2014, when he returned to the *Journal* as a freelance columnist.

Jonathan has written four earlier personal-finance books, and also a novel. He has appeared on ABC's *Good Morning America*, CNBC, CNN, Fox Business, Fox News, MSNBC, NBC's *Today Show*, public television's *Consuelo Mack WealthTrack* and National Public Radio. An avid bicyclist, Jonathan lives in New York City and, on many mornings, can be found pedaling madly around Central Park. He's married, with two children and two stepchildren, all of whom are a source of constant wonder.

You can learn more at JonathanClements.com. Got a suggestion for how to improve the *Money Guide*? Write to ClementsGuide@gmail.com.

DETAILED TABLE OF CONTENTS

Made in the USA
Lexington, KY
06 January 2015